Military Heretics

Military Heretics

THE UNORTHODOX IN POLICY AND STRATEGY

EDITED BY B.J.C. McKERCHER
AND
A. HAMISH ION

Westport, Connecticut
London

Library of Congress Cataloging-in-Publication Data

Military heretics : the unorthodox in policy and strategy / edited by
   B.J.C. McKercher and A. Hamish Ion.
      p.   cm.
   Includes bibliographical references and index.
   ISBN 0-275-94554-5 (alk. paper)
      1. Military policy. 2. Strategy. I. McKercher, B.J.C.
   II. Ion, A. Hamish.
   UA11.M465   1994
   355'.0335—dc20   93–14116

British Library Cataloguing in Publication Data is available.

Copyright © 1994 by the Military History Symposium of the Royal
Military College of Canada

All rights reserved. No portion of this book may be
reproduced, by any process or technique, without the
express written consent of the publisher.

Library of Congress Catalog Card Number: 93–14116
ISBN: 0–275–94554–5

First published in 1994

Praeger Publishers, 88 Post Road West, Westport, CT 06881
An imprint of Greenwood Publishing Group, Inc.

Printed in the United States of America

The paper used in this book complies with the
Permanent Paper Standard issued by the National
Information Standards Organization (Z39.48-1984).

10 9 8 7 6 5 4 3 2 1

Contents

Introduction
    Military Heretics: The Unorthodox in Policy and Strategy
    B.J.C. McKercher and A. Hamish Ion   1

1. Making and Breaking the Rules:
   Orthodoxy, Heterodoxy, and Heresy in Modern War
   John Gooch   11

2. New Wars and Old: Félix Calleja and
   the Independence War of Mexico, 1810–1816
   Christon I. Archer   33

3. From Genius to Intellect:
   Unorthodox Union Officers in the American Civil War
   Carol Reardon   57

4. Alfred von Tirpitz's Heretical Orthodoxy
   Ivo Lambi   83

5. The Youth of General A. A. Brusilov: The Making of
   an Unconventional, Conventional Professional
   David R. Jones   101

6. Hugh Trenchard: Making the Unorthodox Orthodox
   Scot Robertson   123

7. Admiral Katō Kanji: Heretic, Hero, or the Unorthodox in Pursuit of an Orthodox Naval Policy
   Ian Gow   143

8. Moshe Dayan: Above the Rules
   Michael I. Handel   165

9. Afterword: The Mark of the Heretic
   John A. English   197

Bibliography   223

Index   237

About the Editors and Contributors   245

Military Heretics

Introduction

Military Heretics:
The Unorthodox in Policy and Strategy

B.J.C. McKercher and A. Hamish Ion

> If we study the campaigns of great soldiers and examine the causes of their victories, we shall find that in the first instance always moral qualities enforced victory. Superior resolution, boldness, daring, and steadfastness paralysed the energy of the enemy, and carried forward the victorious troops to the performance of extraordinary deeds.
> General Friedrich von Bernhardi, 1914[1]

It is axiomatic that the unorthodox, particularly in conventional organizations like armed forces with their traditions and rigid hierarchy, attracts the interest of historians. When this unorthodoxy affects policy and strategy there is double the interest. Whether military heretics are successful or not—and here the historiographical debate can lead to profound disagreement[2]—is not the issue. For instance, as a comparison of British generalship in the Crimean War shows,[3] the record of unorthodox military leaders is as mixed as those noted for a conventional approach to the art of war and war planning. But what is intriguing about military heretics—or, at least, those charged with heresy—is that they represent a bright thread in what is generally held to be a colorless cloth. And although orthodox generals and admirals, and in this century, air marshals, demonstrate what the Wilhelmine German General Friedrich von Bernhardi once characterized as the necessities for success on the battlefield—superior resolution, boldness, daring, and steadfastness—it is perhaps fairer to say that these are the qualities that distinguish the unorthodox within military leaderships. Heresy is not restricted only to wartime. It has also risen in peacetime when, in preparing for unknown hostilities, some serving officers, writers, and others seek to divine the future in order to guide the development of weapons, tactics, and strategy.

Therefore, in discussing military heretics, historians are talking about a particular subset within the profession of arms: a group comprising commanders, writers, thinkers, and others who were willing to go against the grain to ensure victory. This raises some crucial questions: Does deviation from the normal course, defined by such things as official orders or field manuals, imply that heretical commanders are more willing than their more fixed colleagues to take risks—not only with the lives of their men but with the overall success of the armed forces in which they serve? Does it imply an innate desire to go against the dictates of their superiors and the political leaders—those they serve yet perceive as inadequate to meet new conditions created by advances in weapons, strategy, and tactics? How do heretics apply their different ideas to practical policy both in peace and war, especially since that practical policy is usually the result of the historical development of the state they serve, a seemingly universal political process involving the allocation of funds, and the lessons those in charge have learned from past experience?

One of the difficulties in approaching such a complex issue, as John Gooch and his colleagues show, concerns the precise meaning of the term "heretic." In the first place, what exactly is "orthodoxy"? From this, does deviation from the orthodox explicitly mean "heresy"? Does heresy perhaps imply eccentricity? Does it suggest only the unconventional in thought and action? Does it mean simple dissent? Or does it signify radical departures from the normal course? For the purposes of this book, it is perhaps best to consider that a military heretic can exhibit each and all of these attributes. The issue, then, is the degree to which any one of them, or two of them, or three, might dominate the others. Just as important, given that this book examines military heretics in the modern period—roughly from the end of the eighteenth century—how important is the unique historical context in which the "heretics" developed, functioned as leaders, and either prepared for or fought wars?

It seems clear that time and circumstance largely promote heresy in military thinking—or, as John Gooch deftly puts it, promote a need to rewrite the rules of war. Christon Archer demonstrates that the rise of a new kind of enemy, fighting by new rules—or, at least, without the old ones—can render traditional military responses inadequate. When the Spanish Army confronted effective irregular forces for the first time in early nineteenth-century New Spain, forces that threatened the Imperial edifice in Mexico, it fell to Félix Calleja to devise new tactics and strategy. Set-piece battles concurrently being refined on continental Europe as a result of Napoleon's successes were not going to defeat Mexican insurgents. That ambition marked Calleja's character, that he knew his military success would enhance his career, and that he possessed firm adherence to Madrid's Imperial mission helped shape his military response to insurgency. But what was unique in the context of Calleja's actions became less so as the nineteenth century and then the twentieth unfolded. Other Great Powers also faced insurgency in various parts of the globe, though not necessarily with the disastrous consequences that confronted Spain in the Americas by 1821, and from which Calleja's career emerged unscathed. The course of tsarist Russian arms in Central Asia in the mid-nineteenth century, British efforts in southern Africa for a quarter century after 1880, and Franco-American military adventures in southeast Asia after 1945[4] all showed the need for regular armies to adapt to new situations when irregular forces engaged in wars of independence. The results in these and other instances were mixed; but as Calleja's experience demonstrated when confronting the unexpected, the application of unorthodox tactics and strategy, which might have been seen as heresy, was necessary for victory.

Gooch points out that new technologies, such as armor and air power, also have done much to provoke the writing of new rules for modern warfare. Scot Robertson's examination of the Royal Air Force and the development of its interwar air doctrine under Sir Hugh Trenchard provides eloquent testimony to this. The question for all emerging air forces after 1918 involved whether to be defensive, offensive, or both. Depending on the answer to that question, should they be used solely to assist armies on the land and navies at sea, or should they also have an independent operational role?[5] This is why the matter of aerial bombardment assumed increasing importance between the two world wars of this century. Air power could not be "offensive" without a sizeable bomber force able to carry the war deep into the enemy's homeland. Adolf Hitler understood the deterrent value that long-range bombers could give his foreign policy, quite apart from any tactical and strategic value short-range ones could give German armor on the battlefield. Trenchard and others in Britain—both his supporters and critics—also grasped this essential dichotomy. However, aircraft were expensive. Fighters could protect Britain from aerial attack. Bombers could deter an enemy from launching raids on Britain out of fear of retaliation. The debate about air power fell into the political arena, since it meant determining where Britain's limited financial resources should be directed to produce the most effective air force.

The difficulty that Trenchard faced involved how to convince his critics—in his own service, in the army and the navy, and in the government—about the balance the Royal Air Force should have between its fighter and bomber commands. Indeed, debate hinged on what that balance should be. That the answer was not clear-cut resulted largely from the debate revolving around a new military technology that had not been tested to any major extent in the heat of battle. Thus, Trenchard's challenge involved transforming the unorthodox into the orthodox when the full implications of the weapons under consideration were not known.

Whereas Archer and Robertson essentially analyze external pressures that impinge on conventional military thinking and can create heresy—the rise of an unanticipated military threat and the advances in technology—Carol Reardon, Ivo Lambi, Ian Gow, and Michael Handel consider the role of personality. Their chapters are arresting in that they show that there are degrees of heretical behavior determined by the character of commanders within armed forces: at one end of the spectrum, there are those who can be considered moderate reformers (the younger officers in the Union Army during the American Civil War, epitomized by General Ulysses Grant); there are those in the middle who see the need to revise existing general strategies to ensure that the forces for which they are responsible can fulfill national ambitions (Admiral Alfred von Tirpitz and Admiral Katō Kanji); and at the other extreme, there are men whose personal weaknesses, for better or worse, significantly alter the accepted norms in the planning and execution of strategy and tactics (General Moshe Dayan).

Reardon carefully unravels the various strands that led to the improvement of the Union officer corps between 1861 and 1865. She does this by showing that when antebellum ideals of good military leadership began to erode because of the failure to achieve victory over the Confederacy by the second year of the Civil War, new approaches were called for in the Union Army itself, the political leadership in Washington, and among an array of thinkers who expressed themselves in print. This did not mean that there had to be a full-scale reform of Union generalship; rather, it had more to do with ensuring that technically competent officers were given responsibilities of command in place of those who did not understand the intricacies of an increasingly complex battlefield. It also meant the rise of officers, like Grant, General Sherman, and General Sheridan, who had the intellectual presence to assess a fluid situation and formulate tactics and strategy that could defeat the rebel armies. And not just the rebel armies. As Grant and Sherman understood, the entire political and economic structure of the South would have to be broken up to ensure that a Union military victory could be preserved once General Lee's forces had been rendered useless.

Tirpitz and Katō, on the other hand, were commanders whose branches of their respective armed forces were in many respects junior services: more specifically, they were admirals in states where military tradition involved the possession and use of land forces to meet the foreign and defense policy objectives determined by the Prusso-German and Japanese political leaderships. As Lambi and Gow demonstrate, this translated into Tirpitz and Katō fighting bureaucratic battles in peacetime to improve and expand the fighting capacity of their navies against inroads by politicians, budget-cutters, diplomats, and the entrenched strength of army commanders. In Tirpitz's case, he fought against the army, which, as one of the political and social bases of Prussia and then unified Germany, was the instrument by which Prusso-German greatness had been achieved under leaders from Frederick the Great to Bismarck. In his struggle, Tirpitz had the support of Emperor William II, himself a disciple of Alfred Thayer Mahan. They both looked for the emergence of Germany as a true world power, and the navy was the instrument to be brandished to achieve this ambition. But as Lambi shows, the heresy of Germany building a navy that threatened the British Royal Navy, let alone the diminution of the strength of the German Army caused by the diversion of public funds to the High Seas Fleet, proved ultimately to undermine Germany's national strength when World War I broke out.

Katō, on the other hand, occupied a leading position in the Imperial Japanese Navy, which, by dint of operational brilliance in the Russo-Japanese war of 1904–1905 and the fact that the German High Seas Fleet had been emasculated by the British and their allies during World War I, emerged by 1918 and 1919 as one of the three great navies in the world. But pressures were placed on the Imperial Japanese Navy in the decade after 1920, externally by the British and Americans, who wanted to ensure their own maritime preeminence, and domestically by Japanese politicians, diplomats, and some naval officers who wanted to appease the British and Americans in East Asia. In the view of Katō and his supporters, these pressures amounted to keeping Japanese naval forces inferior to Britain and the United States by arms limitation agreements at the Washington conference in 1921, at Geneva in 1927, and at London in 1930. Such strictures had to be loosened. Added to the traditional importance of the Japanese Army, which saw Japan's destiny on continental East Asia and for which land forces would be indispensable,[6] Katō's purpose involved getting his government to build the Imperial Japanese Navy to its maximum strength—in short, as Gow argues, to establish a naval policy that could be considered part of a new orthodoxy for the extension and protection of Japan's interests in the western Pacific and East Asia. In this, Katō mirrored Tirpitz; but those who have criticized Katō have failed to see that, in their eyes, his was not heresy. Rather, his actions entailed a revision of Japan's existing grand strategy to ensure that the navy could play an equal role in securing the national ambition to dominate in the region. Here, personality was crucial in that Katō, like Tirpitz, sought to enforce his concept of armed strength among less visionary countrymen—people hopelessly orthodox in mouthing traditional ideas about national survival, ideas that bore little semblance to the realities of international politics.

Moshe Dayan represents the most extreme kind of heretic in modern military history. With an innate determination to succeed, Dayan's ambition seems to have fueled his rise within the Israeli Defense Forces where, in 1967 and afterward, he took the leading role in the armed forces to defeat the combined forces of Israel's Arab enemies. Of course, Dayan believed passionately in Israel's destiny to survive in the hostile political and military environment of the Middle East—and not only survive, but prosper—yet he saw clearly that the only way to do this was to ensure that Israeli armed forces constituted a modern equivalent of "the sword of Gideon." In this Dayan was not alone, but in the political process some views dominate others; Dayan was determined that his views should hold the day. Thus, Dayan rose to the upper echelons of the Israeli Defense Forces by 1967 by outmaneuvering his critics, by ignoring their admonitions in his build-up of armed strength, and, based on what he had imbibed from that other extreme heretic, Orde Wingate, the development of tactics and strategies that would ensure Israel's survival against its Arab neighbors. After all, these neighbors vastly outnumbered Israel in population, which meant they had potentially more men to put in the field. A debate has arisen in Israel since Dayan's death in 1981 about the soundness of his ideas—his critics look to his private life, accusing him of salacious behavior with multiple mistresses, for ammunition to denigrate him. Nonetheless, it remains that Dayan played a pivotal role in defending Israel's national existence after 1967—both as the commander of the armed forces and, later, as defense minister. That he did so by giving heretical ideas practical form through the strength of his personality is undeniable.

There seems, finally, to be another sort of heretic. This is the commander who, during wartime, and despite previously being orthodox in his pursuit of the military art, realizes that traditional methods of conducting operations are inadequate. David Jones's discussion of General A. A.

INTRODUCTION

Brusilov is a case in point. Brusilov gained luster as a general by being the strategist who, during World War I, solved the deadly riddle of how to break through heavily defended trenches:[7] by 1916, the static struggles that marked trench warfare, in contradistinction to pre-1914 doctrines about movement and mobility, had become the new orthodoxy in Europe. Although Brusilov's ideas were never used effectively by tsarist armies after the summer of 1916, a result of supply problems that devolved from the chaos of the Russian transportation system, his heresy was used effectively by the German Army in its great—and last—offensive in 1918, which also failed for logistical reasons. Interestingly, until World War I Brusilov outwardly epitomized a traditional Imperial Russian army officer: he came from a military family; he was educated at Court; despite being orphaned, his family connections gave him an entry into the right circles at St. Petersburg; and he served with distinction in military operations against Turkey and in Central Asia in the latter part of the nineteenth century in a cavalry regiment noted for its conservatism. But some traits in Brusilov's character emerged in his younger years—exposed by Jones in what he calls an exercise in "psycho-history"; these paved the way for his conversion to unconventional tactics and strategy in 1916. Like life itself, which had been unkind to Brusilov in the early deaths of his mother and father, the exercise of military power was filled with problems. As a youth and young officer, Brusilov showed a penchant for seeing problems as not unsolvable but, instead, as difficulties that could be surmounted by careful study. He overcame such problems in his personal life by study and, then, by a distinctive boldness; this approach was later translated to the battlefield—in the Caucasus in the 1880s and in Galicia in 1916. Significantly, beginning when he was a young officer and throughout his military career, Brusilov considered himself to be a descendant of the great Russian military thinkers Suvorov and Dragomirov. When he fashioned his unconventional strategy in 1916, he felt that he was only refining what the traditionalists had done before him. That he did so by overcoming the orthodoxies of the tsarist and every other army then fighting in Europe, however, reveals much about his reputation for ignoring the norm and joining the ranks of military heretics.

In this way, these contributions outline the problems that Gooch describes about the making and breaking of the rules in modern war. In his afterword, John English seeks to put this process in the wider perspective by looking at the impact unorthodox military thinkers can have on others in the profession. Largely concentrating on three British "heretics" of the interwar period—J. F. C. Fuller, Basil Liddell Hart, and Herbert Richmond—English examines how their ideas were derided to a degree in

Britain and, yet, how they roused some influential contemporaries outside of Britain. In Fuller's case, in the best example, his conception about how to utilize the new technology of the tank effectively in future warfare had a decided influence on German officers such as Heinz Guderian and Americans such as George Patton. Certainly unconventional in thought, actively involved in dissent over the norms of the interwar British army, offering a radical departure from accepted doctrine, and possessing a forceful personality, Fuller offered a vision of the future that, though prescient, was breathtakingly heretical. In the same way and for the same reasons, Liddell Hart and Richmond deviated from what was felt to be acceptable in Britain, so that their ideas, too, created a sharp reaction. There seemed to be no middle ground for these heretics. Other officers, writers, and thinkers did not simply take or leave what Fuller and his fellow heretics said; they lined up firmly on one side or the other. This has largely been the fate of other military heretics.

This does not mean that orthodox military men were fools. Perhaps no officer in the modern period was more orthodox than the World War II British commander, General Archibald Wavell.[8] He served as the commander of British forces in North Africa from 1940 to 1941 and, beginning in January 1942, of Allied forces to oppose the Japanese in Southeast Asia. In January 1930, as a young brigadier, he had published an article in the *Journal of the Royal United Service Institution* on "The Army and the Prophets." He specifically named the "prophets"—Fuller, Liddell Hart, and General Hans von Seeckt, the commander-in-chief of the German Army during the early years of the Weimar Republic—and sympathized with them:

The problem which faces the reformer of armies in peace might be likened to that of an architect called on to alter and modernize an old-fashioned house without increasing its size, with the whole family still living in it (often grumbling at the architect's improvements, since an extra bathroom can only be added at the expense of someone's dressing room) and under the strictest financial limitations.[9]

Nonetheless, Wavell argued cogently that "military thought and ideas of all kinds ('lucid, average, incoherent' . . .) are being poured forth, far ahead of the possibilities for re-organization and re-equipment." It was not that the existing military high command in Britain failed to appreciate the changes in strategy and tactics that arose with World War I; quite simply they did appreciate them: machine-gun fire that reduced the effectiveness of infantry assault; increased artillery fire and the use of armor to "neutralize" the machine gun; advances in air power; the employment of poison gas; and the need for the civilian populations and industrial strength of the belligerents to support the men in the field to achieve victory. But the high command could not function in a political or financial vacuum. The bloodletting between 1914 and 1918 had led to a public revulsion of war that translated into postwar reductions of military spending beyond garrisoning the Empire and ensuring internal security. There were also fiscal restraints put on governments by the electorate to reduce arms spending in order to transfer public monies to social and other programs. Finally, "military administrators stood too close to the event to judge clearly the lessons of the war," so that "a period of assimilation was necessary before the true teaching of the war could be seen."

Thus, Wavell opined, "post-war armies came to differ from those of 1914 in detail rather than principle." Those responsible for the administrative, tactical, and strategic policies on which the army would function in the future did not differ from "the prophets" in the purpose for which the British armed forces were being readied—and, it was hoped, not to be employed. But Wavell cautioned: "Military progress follows civil progress, though at considerable distance." Given the political and financial climate in which the existing leadership—Wavell did not use the term, but he could have said "the orthodox"—had to plan and improve the British armed forces, the admonitions of "the prophets" were not unheeded. Instead, they were balanced with the military requirements that those responsible for armed forces had to consider in their planning. The difficulty was that no people in responsible positions in the government and the Imperial General Staff were willing to stake the future on what might occur; they had to consider what had occurred already, how this had altered the details of planning, and how armed forces *in situ* could be made more responsive to the anticipated problems. No one, least of all "the prophets," could guarantee how a future war might develop.

Wavell's article points nicely to the process that the contributors to this book have worked to understand and explain. Over the past two hundred years, and probably before, there has existed a dialectic through which military policy and strategy have been fashioned in a range of armed forces from those of the old Spanish Empire to Civil War America to Imperial Japan and the European Great Powers: an entrenched orthodoxy and the challenge of heretics. Heretical ideas have not always proved to be correct; orthodox ones have not always been based on the myopia and intransigence of conservative die-hards. Like any other human endeavor, the development of military policy and strategy has largely been an intellectual process. However, its controversy resides in the fact that it is a process that can have deadly consequences for soldiers, sailors, and airmen, and the nations they serve, if the surmises are incorrect. John Gooch and his colleagues have contributed markedly to the body of knowledge about modern military history, and they have done so in a way that seeks to put military heretics in an understanding but critical light.

NOTES

1. Friedrich von Bernhardi, *How Germany Makes War* (London, 1914), 11.
2. Compare P. Carell, *The Foxes of the Desert* (London, 1960); J. M. Fitère, *Panzers en Afrique: Rommel et l'Afrikacorps* (Paris, 1980); W. Heckmann, *Rommels Krieg in Afrika* (Garden City, NY, 1981); S. W. Mitcham, *Rommel's Last Battle: The Desert Fox and the Normandy Campaign* (New York, 1983); S. W. Mitcham, *Triumphant Fox: Erwin Rommel and the Rise of the Afrikakorps* (New York, 1984); and H. Speidel, *Invasion 1944: Ein Beitrag zu Rommels und des Reichs Schicksal* (Tübingen, 1949).
3. Compare A. J. Barker, *The Vainglorious War, 1854–56* (London, 1970); R. L. V. ffrench Blake, *The Crimean War* (London, 1971); Hew Strachan, "Soldiers, Strategy, and Sebastopol," *Historical Journal*, 21 (1978), 303–25; and P. Warner, *The British Cavalry* (London, 1984).
4. Compare Byron Farwell, *The Great Anglo-Boer War* (New York, 1976); T. Pakenham, *The Boer War* (London, 1979); Bruce Palmer, *The 25-Year War: America's Military Role in Vietnam* (Lexington, KY, 1978); Harry Summers, *On Strategy: A Critical Analysis of the Vietnam War* (San Francisco, 1982).
5. Compare Uri Bialer, *The Shadow of the Bomber: The Fear of Air Attack and British Politics, 1932–1939* (London, 1980); R. Higham, *Air Power: A Concise History*, rev. ed. (Manhattan, KS, 1984); H. M. Hyde, *British Air Policy between the Wars, 1918–1939* (London, 1976); Barry Powers, *Strategy without Slide-Rule: British Air Strategy, 1914–1939* (London, 1976); and Malcolm Smith, *British Air Strategy between the Wars* (Oxford, 1984).
6. On the argument that Japan was a "continental" Power, see A. D. Coox, *Nomonhan. Japan Against Russia, 1939* (Palo Alto, CA, 1985).
7. See Norman Stone, *The Eastern Front, 1914–1917* (London, 1975), 232–63.
8. See C. Barnett, *The Desert Generals*, new ed. (Bloomington, IN, 1982); J. R. Colville, *Wavell, Scholar and Soldier: To June 1941* (London, 1964); and J. R. Colville, *Wavell, Supreme Commander, 1941–1943* (London, 1969).
9. A. P. Wavell, "The Army and the Prophets," *Journal of the Royal United Service Institution*, 75 (1930), 666–75.

1

Making and Breaking the Rules: Orthodoxy, Heterodoxy, and Heresy in Modern War

John Gooch

On 31 October 1963, the Royal United Services Institution honored with its Chesney Gold Medal two of the most provocative military thinkers of the interwar years: Major-General J. F. C. Fuller and Captain Basil Liddell Hart. On such an auspicious occasion it is perhaps not surprising that neither man was congratulated for propounding a heresy, although that was the reaction of many of their contemporaries to the books and articles that eventually brought them acclaim. In his speech of reply, Fuller denied being a prophet—a laurel with which the chairman had not adorned him—on the grounds that he had "too much common-sense"; but he was prepared to label himself a missionary. His fellow prize winner characterized himself somewhat more aggressively as a crusader for military progress.[1]

Both men had made their careers in the quest for innovation in military thought and practice. Defining their status illustrates the distinctions in the taxonomy of change. The ideas of both men were too far removed from the accepted practices of the British military establishment of the 1920s merely to be labeled "unorthodox," and too well considered to be dismissed as simply "eccentric." Together, they constituted a strident challenge to a long-established concept of strategy. The environment into which they were introduced was nonpermissive, in the sense that it did not encourage radical re-thinking and change; and the system under which the British army operated in the 1920s was equally nonpermissive by virtue of its inflexible cast of mind.[2]

Barriers to change were erected in the nineteenth century in the shape of the rules or norms of strategic thought and tactical doctrine. The former tended more often to be universalistic and unchanging, the latter to be localized and varied. The permeability of these barriers largely depended—and still depends—on the degree to which circumstances created "permissive environments" and national military cultures represented "permissive systems" in which flexibility of thought and practice were allowed and encouraged. Since there were many varieties of military culture, and since perceptions of the need to respond to technological change varied, there were anticlericals of many kinds in the church of war.

In 1521 Machiavelli proposed in his *Arte della guerra* the existence of "general rules" of warfare, and from the early eighteenth century, writers began to seek to identify them, fueled by Baconian and Newtonian ideas of scientific inquiry. At the same time, Aristotelian neoclassicism reserved a place in war for the creative imagination and the actions of genius. De Saxe, Maizeroy, Guibert, and others sought definitive rules and systems in both spheres.[3] But principles and pragmatism could be uneasy bedfellows: the work of theorists such as E. H. Lloyd emphasized the changeability of war, on the one hand, while suggesting general rules of conduct on the other.[4] Theory was working toward a central problem—how much of military success depended upon the correct identification and application of right principles and how much upon individual mastery of contemporary circumstances—when Napoleon burst upon the scene.

Although the wars of the French Revolution and Empire were regarded by contemporaries as turning the military world upside down, they were in some ways less revolutionary than they seemed at the time. It is worth remembering that Napoleon was beaten on the field by a quintessentially conservative Wellington, and that the attack column dissolved before the withering fire of the line, a formation with a long pedigree by 1815. Nor were Napoleon's successes, remarkable though they must have seemed to contemporaries and as impressive as they remain today, won by the imaginative use of new military technologies. Weapons had changed little in their fundamentals since Marlborough's day. But Napoleon's battlefield virtuosity focused a process that had started not long before he first took up the sword and with it both set Europe on the path to general orthodoxy and opened up the possibility of heresy.

By his actions and by his example, Napoleon gave decisive support to the quest for a strategic orthodoxy. A firm believer in guiding principles of strategy, if not of tactics, he based what he liked to call his "strategimatical manoeuvres" on late eighteenth-century physics.[5] In analyzing the reasons for his success, his two great interpreters produced a strategic orthodoxy that ruled the nineteenth century and much of the twentieth. Jomini, who could fairly be labeled a reductionist, turned Napoleonic maxims and precepts that were meant for guidance into strategic commandments that, if neglected, exacted the supreme penalty of failure. Clausewitz produced in *On War* a work that was read as holy writ.

By the middle of the nineteenth century, the content and meaning of Napoleon's ideas and actions had been mediated through the works of these writers, establishing the belief that determinable and immutable principles of strategy existed. Mass, concentration, superiority of numbers at the decisive point, surprise, and the like became the canon laws of war. Differing weight might be put upon one or another, and points of interpretation were much debated, but it became a heresy to suggest that there were no principles of war at all and that everything depended upon the circumstances of the time and the actions of the day. Occasionally a challenger arose to question the general orthodoxy. M. I. Dragomirov, the Russian theorist of the late nineteenth century, doubted the existence of a military science, saying that that was as unthinkable as a science of poetry, painting, or music; but his was a rare voice.

Perhaps the most potent legacy of Napoleon—and one to which contemporary readings of Clausewitz contributed considerable force in the latter half of the century—was the belief that the decisive battle was the goal of the practical strategist.[6] The seductive notion that a correct application of the rules of strategy could permit a short campaign culminating in a definitive encounter was given considerable force in mid-century by the rapidity with which the Prusso-German wars of reunification of 1864 and 1866 were brought to victorious conclusions, and by the Italian wars of 1859, 1866, and 1870 that, if somewhat less glorious, were equally short and no less decisive.

By the second half of the nineteenth century orthodox strategic thinking propounded a belief in the short war. The Franco-Prussian war, however (which was not one campaign but two, in which the German armies took less than a month to rout the Second Empire and then another five months to defeat the people in arms raised by Leon Gambetta and Charles de Freycinet), suggested an alternative paradigm. Alert to the passions of the masses and the power of modern states, Helmuth von Moltke the elder uttered his celebrated warning to the Reichstag in May 1890 that the next war might last seven years or thirty.[7] In an age when principles and practice appeared to point to a quite different scenario, this was military heresy indeed. However, the German example embedded the orthodoxy of the short war in the minds of Europe's soldiers and politicians. So Kitchener's remark in August 1914, that the war that had just begun might last two years, was a private heresy that had little hold on either the military mind or the popular imagination. At the start of the twentieth century, strategic theory and the lessons of history appeared to converge appropriately enough—on the ghost of Napoleon.

Orthodoxy of a different kind characterized the world of early nineteenth-century military tactics. As John Mitchell put it in 1838 in his *Thoughts on Tactics*, tactics was "a poor and puny science," since there was little pressure to extend and rigorize it.[8] The frozen state of military thought was largely due to the preeminence of drill—indeed, tactics were widely viewed as being little more than field drill. Drill itself was a repetition not merely of movements but of the ideas of previous generations or of other people. The French army went back to the drill book of 1791, which it reproduced in 1831 and again in 1862. An attempt to revise it in 1844 was obstructed by the Infantry Committee "with religious fervour."[9] In 1838 the Sardinians, seeking a guiding corpus of tactical rules, merely copied the French regulations. What counted in their book was simply the regularity and precision of movement.[10]

In a world where little had changed in terms of weaponry, the small professional armies of Britain, France, and Prussia simply reverted to eighteenth-century practices. The British did not feel the need to try to agree on a theory of tactics suitable for the age, and the French were not able to do so. Tactics were largely overlooked in French military writing between 1830 and 1870. When they were accorded attention, complex taxonomies were created that sought to predict the outcomes of all possible combinations of arms in combat, with the result that the French were unable to agree on anything very precise. What prevailed in the first half of the nineteenth century, then, was a kind of unsystematized orthodoxy in which generals simply ransacked their memories for whatever feature of eighteenth-century practice looked best suited to their circumstances and laid down their own personal guidelines. Unified doctrine—and with it the possibility of heresy—was nonexistent. General Ambert's observation in 1841 that "One goes into battle as if to one's mistress: the same palpitations, the same embraces, same hopes and same uncertainties" was another, and less cerebral, way of putting Voltaire's observation that the art of war, like that of medicine, was murderous and conjectural.[11]

In Prussia the uncomplicated tactics of the early nineteenth century, embodied in the Prussian infantry regulations of 1847 and 1853, prescribed first the fire-fight and then the decisive attack by closed columns, the whole covered in its preparations by squads of skirmishers.[12] These were tactics born in the age of the musket, and they were employed with success during the Austro-French war of 1859 by French troops in Italy and also by Garibaldi, who, if imaginative in the use he made of surprise, mobility, and reconnaissance, was certainly no heretic in his preference for mass column attacks with the bayonet when in combat.[13]

The tactics of the eighteenth century proved to be costly in the war of 1859—but successful. The result, as far as the infantry was concerned, was a decade of tactical orthodoxy, although the change from smoothbore to rifled guns created so many uncertainties that artillery doctrine was quite unclear. On the eve of the Franco-Prussian war, technological innovations were slowly beginning to transform tactical practices; but no unambiguous challenge to orthodoxy had as yet appeared. An official French committee mused: "The more one studies the improvements recently introduced into the armaments of various powers, the more one is inclined to ask if the prescriptions of our training instructions can still suffice to meet the exigences [sic] of the new situation."[14] The answer lay in the belief that the tactical orthodoxies of the Napoleonic age would still work. It took the Franco-Prussian war to demonstrate the backwardness of the old European tactics when used against modern armaments.

The one possible source from which to derive an apparently much needed dose of the unorthodox in the nineteenth century appeared to be colonial warfare. Here was a permissive environment quite unlike that on the continent, where the unorthodox, the eccentric, and the unwanted could be allowed free rein. Some historians have spoken of the "drawbacks of . . . prolonged immersion . . . in colonial warfare," and of the advantage conferred on Prussia-Germany, the only country that did not have to fight colonial wars in the nineteenth century, thereby avoiding an experience in which "morale and mystique could acquire disproportionate importance."[15] Certainly men like Bugeaud liked to portray themselves—and were frequently portrayed—as practitioners of new, unorthodox, and effective methods. They were far from averse to charges of heresy, and such charges were frequently leveled at them.[16]

In practice, however, much colonial warfare simply involved making effective use of classic eighteenth-century practices. Bugeaud favored close-range fire and he, St. Arnaud, and the Africans sought to recapture the great days of Napoleon before his art had been corrupted by "gigantism." British generals, too, transported classic methods abroad, relying heavily on their skills at logistics and resorting to echelon attacks and shock tactics. Even skirmishing was extended to the colonies.[17] In 1879 and 1882, the British army used the line and square, long obsolete in European warfare, in colonial campaigns.

The appearance of the unorthodox in colonial warfare was perhaps greater than the reality. In 1870, the contrast between the Jominian formalism of European armies and the stress of the "Africans" on the morale elements of war gave the appearance of two traditions coexisting uneasily; but, in fact, the idea of the importance of the morale element in war and of mobility dated back to the French Revolution and had been present in metropolitan thinking, though not as prominently as in the colonies.[18] What colonial soldiering appears to have provided was an alternative model for European armies mired in routine. How great the differences between colonies and continent really were remains to be explored properly, but they may well have been exaggerated by contemporaries on both sides. The Russian army, after all, fought mobile campaigns in the Caucasus yet in the Crimean War reverted to close-order drill and mass tactics. In theory, colonial campaigns could function as experimental laboratories in which to devise and test new methods. In practice, they were unnecessary in armies that operated "permissive systems," and ineffective in those that did not.

In Germany, the rapidity with which pre-1870 tactical forms were abandoned demonstrated the flexibility of a permissive system. Disorder was deliberately practiced at the tactical level "so that, when reduced to that condition, we may be able to move and fight."[19] In 1876 the column of attack was renounced in favor of deploying infantry in extended formations, and by 1896 frontal attacks had been abandoned for extended fronts and envelopment.[20] The stress laid on discipline, conscious commitment, and the development of "self-assertiveness" was paralleled by the growing emphasis on the responsibility of officers to act on their own initiative if the orders they had received were not issued with full knowledge of the situation. In an army dedicated to tactical pragmatism there could be no heretics: there was neither the need nor the place for them.

In Italy, "controlled permissiveness" degenerated into something more chaotic. Regulations were repeatedly altered in the decades before World War I and, in any case, were devised as the loosest of guidelines: in 1885, the *General Regulation for the Employment of the Three Arms in Combat* announced that regulations were a guide only and that commanders were free to choose the mode of execution best calculated to gain the desired ends. Until 1913, there were no regulations at all for formations larger than a division. The result was an army with no real doctrine and one that permitted, encouraged, and even relied upon common-sense variations in the official "norms" at the whim of the commanding general.[21]

France presents a third model that somehow managed to fuse a covering dogma—the efficacy of the attack—with a lack of any set of logical rules. Seizing with enthusiasm on a Clausewitz in whom contemporaries saw the "incomparable merit" of informality, the French emphasized the decisive factors that would overcome firepower—speed, initiative, and, above all, will.[22] The French took from their reading of Clausewitz and Napoleon the idea of will as the objective and added to it the traditional concept of will as the means, jettisoning on the way the weapons technology lessons of the war of 1870 to 1871. The transformation took no more than a dozen years: the infantry regulations of 1875 spoke eloquently of the effects of the range, accuracy, and rapidity of rifle fire on the battlefield and advised that troops be broken up in dispersed order, whereas those of 1887 announced the gospel of the attack pure and simple.[23]

The offensive became a dogma deeply ingrained in the psyche of the French army. Thus, shortly before World War I, when Lanrezac lectured at the École Militaire, he chose momentarily to depart from the orthodox line: "Gentlemen, the windows are closed, no one is listening at the doors. . . . very well, I'm going to talk to you for a moment about the defensive."[24] Skeptics included Carey de Bellemare, who opposed the idea that leadership would conquer firepower. His heresy was so great that in the interwar years, he was compared to de Gaulle, Negrier, and Kessler, each of whom saw the need to avoid certain losses by flank envelopment, and, most famously, to Pétain, with his pragmatic challenge to orthodoxy: "Firepower kills." The existence of such critics suggests that the French army possessed a degree of tolerance toward those who did not profess the common faith; its failure to effect any significant alteration in the ruling dogma demonstrates that the system in which it operated was not genuinely permissive.

Whether it sprang from the lower reaches of the armed forces or was a more complex organizational and institutional response to the needs of the time, the offensive became the goal of the army.[25] It was, however, a jewel without a crown, for there was no body of doctrine of any scientific kind to support putting the offensive into practice. The social and political strife that characterized the French army after 1900 reached its nadir under the liberal hand of General André, who encouraged everyone to "select a system in harmony with his own character, energy, temperament, aptitudes."[26] Recognizing that orthodoxy in France was nothing more than chaos, Joffre announced on his appointment as chief of staff in 1911 that his first task was to create and impose a coherent doctrine; but Plan XVII represented unconsidered obeisance to the god of the offensive.

Whereas Germany operated a permissive system, pre-1914 Britain presented a permissive environment. The range of tasks that the British army might be called upon to fulfill negated the idea of any single doctrinal orthodoxy, and the absence of any intellectual consensus about the nature of strategy helped to generate a multiplicity of opinion. Empiricists professed skepticism over the existence of immutable principles or doubted their value: G. F. R. Henderson thought the rules of strategy were few and of little value in teaching generals; J. F. Maurice believed that there never was and never would be an art of war "which was something other than the resultant of accumulated military experience"; and Spenser Wilkinson believed that no two wars were alike. Rejecting these views, "Continentalists" such as Maude and Lonsdale Hale saw Germany as their model and pinned their tactical faith to the offensive and the importance of the morale factor. Meanwhile the imperialists of the Wolseley ring, who believed that Britain would never again fight in Europe, snapped at "slavish imitations from the Prussians."[27]

The long drawn out and bitter feud over cavalry doctrine demonstrated the doctrinal confusion that such an environment could encourage. Supporters of a mounted infantry, armed with rifles, and proponents of the *arme blanche* each accused the other of the deepest heresy. The latter group were themselves riven between those who favored the lance and those whose preference was the sword, thereby creating room for true eccentrics such as Major-General Brabazon, who solemnly informed the members of the Royal Commission on the War in South Africa of his "life-long mistrust of the weapons supplied to the cavalry, and of his preference for shock tactics by men armed with the Tomahawk."[28]

By the close of the nineteenth century, land warfare was conceived in terms of a commonly accepted strategic dogma but regulated by a variety of tactical systems. At sea, naval strategy and tactics were in a state of flux until the arrival of Mahan in 1890 provided a strategic dogma. In the half-century before, technological change in propulsion and armaments came at such a pace that the operational capacities and capabilities of ships of war were difficult to fathom. Perpetual novelty was not an environment that favored any single orthodoxy. The impossibility of working out any fixed body of thought in these circumstances was concisely summed up in the observation made, in the face of much confusion, by a tactical commission of the French navy in 1853: "*Le mot ne vient qu'après la chose.*"[29]

In the absence of an established body of specifically naval thought, professionals and amateurs were applying land tactics and methods to sea warfare by the middle of the century. Sharp differences between national orthodoxies were evident in the contrasting theories of the Russian navy under Admiral Boutakoff, characterized by strict centralized control of the fleet in battle, and the "chaos" theory favored by the French in which command was delegated from the fleet to divisions, squadrons, and even individual ships. Naval warfare, in short, was in the grip of profound uncertainties about the ends for which it existed, the means to bring those ends about, and the methods to employ in battle.[30] To sailors who did not know what to believe or where to look for true guidance, Mahan offered certitude. To him, the fact that the "rapid, many sided activity in the development of weapons produces a confusion in the mind which must by all means be ended" made it imperative that an art of naval warfare be developed.[31] Steam made that art possible by producing precision and certainty in the movement of fleets. The result is described in *The Influence of Sea Power upon History, 1660–1783*, published in 1890, and the flood of books and articles that followed.[32]

The eagerness with which Mahan's work was received by navies and politicians around the world was a reflection of the fact that he had in one stroke provided the answers to many of the questions of the previous half-century. The goal of seapower was command of the sea; the means to achieving that goal was the decisive naval battle; the instruments were the new capital ships; and the method was concentration. These were the rules of naval strategy according to Mahan. From them, his readers drew the corollary that there was an orthodox naval battle in which capital ships contested command of the sea. By making this the objective, Mahan closed the door that had previously allowed freedom of action at sea. Mahan's ideas effected a Pauline conversion on his generation. Not only had the naval purpose of battle fleets at last been made clear but so, too, had their broader political function. The American Rear Admiral Bradley Fiske was one who experienced the revelation. After a talk with Admiral Stephen Luce, Mahan's patron and mentor, at the Naval War College in 1903, Fiske wrote: "Before hearing Luce talk that bright summer morning, I had had a vague idea that war was merely a situation in which great numbers of men or of ships fought one another. I had had no clear idea connected with war except that of fighting."[33] Like Fiske, naval officers the world over raised their eyes from the barrels of their guns and the decks of their ships to greater visions. That they were able to do so was the direct consequence of Mahan's remarkable feat of creating a naval orthodoxy virtually overnight. In Henry Stimson's memorable simile, Mahan became the true prophet, and the navies who adopted his commandments became the church assembled.

Mahan's firm and uncompromising dogmas invited challenge, not least because they were based on an interpretation of historical evidence and history that was too varied and too complex to be a secure foundation for certain faith. Scarcely twenty years passed before Julian Corbett challenged almost every part of the Mahanian catechism. Dispersion, not concentration, was the key to success at sea; the primary object of a fleet was not to seek out and destroy an enemy fleet but to secure and use sea communications; the main instrument of naval action was not the capital ship but the cruiser—a heresy Corbett compounded by talking of "intermediate ships" (battle cruisers) and the "structureless fleets."[34] It is therefore hardly surprising that the naval officers to whom he lectured frequently found his ideas "contrary to those generally accepted."[35]

Corbett did not directly substitute one dogma for another; the range of activities he prescribed in order to secure, dispute, and exercise command of the sea was too varied. But he did come very close to doing so by replacing the Mahanian orthodoxy of the decisive battle with his own ark of the covenant: the use of sea power to carry out overseas expeditions. Corbett's ideas found great favor with Admiral "Jacky" Fisher, the British first sea lord from 1904 to 1910, who often declared in ringing tones that the army was a projectile to be fired by the navy; but it did not greatly endear itself to many others. At a broader level, Corbett's ideas were heresy for many of his contemporaries because they challenged the shibboleths of every major navy that was—or fancied itself to be—a bluewater battle fleet.

The convergence of technological development and Mahanian thought reconfirmed the traditional value put on capital ships and decisive battles. It was on this ground that a contest developed in the early years of the twentieth century between the orthodox, whose vision of naval warfare hinged on central control of a stereotypical battle, and the unorthodox, who demanded a mere permissive and flexible operational doctrine. Both Tirpitz and Fisher believed in the importance of hitting power and of the battleship (although Fisher began to favor the battle cruiser toward the end of his career).[36] Both hallowed the line of battle as the centrality of naval operations and the maneuver of "crossing the T" as the commanding rite of battle. War at sea, unlike war on land, was under the sway of a common dogma at a time when extensive technological innovation cast into question many of its central tenets. In these circumstances, both in Britain and in Germany, men arose to challenge the new orthodoxy.

In Britain, Custance, Bridge, Noel, and Richmond opposed the "big ship" mentality and the single line of battle; and in Germany, Hollman, von Koerster, and Oldekop advocated cruiser warfare. Dewar, an archheretic in Britain, even wrote of "this highly artificial conception of two fleets meeting in massed formation, rapidly deploying into line and solemnly engaging in a methodical artillery duel at long range"; and a German contemporary, Admiral von Mentey, spoke scornfully of the exercises in which such fleet tactics were regularly practiced in peacetime as "*à la polonaise.*"[37] The heretics were reacting against the straightjacket of strategic orthodoxy and the interpretation of the benefits of technology for a war at sea, and seeking a return to what they saw as an earlier Nelsonic tradition of divisional control.

Fisher, who was in some respects highly conventional, accepted as orthodoxy the doctrine of centralized control. He was quickly challenged by heretics such as Dewar, Richmond, and Sturdee, who sought devolved divisional control.[38] The attempt to introduce a more permissive system into fleet operations can be seen in Admiral Sir David Beatty's battle-cruiser tactical notes of 1913; in them he emphasized the need for individual captains to use their initiative without fear of accepting responsibility and allowed them to exercise their own discretion in conditions the admiral could not be expected to anticipate.[39] The centralization of control is apparent in Admiral Jellicoe's "Battle Orders for the Grand Fleet" from August 1914, which permitted individual captains, or even divisional admirals, to exercise only very limited discretion and emphasized the lead that was to be given and accepted by the admiral's flagship.[40] However, what seems to have been a clash of doctrines more properly represents a differentiation of function, Jellicoe's apparently impermissive operational system being the necessary consequence of the need to get all the guns of the fleet into action simultaneously in any engagement if he was not to run a serious risk of defeat.

With the outbreak of war in 1914 came the moment of truth for prewar military and naval orthodoxies. Although all parties suffered early setbacks on land, the generals stuck to their strategic guns. Rigidly hierarchical systems of command meant that Joffre, French, Haig, and Cadorna were not only untroubled about the correctness of their ideas, but they were untouched by pressure from subordinates to reconsider their methods and recalculate their plans.[41] In such circumstances, and since the generals either retained the confidence of their political masters or were too powerful to be removed, only massive and inescapable military failure could cause orthodoxy to buckle. This had to wait until 1917, when the triple agonies of the Ainse offensive, the Passchendaele campaign, and the battle of Caporetto forced changes at the top of two armies and alterations in the operational methods of all three.

Elsewhere more permissive environments enabled the unorthodox to experiment with new ways of doing old things. Although their individual circumstances were entirely different, Brusilov in Russia and Lawrence in Arabia were in positions that were not entirely dissimilar. The creation of autonomous "fronts" in Russia in 1914 produced a permissive environment that offered Brusilov the freedom to experiment in a way in which no British or French army commander on the Western Front could ever hope to do. In Brusilov's case necessity, in the shape of a shortage of artillery ammunition, was the midwife of the unorthodox.[42] Far from G. H. Q. in Cairo, and given free rein by Allenby, Lawrence, too, could experiment to his heart's content—with the added advantage that using the methods he had devised did not involve converting his followers from one military doctrine to another. But opportunities such as these were relatively uncommon.

As the world war drew on, armies learned how to fight better in the new conditions they faced. They learned at different speeds and in different ways, with the result that established orthodoxies were often difficult to modify and impossible to overturn. Their success—or otherwise—seems to have depended to a considerable degree on the philosophies with which they entered the war and on the command systems that expressed those philosophies: some encouraged flexibility, others did not.[43] The best example of a permissive system was the German army. Here observation, learning, and change were the order of the day as much in war as in peace. Operational innovations were more or less continuous, beginning with the complex trench systems constructed in 1914 and reaching their apogee with the dissemination of "storm troop" tactics throughout the army after Ludendorff had inspected a company of the assault battalion "Rohr" in September 1916.[44] By the later stages of the war, specialist units in most armies were using the new combat methods; only the Germans institutionalized them.

At sea, technological developments both fragmented navies and forced them to become less rigid and more permissive. The tyranny of the Mahanian capital ship encounter was not exorcized from the Royal Navy, but its experience at Jutland stimulated a move away from strict battle orders toward greater flexibility and some devolution of command. As far as Germany was concerned, circumstances altered cases, and early U-boat successes gave powerful support to the proponents of a *guerre-de-course* strategy. A combination of submarine opportunities and surface anxieties converted Tirpitz to the cause of the submarine in the winter of 1915–1916, and in February 1917 the heretics won the day with the introduction of unrestricted U-boat warfare. However, the naval system had not become a permissive one: Bauer and Michelson, successive U-boat commanders, sought in vain to be allowed to hunt in "wolf packs" but were unable to dent the adamantine doctrinal shell of the Admiralty Staff.[45] In the Mediterranean, the dramatic successes of the MAS torpedo boats and the "human torpedoes" of the Italian navy demonstrated the challenge that technology now posed to Mahanian orthodoxies.

Before World War I, the orthodox and the unorthodox were rivals in speculation; after the war ended, they disagreed on the interpretation of experience. On land, Maginot, Metaxas, and Mannerheim gave their names to lines of fortification that embodied a belief in the strength of the defensive and in the need for massive supremacy and careful preparation before any attack could reasonably be launched. The "short-war" illusion had been replaced by the "long-war" scenario. The difficulty of mastering the modern battlefield, and the high cost that faulty or inadequate doctrine would be likely to exact, led the French army to develop a rigid operational orthodoxy that revolved around the *bataille conduite*, stressing preparation and not improvisation, the employment of carefully constructed timetables, and the imposition of centralized command. Since the goal of France's armies would not be to break through the enemy's lines, but methodically to destroy its equipment in slow, remorseless battles, tanks were allocated the subordinate role of accompanying the infantry.[46]

The image of war that bred such a cautious professional orthodoxy did not unnaturally alarm the political leaders of the Western democracies, many of whom were inclined through personal experience to believe in it and, therefore, put much of their energy during the interwar years into averting the reality. It also encouraged the unorthodox to revise the paradigm by demonstrating that its proponents underestimated the potential of motorization and mechanization. In the late 1920s and early 1930s a cohort of revisionists went into action across Europe: Collins and Hobart in England; Gamelin and Weygand in France; Grazioli, Visconti Prasca, and Zoppi in Italy; and Tukhachevsky in Soviet Russia.

Whether or not the new ideas were transmuted into orthodoxies depended to a considerable extent on the political environment into which they were released. In Russia, Tukhachevsky was able to fasten his ideas onto a prerevolutionary military tradition of deep penetration raids, the lessons of the civil war, and the aggressive dimensions of Marxist-Leninist dogma, with the result that military and political revolution marched hand-in-hand until 1937. Then a conservative reaction swept away both the new ideas and their chief progenitor.[47] In Fascist Italy, the modernizers who sought to make the army mobile, offensive, and hard-hitting— by no means all of whom were active party members—collided with the inflexible conservatism of the military high command and the Fascist conception of a mass army that militated against an elite, professional mechanized force. In this largely nonpermissive environment, progress was patchy but complete by the time that war came in 1940.[48]

In England, Fuller and Liddell Hart—"the scientific visionaries"— propounded theories that went so far beyond the bounds of orthodoxy as to qualify them as heretics, not least because their works were abstractions that were not based on experiment. Overturning one of the central canons of strategic orthodoxy, they both argued that the object to be attacked in war was not the enemy's physical mass but its psychological center of balance. Their ideas about the decisive role to be played by tanks and mechanized infantry—which were not as different from one another as Liddell Hart afterwards liked to make out—failed to revolutionize the attitudes and activities of the British army. This was not so much because of innate military conservatism but because they were, for a variety of reasons, impractical.[49] In interwar Britain, cuts in the defense budgets did much to create a nonpermissive environment that was at least as significant a barrier to Fuller and Liddell Hart as the nonpermissive system that neglected the lessons of the Great War.

In *Vers l'armée de métier*, published in 1934, Charles de Gaulle went further than either Fuller or Liddell Hart in challenging accepted orthodoxies. His heresy was not merely technological but also social and political, for in propounding his beliefs on the supreme importance of mechanization, he attacked the fundamental shibboleths of *la France militaire* that had grown up since 1871 and even the traditions of the Revolution itself. De Gaulle challenged the spirit of 1792 by arguing that the French did not have an aptitude for mass action: "It does not seem as though the spirit of discipline, the taste for being herded together, the capacity for acting in waves, in which consist the massive strength of hordes, has been given to us to any large extent," he declared.[50] To fill this national lacuna, and to master the revolution in tactics heralded by the advent of the tank, de Gaulle proposed the creation of a small, long-serving professional army that would be able to use the mobility and speed of the new machines to achieve what had eluded the generals of the Great War—operations in depth, penetration, and exploitation.[51]

Here was massive heresy, for de Gaulle was coupling advocacy of the technologically new with rejection of established French military tradition and, at the same time, denying national conceptions of France's military virtues. Politically his ideas threatened the basis of the Third Republic, which by the 1930s was demonstrating a profound suspicion of generals and standing forces as potential tools of the right. They carried alarming undertones of Boulangisme with their author's assertion that to institute them would require a leader of irreproachable military authority and public popularity, and this did not increase their attractiveness in many political quarters. The army responded by smothering de Gaulle with arguments for administrative caution and strategic passivity: the expense of adding an all-professional force to a cadre of 106,000 was too great, and tanks were in any case aggressive weapons when France had adopted a defensive posture. By proclaiming the overriding merits of professionalism, de Gaulle had attacked not merely one orthodoxy but two. In this case the consequence of heresy was that orthodox conservatism was able to resist mechanization even more strongly than it could otherwise have done.[52]

In Germany there were no properly defined heretics, despite Guderian's attempt after the war to claim the starring role in a lonely drama and falsely recruit an overseas mentor—Liddell Hart—and thereby reinforce his heresy.[53] Ever flexible, the German army amalgamated mechanization with mobile war and people's war so that, in Michael Geyer's words, by 1929 tank warfare was the "main thrust of army modernization."[54] Doctrinal flexibility, traditional in the German army, exactly suited the needs of machine age warfare in which mobility, concentrated firepower, and the possibilities of devolved command through radio nets played to the very virtues that the Kaiser's army had encouraged. The permissiveness of the German military system was reinforced by army officer training in the 1920s that, under von Seeckt's determined guidance, emphasized qualities of character, independence of judgment, and initiative; discouraged the search for "school solutions"; and fought against formalism in tactical and operational thought.[55] Albert Wedemeyer found on being ordered to Kriegsakademie in 1936 that the same basic attitudes still flourished there. The emphasis on practical problems and individual decisions was a strong contrast to the extreme theoreticism of Fort Leavenworth.[56]

In Nazi Germany, unlike Fascist Italy, a forward-looking group of modernizers was able to join forces in 1933 with a galvanizing political regime—ultimately to their own and everyone else's detriment. Political circumstances permitted, and military preferences encouraged, a marriage of conventional tactical flexibility, innovative thinking, and material development. To be sure, there were conservatives in Germany in the 1930s, both political and military, but they did not thrive in the atmosphere of re-armament. In the topsy-turvy world of the Third Reich, to utter caution and calculate in conventional terms in the face of diplomatic and military opportunism was heresy.[57]

If technology threatened the orthodoxies of land war in the 1920s and 1930s, it doubled the uncertainties in naval circles. Sometimes the potential of the new technology was exaggerated to the point of individual or collective eccentricity: in the late 1920s, the French navy was toying with the idea of giant 1500-ton submarines, while at the beginning of the decade the Royal Navy's director of naval construction had proposed building submersible battleships. However, even in politically favorable environments, unorthodoxy was reined in by caution. In Italy, radical innovators argued that the capital ship had no future and sought to replace it with a fleet of submarines, MAS boats, and airplanes. Since they offered a cheap way to contest British domination of the Mediterranean, their ideas appealed to Fascism's "strategic adventurism"; however, the conservative naval high command aimed at building a balanced fleet in its construction programs in the 1930s.[58]

The same attitude of naval orthodoxy was also visible in Nazi Germany. Under the command of Admiral Raeder—the naval traditionalist *par excellence*—plans for a balanced fleet went ahead until 1938.[59] Then, in the face of war with Britain, Raeder was prepared to abandon battleship construction in order to have four battle cruisers ready by 1943. On this occasion, a conservative politician overruled an unorthodox proposal: Hitler recalled Raeder to the balanced fleet concept embodied in the Z-Plan in January 1939.[60]

Unorthodox ideas made relatively little headway in any of the major navies before 1939. This was partly a function of professional uncertainties about whom each navy would be called on to fight, and when and where. But it was no less a function of uncertainty about how the fighting would take place. The line of battle still held sway and "crossing the T" was still the holy grail of naval battle; but sailors now recognized what they had not realized before 1914—that orthodox engagements in which battle fleet met battle fleet were likely to be rare. Different circumstances, different conditions, and even different places would shape the "mix" of units that would be used. Navies were therefore commonly permissive in their outlook in the sense that they felt they had to be ready for anything.

Nothing, of course, challenged conventional thinking between the wars as much as the advent of the airplane and the ideas of its most radical theorist, Giulio Douhet. In the space of little more than four years, he moved from the unorthodox to the visionary. In a series of articles written in 1910, he had pointed to the fact that the skies were about to become "a battlefield as important as the land or the sea," and before World War I was six months old, he was making prophetic claims for air power: "To shoot down enemy airplanes, to gain the command of the air is to render the enemy harmless in the air ... to gain command of the air is to be able to attack with impunity any point of the enemy's body."[61] Douhet was not alone in foreseeing a major role for airplanes in modern war. In November 1917, Trenchard was already emphasizing the need for sustained and aggressive long-distance bombing in order both to weaken enemy morale and inflict material damage.[62] However, Douhet's theory of the primacy of air power, put forward in *The Command of the Air* in 1921, offered a comprehensive challenge to the most basic rationales of both land and sea power.

The doctrines developed by airmen in the 1920s and 1930s were self-consciously new and avowedly heretical. They even denied the canons of strategic orthodoxy that had been established during the course of the nineteenth century: "The principles of war do not apply to the air," Trenchard once remarked at a chiefs-of-staff meeting.[63] In one sense, Douhet's ideas did not depart radically from that orthodoxy: the emphasis on the air fleet and on the strangulation of the enemy's economy had, it has been claimed, Mahanian undertones.[64] Yet in another more fundamental sense, Douhetian doctrines were revolutionary to the point of heresy: they challenged the classic belief that victory was won by the direct clash between armed forces for mastery of the field. Air power, used in a preemptive strike, could cripple an adversary before it had time to recover. It could bring a war to a victorious conclusion at a low cost and in a short time. And it could do so unaided, or virtually so: the operations of armies and navies were henceforth of no more than secondary importance. Pétain detected this interweaving of the conventional and the radical, remarking on it in his preface to the French edition of *The Command of the Air*: "Profoundly classic in its starting point and in its method, it reaches conclusions which are unorthodox. Take care in treating lightly as a utopian dreamer a man who perhaps will be regarded, in the future, as a prophet."[65]

For Douhetian heresies to transmute into orthodoxies, they had to be institutionalized. The creation of the Royal Air Force in April 1918 provided an independent institutional vehicle wherein Trenchard could forcefully propound his theories of independent air power. The interservice rivalries that ensued were bitter. Trenchard's claim that air substitution could police the empire more cheaply and more effectively than land forces challenged the deepest tenets of imperial military control; and the proposition that aircraft and not big guns offered the best defense for Singapore was so heretical to the Royal Navy that they called on Mahan in their successful attempts to refute it. British air power survived and flourished in the 1930s largely thanks to external political support in the person of Neville Chamberlain. In Germany, France, and Italy, Douhetian ideas failed to flower, even when independent air forces were created, because of a combination of the preeminence of land power and the lack of external political support powerful enough to overcome the innate orthodoxy of the airmen.[66] In the United States, Billy Mitchell's demands for an independent air arm led to his court martial and conviction.[67] To the United States Navy he was guilty of heresy; to the United States Army he was guilty of the deeper sin of apostasy. The feeling in the army establishment that proponents of air power were traitors was one that lingered in the minds of American airmen.[68]

Technology and theory alike were put to the test between 1939 and 1945. The result was the triumph of orthodoxy. Lightning attacks by the armored spearheads of the *Wehrmacht* dislocated and defeated a physically and intellectually disorganized opponent in the West but failed when faced with the vast spaces of the Russian steppes.[69] In the skies, the classic principle that the enemy's forces must be defeated before the air could be freely used was confirmed in 1943 and 1944, and the Anglo-American bomber offensive began to inflict major damage on Germany only in the closing stages of the war. The war at sea was more protean, which is what most prewar sailors had anticipated, but the battle of the North Atlantic confirmed that control of the sea, like command of the air, had first to be won before it could be used to defeat an opponent.

The political leaders took a greater hand in running World War II than their predecessors had done in World War I. Franklin Roosevelt intervened in strategic issues, though he generally left his commanders to get on with the fighting. Hitler interfered with the land war with increasing frequency, eventually taking it over and fighting it like the corporal he had once been. Churchill, who was liable to flights of strategic fancy that generally seemed to those around him less heretical than wildly impractical, finally put his trust in a general of almost impeccable orthodoxy—Bernard Montgomery.

Many of the challenges to orthodoxy mounted in the second half of the nineteenth century and the first half of the twentieth century, whether in strategic thought or tactical norms, were generated by differing responses to technological change. Whether those challenges have been regarded as evolutionary developments, which are to be accommodated, or revolutionary developments, which new regimes may be inclined to embrace and established regimes moved to reject, has in turn depended upon the environment into which they were injected and the systems of operation of the armies, navies, and air forces confronted by them. Strategic rules in their modern form were the creation of the nineteenth century. Distinctive military cultures, which may foster and encourage some qualities in preference to others, have a longer history.[70] Although the nature of warfare has changed since 1945, these underlying factors have not—suggesting that orthodoxy and heresy in military policy and strategy are likely to confront one another in the nuclear age just as they did in the century that preceded it.

NOTES

1. A. J. Trythall, *"Boney" Fuller: The Intellectual General* (London, 1977), 259–60; see also Brian Holden Reid, *J. F. C. Fuller: Military Thinker* (London, 1987), 217.
2. For a vivid depiction of the collective mentality of the British officer corps in the 1920s, see Brian Bond, *British Military Policy between the Two World Wars* (Oxford, 1980), 35–71.
3. Azar Gat, *The Origins of Military Thought from the Enlightenment to Clausewitz* (Oxford, 1989). See also John I. Alger, *The Quest for Victory: The History of the Principles of War* (Westport, CT, 1982). B. H. Liddell Hart, *The Ghost of Napoleon* (London, 1933), though dated, remains useful.
4. The best general discussion of Lloyd's work is Franco Venturi, "Le avventure del generale Henry Lloyd," *Rivista storica italiana*, 91 (1979), 369–433.
5. Carolyn Shapiro, "Napoleon and the Nineteenth Century Concept of Force," *Journal of Strategic Studies*, 11 (1988), 509–19. For an excellent description of Napoleon's system of command, see Martin van Crefeld, *Command in War* (Cambridge, MA, 1985), 58–102.
6. Lorenzo Crowell, "The Illusion of the Decisive Napoleonic Victory," *Defence Analysis*, 4 (1988), 329–46.
7. Stig Foerster, "Facing 'People's War': Moltke the Elder and German Military Options after 1871," *Journal of Strategic Studies*, 10 (1987), 209–30.
8. Hew Strachan, *From Waterloo to Balaclava: Tactics, Technology and the British Army, 1815–1854* (Cambridge, 1985), 10.
9. Paddy Griffith, *Military Thought in the French Army, 1815–51* (Manchester, 1989), 122.
10. Filippo Stefani, *La storia della dottrina e degli ordinamenti dell'esercito italiano*, Vol. I (Rome, 1984), 30, 33–34.
11. J. Ambert, *Equisses Historiques de l'Armée Françaises* (Brussels, 1851), 590; and Griffith, *Military Thought in the French Army*, 121.
12. Dennis E. Showalter, *Railroads and Rifles: Soldiers, Technology, and the Unification of Germany* (Hamden, CT, 1975), 102.
13. Stefani, *La storia della dottrina*, 137–39.
14. Richard Holmes, *The Road to Sedan: The French Army, 1866–70* (London, 1984), 211–12.
15. Edward M. Spiers, *The Army and Society, 1815–1914* (London, 1980), 211; and Dennis E. Showalter, "Army and Society in Imperial Germany: The Pains of Modernization," *Journal of Contemporary History*, 18 (1983), 597.
16. Eugene Carrias, *La pensée militaire française* (Paris, 1960), 252.
17. Griffith, *Military Thought in the French Army*, 32–43; and Strachan, *From Waterloo to Balaclava*, 1–2, 12–14.
18. Griffith, *Military Thought in the French Army*, 244–46.
19. A. von Boguslawski, *Tactical Deductions from the War of 1870–71* (London, 1872), 168.
20. Kraft Carl zu Hohenlohe-Ingelfingen, *Letters of Infantry* (London, 1889); and Showalter, "Army and Society," 592–94.
21. Stefani, *La storia della dottrina*, 379–80, 419–38.

22. J. Colin, *The Transformations of War* (London, 1912), 298.

23. D. D. Irvine, "The Origin of Capital Staffs," *Journal of Modern History*, 10 (1938).

24. M. G. Merlier, "De Grandmaison—penseur et écrivain militaire," *Actes du quatre-vingt-septieme congrés national des savantes: Poitiers 1962* (Paris, 1963), 532.

25. Douglas Porch, *The March to the Marne: The French Army, 1871-1914* (Cambridge, 1981), 216, for the belief that it came from the middle ranks. See also Jack Snyder, *The Ideology of the Offensive: Military Decision Making and the Disasters of 1914* (Ithaca, NY, 1984), 57-106.

26. Porch, *The March to the Marne*, 215.

27. Howard Bailes, "Patterns of Thought in the Late Victorian Army," *Journal of Strategic Studies*, 4 (1981), 29-45. Also see Jay Luvaas, "European Military Thought and Doctrine, 1870-1914," in M. E. Howard, ed., *The Theory and Practice of War* (Bloomington, IN, 1975), 69-94.

28. M. V. Brett and Viscount Esher, *Journals and Letters of Reginald, Viscount Esher*, Vol. I (London, 1934-38), 362-63. For a concise summary of the cavalry debate, see Brian Bond, "Doctrine and Training in the British Cavalry, 1870-1914," in Howard, *The Theory and Practice of War*, 97-125.

29. C. E. Hamilton, "The Royal Navy, *la Royale*, and the Militarisation of Naval Warfare, 1840-1870," *Journal of Strategic Studies*, 6 (1983), 184.

30. D. M. Schurman, *The Education of a Navy: The Development of British Naval Strategic Thought, 1867-1914* (Chicago, 1965). On technological change, see Bernard Brodie, *Sea Power in the Machine Age* (Princeton, NJ, 1941); and Karl Lautenschlager, "Technology and the Evolution of Naval Warfare," *International Security*, 8 (1983), 3-51.

31. John B. Hattendorff, "Alfred Thayer Mahan and His Strategic Thought," in John B. Hattendorff and R. Jordan, eds., *Maritime Strategy and the Balance of Power* (London, 1989), 87.

32. See John B. Hattendorff and Lynn C. Hattendorff, eds., *A Bibliography of the Works of Alfred Thayer Mahan* (Newport, RI, 1986).

33. Bradley Fiske, *From Midshipman to Rear-Admiral* (New York, 1919), 362.

34. Julian Corbett, *Some Principles of Maritime Strategy* (London, 1911), 113ff.

35. D. M. Schurman, *Julian S. Corbett, 1854-1922: Historian of British Maritime Policy from Drake to Jellicoe* (London, 1981), 45.

36. Holger H. Herwig, *Luxury Fleet: The Imperial German Navy, 1888-1918* (London, 1980), 86.

37. A. J. Marder, *From Dreadnought to Scapa Flow*, Vol. I (Oxford, 1961), 396-97; and Herwig, *Luxury Fleet*, 146.

38. It is significant that Custance, one of the rebels against the "big ship" orthodoxy, here became a rebel by arguing that there were no principles for tactics, undercutting the efforts of the group to develop more complex ones.

39. See "Functions of a Battle-Cruiser Squadron," 5 April 1913; and "Confidential Battle Orders for the 1st BCS," 17 July 1913, both in B. Ranft, ed., *The Beatty Papers*, Vol. I (London, 1989), 59-64, 73-75.

40. "Extracts from Grand Fleet Battle Orders," 18 August 1914, in A. T. Patterson, ed., *The Jellicoe Papers*, Vol. I (London, 1966), 52-63.

41. For an excellent analysis of one aspect of this problem, see T. H. E. Travers, "A Particular Style of Command: Haig and the GHQ, 1916-1918," *Journal of Strategic Studies*, 19 (1987), 363-76.
42. David Jones, "Imperial Russia's Forces at War," in A. Millett and W. Murray, eds., *Military Effectiveness*, Vol. I (Boston, 1988), 297, 300, 306-8.
43. For a model study of a comparative study in this field, see Martin Samuels, *Command or Control? Command, Training and Tactics in the German and British Armies, 1864-1918* (Ph.D. diss., Manchester University, 1992).
44. Bruce I. Gudmundson, *Stormtrooper Tactics: Innovation in the German Army, 1914-1918* (New York, 1989); and Holger H. Herwig, "The Dynamics of Necessity: German Military Policy during the First World War," in Millett and Murray, *Military Effectiveness*, 93-104.
45. Herwig, *Luxury Fleet*, 228-29.
46. Robert A. Doughty, *The Seeds of Disaster: The Development of French Army Doctrine, 1919-1939* (Hamden, CT, 1985); and L. Mysyrowicz, *Autopsie d'une défaite: Origines de l'effondrement militaire française de 1940* (Lausanne, 1973).
47. John Erikson, *The Soviet High Command* (London, 1962); Bruce W. Menning, "Deep Strike in Russian and Soviet Military History," *Journal of Soviet Military Studies*, 1 (1988), 9-28; Vitaly Rapoport and Yuri Alexeev, eds., *High Treason: Essays on the History of the Red Army, 1918-1939* (Durham, NC, 1985); and Richard Simpkin, *Deep Battle: The Brainchild of Marshal Tukhachevskii* (London, 1987).
48. Massimo Mazzetti, *La politica militare italiana fra le due guerre mondiali (1918-1940)* (Rome, 1982); Brian R. Sullivan, "The Italian Armed Forces, 1918-40," in Millett and Murray, *Military Effectiveness*, 187-88; and Brian R. Sullivan, *A Thirst for Glory: Mussolini, the Italian Military, and the Fascist Regime, 1922-1936* (Ph.D. diss., Columbia University, 1984), 366.
49. Bond, *British Military Policy*; J. P. Harris, "The British General Staff and the Coming of the War, 1933-1939," *Bulletin of the Institute of Historical Research*, 59 (1986), 196-211; and J. P. Harris, "British Armour and Rearmament in the 1930s," *Journal of Strategic Studies*, 11 (1988), 220-44.
50. Charles de Gaulle, *The Army of the Future* (London), 80.
51. De Gaulle, 36, 57, 133-35.
52. Peter Paret, ed., *Makers of Modern Strategy from Machiavelli to the Nuclear Age* (Princeton, 1986), 615.
53. John Mearsheimer, *Liddell Hart and the Weight of History* (Ithaca, NY, 1988), 189-91.
54. Paret, *Makers of Modern Strategy*, 538. See also Malcolm Cooper, *The German Army, 1933-1945* (London, 1978).
55. David N. Spires, *The Making of the German Officer, 1921-1933* (Westport, CT, 1983).
56. Albert C. Wedemeyer, *Wedemeyer Reports!* (New York, 1958), 51.
57. Paret, *Makers of Modern Strategy*, 585.
58. Walter Polastro, "La marina militare italiana nel primo dopoguerra (1918-1925)," *Il Risorgimento*, Pt. 3 (1977), 127-70. Compare Mazzetti, *La politica militare*; Sullivan, "Armed Forces"; and Sullivan, *Thirst for Glory*.
59. Charles S. Thomas, *The German Navy in the Nazi Era* (London, 1990), 178.
60. See Wilhelm Diest, *The Wehrmacht and German Rearmament* (London, 1981), 70-85.

61. Frank J. Capelluti, *The Life and Thought of Giulio Douhet* (Ph.D. diss., Rutgers University, 1967), 36, 70.

62. Neville Jones, *The Origins of Strategic Bombing: A Study of the Development of British Air Strategic Thought and Practice up to 1918* (London, 1973), 162.

63. Richmond to Freeman, 14 October 1942, quoted in Barry D. Hunt, *Sailor-Scholar: Admiral Sir Herbert Richmond, 1871–1946* (Waterloo, Ont., 1982), 161.

64. Michael S. Sherry, *The Rise of American Airpower: The Creation of Armageddon* (New Haven, CT, 1987), 27.

65. Capelluti, *Giulio Douhet*, 230–31.

66. On the German air force, see Manfred Messerschmidt, "German Military Effectiveness between 1919 and 1939," in Millett and Murray, *Military Effectiveness*, Vol. I, 241–42, 245–48; and Williamson Murray, *Strategy for Defeat: The Luftwaffe, 1933–1945* (Maxwell, AL, 1983).

67. See Alfred F. Hurley, *Billy Mitchell: Crusader for Air Power* (Bloomington, IN, 1975); and Burke Davis, *The Billy Mitchell Affair* (New York, 1967).

68. See Curtis LeMay, with Mackinlay Kantor, *Mission with LeMay: My Story* (New York, 1965), 141.

69. Martin van Crefeld, *Supplying War: Logistics from Wallenstein to Patton* (Cambridge, 1977), 142–80.

70. See Stephen Forde, "Thucydides on the Causes of Athenian Imperialism," *American Historical Review,* 80 (1986), 433–86.

2

New Wars and Old: Félix Calleja and the Independence War of Mexico, 1810–1816

Christon I. Archer

[I]f Spain should not have lost her dominion over these countries through later events, Calleja would have been recognized as the reconqueror of New Spain, and the second Hernan Cortés.

Lucas Alamán[1]

Today, over 170 years after national independence, Félix Calleja ranks in the top echelon of Mexico's intellectual black pantheon that commemorates historic figures condemned to eternal damnation as inexorable enemies of the nation. The inscription would describe him as "rigid," "severe," "rapacious," "ferocious," "violent," and "arrogant"; and the word "sanguinary" would appear as often as his name. The early postindependence historian Carlos María de Bustamante described Calleja as "the most terrible scourge of Mexican America."[2] Calleja was "a torrent of desolation that laid waste to and consumed everything, and America looked upon him correctly as one of the greatest plagues that heaven in its anger wished to inflict."[3] Even in the late nineteenth century, the Mexican historian Julio Zárate noted that Calleja's name "is still spoken today with terror."[4] In Zárate's view, Calleja conceived no strategy on how to combat revolution except mass extermination, extreme rigor, and a program that granted "not one stroke of clemency to the vanquished." Exerting leadership over subordinate commanders who possessed similar "sanguinary instincts," Calleja's forces "trampled human rights and fought a devastating and horrible war." Here was a most negative portrait of the most famous or infamous general of the side that eventually suffered defeat in the decade of war. In the view of most Mexican historians, in his diabolical strategies and policies to counter revolution, Calleja absolutely transcended the boundaries of military heterodoxy. Recently, Xavier Tavera Alfaro summed up Calleja's career as "tyranny, cruelty, despotism, and greed."[5]

Paradoxically, Calleja earned his reputation as the antichrist of Mexican independence because he was much too successful in his responses to rebellion and in convincing a significant segment of the Mexican population to support the royalist cause. Unlike the vast majority of Spanish army officers trained in the eighteenth century and stationed in the Americas in 1810 who failed in their attempts to confront the specter of mass popular or elite rebellions, Calleja devised ways to defend the Spanish regime, to win all of his conventional battlefield engagements and sieges, to conceive a thoroughgoing counterinsurgency program backed by a militarized regime, and to rule that regime as viceroy (1813–1816). When he returned to Spain in 1816, Calleja recognized that although his approaches to war might not in themselves achieve final victory in a prolonged struggle, he had left in place an effective system to combat popular insurgency and guerrilla warfare. Notwithstanding the inherent difficulties for the Spanish colonial regime that he was the first to acknowledge, Calleja molded and manipulated the creation of a Mexican army and a military-political system that until 1821 withstood regional insurgency and debilitating guerrilla warfare.

Beginning the war as commander of the small Tenth Provincial Militia Brigade based at the northern town of San Luis Potosí, Calleja responded to each insurgent challenge—from their attempts to assemble conventional armies to the emergence of fragmented rural guerrilla bands scattered in isolated regions that attacked agriculture, stock raising, mining, and interdicted essential commerce, transportation, and communications. Beyond his capacity to develop unorthodox approaches to revolutionary war, Calleja grasped the political dimensions required for military victory. He emerged as a highly successful military-political commander, a charismatic generalissimo, and a profoundly effective counterinsurgency strategist. Calleja militarized Mexican society, reorganized the country to combat insurgency, and comprehended the essential weaknesses of counterinsurgency that have had to be relearned time after time in many twentieth-century peoples' wars against colonialism. Trained as an eighteenth-century Spanish infantry officer in an army modeled after that of Frederick the Great, Calleja transcended his background to combat nearly impossible military challenges—confronting revolutionary struggle, insurgency, and civil war.

Calleja may have received greater recognition for his unorthodox approaches to war rather than for his alleged cruelties had it not been for the fact that the Independence era left Mexico prostrate, fragmented, and exhausted. Once unleashed, the divisive forces of insurgency, militarism, guerrilla warfare, regionalism, and ideological conflict could not be curbed. Throughout the nineteenth century, as Mexicans struggled unsuccessfully to construct a modern nation, those intellectuals, writers, and politicians who adopted liberal ideologies and causes associated Calleja's name with the evils of militarism, praetorianism, privilege, and reactionism. The nineteenth-century generals intervened in politics, set up nearly autonomous satrapies in the regions, and protected the military through an *espíritu de cuerpo* (corporate mentality) and the privileged *fuero militar* (separate legal jurisdiction for the army). Liberals condemned the army commanders for their praetorian attitudes and described them as "depraved," "corrupt," "pernicious," and "destructive."[6] Looking back to the Independence decade, many historians blamed Calleja for having initiated situations that created the ailments of the new nation.

What was even worse, Lucas Alamán, the great conservative ideologue and historian of Mexico's Independence period, damaged Calleja's military reputation further by generating fanciful flights of hyperbole about his innovations and martial excellence. No matter what Calleja's talents might have been as a general and military-political leader, it was quite preposterous to describe him as Alamán did: as a second Hernan Cortés. Unfortunately, however, Alamán's image of Calleja the *reconquistador* absolutely infuriated the liberals who went on to dominate the nation.[7] Because much of Mexican historical writing on the Independence era until recently has been based upon reinterpreting the early historians, Lucas Alamán, Carlos María de Bustamante, Lorenzo de Zavala, and José María Luis Mora, rather than upon fresh archival research, the ideological battles of the nineteenth century continued. While both Bustamante and Alamán interpreted documentary evidence accurately before they developed conclusions to reflect their own political ideologies, most historians who followed them did not conduct the same sort of careful research despite the fabulously rich Archivo General de la Nación or the other outstanding documentary collections of the country. As a result, Calleja most often has remained "the Butcher" of Mexicans—a heretic of sorts, but one whose major innovations lay in sowing death and destruction.

Julio Zárate blamed Alamán directly for having created a false and idealized Calleja.[8] After all, Alamán accepted Calleja's own inflated statements about how he had foiled six million Mexicans—even judges, ecclesiastics, writers, women, the youth of the country, and the wealthy classes—all of whom shared a deep desire for national independence. Calleja dealt with priests who used the confessional and even the pulpit to argue for Mexican separation; he suppressed women who used seduction and prostitution to lure royalist soldiers to support the rebel cause; he punished young men who took up arms against the regime; and he made life miserable for old men who spread false news and carried insurgent dispatches.[9] While Calleja might not have altered the opinions of these Mexicans, Alamán concluded that as a royalist general and later as viceroy-captain general of New Spain (1813–1816), he "discredited, conquered, and debased" the Independence revolution. Even though some fortified points and insurgent bands remained in 1816 when Calleja returned to continue his military career in Spain, Alamán argued that he passed on to his successor, Juan Ruíz de Apodaca, "a numerous and select army composed of troops who were accustomed to the incessant fatigues of the campaign, and more accustomed yet to conquering."[10] Alamán went on to state that Calleja left the Mexican treasury in a good state and that he reestablished commerce with regular protected convoys. Although he did not deny that eggs had been broken to produce this omelet, Alamán's portrait of a victorious and brilliant General Calleja drove the liberal historians into a near frenzy of anger and condemnations.

Born in 1757 of poor but noble blood in the Spanish province of Castilla la Vieja, Félix Calleja became a cadet at the age of fifteen in the line Infantry Regiment of Savoy. He served almost seventeen years—until 1789, when, at the age of thirty-two, he earned a promotion to company command with the rank of captain. By this time, his service record included combat in the abortive 1775 expedition against Algiers, during which he won accolades for his part in a bloody action on the landing beach; in the disastrous floating artillery batteries deployed during the 1779–1783 siege of Gibraltar; in the successful siege to liberate the island of Minorca from British control; and later in a series of campaigns along the Spanish coast to root out entrenched contrabandists. Although his career profile was ordinary enough considering the many opportunities for combat during the period, Calleja earned a reputation for high intelligence, devotion to duty, and leadership.

Even as a young cadet officer Calleja trained junior cadets, and from 1784 to 1788 he was director of studies of the cadet companies at the Colegio Militar of Puerto de Santa María. As was essential in the Spanish army, he became the follower of well-connected senior officers such as Lieutenant General Juan Vicente de Göemes Pacheco, Conde de Revillagigedo, and Brigadier Pedro de Gorostiza, all of whom recognized his military aptitude and assisted his career. In an army in which promotions and good appointments depended directly upon personal connections and patronage, Calleja attached his fortunes to these officers who helped to advance his career. In 1789 when Revillagigedo was appointed Viceroy of New Spain and Gorostiza became the powerful Sub-Inspector General of the Mexican army, Calleja transferred with them to Mexico as a regular army captain and training officer in the newly established Infantry Regiment of Puebla.[11] If Calleja shared the qualms of many ambitious army officers about the dangers of duty in an overseas backwater that might separate him from the grasping patronage and promotional structure of the metropolitan army, these were offset by his close connections with the Mexican viceroy. What with (1) military reforms in Mexico to establish an effective defense force against a possible foreign invasion, (2) repercussions from international disputes beginning with the 1789 Nootka Sound Controversy with Great Britain, and (3) the coalition wars and the restoration of the old military alliance with France, Calleja enjoyed numerous opportunities to advance his career.

Until 1810, Calleja won recognition as one of a very few dynamic army officers in Mexico capable of planning the defenses. Each successive viceroy praised his superior aptitude, assigned him to conceive and to implement plans for coastal and northern frontier defenses, and sent him to organize Mexican provincial militia forces. In 1790, Viceroy Revillagigedo commissioned Calleja to survey the northern frontier of Colotlán and the Pacific coast province of Nayarit, which commenced his lengthy association with the Mexican north. He studied the unpacified Colotlanes Indians who defended their rugged territory with guerrilla-style warfare, and he negotiated alliances with the even more warlike tribes of Tarahumaras, Tepehaunes, and Apaches further to the north.[12] In addition to exercising duties that fell specifically into the military sphere, Calleja prepared accurate maps, studied indigenous political organizations, and gathered data about regional history, demography, and ethnology.[13] Success with his first assignments led rapidly to a succession of northern commissions including an inspection and survey of frontier Nueva Galicia (1792); command of Tampico and Panuco on the Gulf coast, where he raised new militia forces (1793); and military surveys of the enormous frontier provinces of Nuevo León and Nuevo Santander (1794–1795).

With increasing anxiety in Spain about possible invasion of the Mexican north by Britain, the United States, or even by forces led by Spanish American revolutionary agents such as Francisco Miranda (1797), Viceroy Marqués de Branciforte (1794–1798) depended upon Calleja. He was appointed to command the regular army frontier companies of Nuevo León and Nuevo Santander, the dispersed militias of both provinces, the militia companies of the Gulf coast, and the two Provincial Dragoon Regiments of San Luis and San Carlos based in the jurisdiction of San Luis Potosí. As the commander of a much dispersed frontier force of over 3,000 troops, Calleja developed a network of personal connections, loyalties, and followers that extended throughout the Mexican north.[14] As subinspector of the militia units he recruited, inspected, and raised frontier forces and reorganized the cavalry and dragoon units of San Luis Potosí. Viceroy Branciforte recognized the critical importance of Mexican provincial militia regiments and battalions—in an age of Atlantic warfare they would have to replace regular Spanish regiments no longer available from the metropolitan army or raised at prohibitive expense in Mexico. Branciforte projected the organization of ten regional provincial militia divisions and assigned the few remaining regular infantry and dragoon regiments, artillery companies, and army engineers to duties in a few strategic coastal and interior garrisons. In theory, the regular forces were to act as a leadership cadre for a militia-based provincial army. In fact, these units failed to recruit Mexicans, who generally viewed service in them as only one step removed from penal servitude.

Given his experience in the north, Branciforte appointed Calleja to command the Tenth Militia Division based at San Luis Potosí.[15] Beginning in 1797, he visited towns and missions throughout the Mexican north, filed detailed reports on governance, surveyed ports, and completed studies on the Indian populations. In the process, Calleja enhanced his knowledge and strengthened a network of connections that culminated in his marriage to Doña María Francisca de la Gándara, the scion and wealthy widow of a leading family of San Luis Potosí.[16] This background, and the opportunities to command the Royalist Army of the Center commencing with the 1810 Rebellion of Father Miguel Hidalgo, permitted Calleja to emerge as the first regional *caudillo* of many in the nineteenth century who worked from a provincial base to capture control of the entire nation. Beforehand, however, Calleja strengthened his northern command and developed policies designed to improve the militia-based army. Although his ideas on maintaining army control over patronage in terms of militia commissions ran counter to official thinking within the Spanish bureaucracy, at the outbreak of revolutionary civil war Calleja possessed the infrastructure and the strong personal regional support necessary to combat a mass movement directed to attain independence.

Prior to the Hidalgo Revolt, Calleja was a leading example of the hardworking Spanish immigrants to New Spain who dominated the military, the bureaucracy, business, and mining in the late Bourbon era. Through the viceregal administrations of Revillagigedo (1789–1794),

Branciforte (1794–1798), Miguel José de Azanza (1798–1800), Félix Berenguer de Marquina (1800–1803), José de Iturriagaray (1803–1808), and the interim administrations (1808–1810), Calleja received almost unanimous praise for his military and civil contributions. All the viceroys and senior army commanders described him as an officer of unusual abilities who deserved rapid promotion. Viceroy Azanza recommended Calleja for the rank of brigadier, and Viceroy Marquina described him as one of only two truly outstanding officers in the Mexican army.[17] In 1806, Viceroy Iturriagaray expressed great satisfaction at Calleja's energy in mobilizing Mexican forces to reinforce the Province of Texas against a feared invasion from the United States.[18] In almost every respect, Calleja appeared to have achieved high success in his military career through intelligence, dynamism, and attention to patronage appointments through his political connections.

Following his marriage to Doña María Francisca de la Gándara, he took up residence on her property at the hacienda de Bledos south of San Luis Potosí near Valle de San Felipe. But despite his successes, Calleja nursed a burning ambition for high office that could not be satisfied by a comfortable life in the provinces. Even with his knowledge of the Mexican north and the fact that he held the esteem of his superiors, Calleja pursued a restless search for fame, higher rank, and power. Throughout his army career, he pressed hard for promotions and assignments that might win him even greater recognition. Shortly after his transfer to Mexico, while he was still a captain in the Infantry Regiment of Puebla, he requested and was denied advancement to the rank of lieutenant colonel in any regular infantry regiment.[19] In 1800, the crown refused Viceroy Azanza's petition to promote Calleja from the rank of colonel to brigadier. Since at that time Calleja was inspector of regular army forces in Mexico, the Viceroy argued that the promotion was necessary so that he would be equal in rank to most of the senior regimental commanders.[20] In 1802, he applied again without success to make the difficult career promotion from colonel to brigadier.[21] With this failure, Calleja requested a two-year paid medical leave to visit Spain—probably with the idea of cultivating his patronage connections in Madrid. As justification for his application to return to Spain, he claimed that the hard frontier life in northern Mexico had damaged his health and the only known cure was to get him out of the country. A royal order of 13 April 1804 granted him permission to travel, but by this time renewed war with Britain, growing fears of an invasion from the United States, and other factors prevented his departure. A later nationalist historian, enraged that circumstances prevented the departure of the man many considered to be Mexico's destroyer, scribbled on the margin of Calleja's royal permission: "Only if he could have used it! He would have freed this America from so many evils."

Calleja's commitment to militia reforms or autonomy commenced during his years in command of the Tenth Militia Brigade, where he struggled to remove patronage appointments that had been dominated by the urban municipal councils (the *cabildos*) that represented the local elites. Since local taxation and donations funded most of the costs of provincial militia units, the urban authorities were permitted to nominate officer candidates pending royal approval and to recommend promotions—sometimes weakening the officer corps with more wealthy but less capable commanders. In addition, many regular officers and non-commissioned officers (NCOs) assigned to the training cadres and as administrators of militia regiments gradually lost their martial vocations and became identified with the districts in which they served. Without competition or the possibility of promotion within a small training cadre, many regular officers assigned to militia units married locally, developed business interests, and neglected their military duties. Some spent their time drinking and gambling, others sold weapons and uniforms, and a few even turned their barracks into brothels, theaters, or bars. In one such case, an inspection report described regular army Sergeant Francisco de Estrada of the Frontier Militia de Colotlán as "a complete drunk, always asleep, and good for nothing." Of fifteen corporals in the unit, eight drank to excess and the rest were medically unfit for duty.[22] Without any specific retirement age, some septuagenarian and octogenarian officers, despite physical disabilities, continued to collect their pay. Some were too weak or overweight to mount their horses, and others suffered chronic illnesses that prevented them from actually commanding their units.[23] In the case of provincial militia officers, many purchased commissions because they aspired to social advancement and wore their uniforms at social occasions without any intentions of actually taking up the duties attached to company, squadron, battalion, or regimental command. Some resided far away from their units or had business obligations that required extensive travel to distant provinces. Such officers neglected training, failed to appear at monthly exercises, and wanted little more from the army than the privileges and enhanced social standing granted by their uniforms.

In the Tenth Militia Brigade, Calleja made every effort to remove inept or absent commanders and to bypass those who lacked martial zeal by promoting talented officers rather than those who enjoyed greater seniority. Unlike other provincial brigade commanders, he exercised great care to make certain that officers resided within close proximity to their units and that they had sufficient income to pay their own expenses. In the region of San Luis Potosí, the ranchers, itinerant merchants, and others who could afford militia commissions often suffered financial misfortunes that prevented them from continuing to pay the costs associated with their militia ranks. Some possessed sufficient wealth to serve as sub-lieutenants or lieutenants, but they lacked the personal income or status needed for promotion to company command. In his brigade jurisdiction, Calleja took care to maintain guard-duty rotations, monthly training programs, firing practices, and annual maneuvers. Stressing the recruitment and training of mobile dragoon units and maintaining a military census of the provincial population, Calleja organized the core of what emerged after 1810 as a well-commanded fighting force.[24]

Convinced that many errors within the provincial army stemmed from civilian direction and interference, Calleja attempted to strengthen the powers of the brigade commanders and the autonomy of the army. With the death in 1805 of the Conde del Peñasco, commander of the Dragoon Regiment of San Carlos, Calleja rejected the *terna* (list of three candidates) proposed by the urban government of San Luis Potosí. Quoting a number of military ordinances from Spain and other Spanish American provinces, Calleja concluded that the crown wanted senior commanders who knew the qualities and abilities of officers to recommend promotions and to evaluate candidates for commissions. In his opinion, the selection of officers by merchants, land owners, and other civilians served no purpose other than to debase military honor and efficiency.[25] Although in 1805 the regime rejected any expansion of military autonomy,[26] when the opportunity emerged Calleja was ready to exclude civilian interference. With mass rebellion in 1810, he moved quickly to establish full military control over his forces. Without any reference to the civil bureaucracy he mobilized ranchers, vaqueros, miners, artisans, and merchants.

The Hidalgo Rebellion was nothing short of a catastrophe for the sedentary colonial army of New Spain. Although there had been signs of unrest since the Napoleonic invasion of Spain in 1808, few observers could have predicted a mass popular uprising. Indeed, internal bickering and backbiting between European-born Spaniards and Mexican creoles of the elite appeared more likely to cause some kind of coup d'état rather than an attempt at social revolution involving the lower classes. In September 1808, a group of European merchants and officers of the Urban Regiment of Commerce of Mexico City deposed Viceroy José de Iturriagaray under the pretext that he was too friendly with Mexican causes and supportive of some form of political autonomy or separation. The explosion of the mestizo and Indian population of the fertile Bajío provinces to the north and west of Mexico City caught the army completely by surprise. Conceived primarily to repel a possible European invasion at Veracruz, an assault inland against Mexico City, or to defend settled regions against the incursions of frontier Indians, there was no military force available to crush internal insurrection before it got out of hand.

Beginning on 16 September 1810, Hidalgo's inchoate masses swarmed from town to town capturing Dolores, San Miguel, and within a few days surrounding the mining capital of Guanajuato. Encouraged by elements of messianism and millenarianism preached by village curates and fueled by rumors of massacres perpetrated by Spaniards against Mexicans, the insurgent forces swelled to a point at which they simply overpowered existing authorities and incorporated elements of the Eighth Militia Brigade commanded by an ancient officer, Brigadier Ignacio García Revollo, who had served in the army of New Spain since the 1760s.[27] In a matter of days, the insurgents won a reputation for invincibility. Although most men and women joined for pillage and armed themselves with lances, slings, and agricultural implements rather than muskets, swords, or other weapons of war, without opposition their great numbers gave them the impression of invulnerability. The rebel capture of Guanajuato followed a siege of the fortified urban granary and a massacre of European Spaniards on 26 September 1810; this shocked most army commanders to the degree that they assumed purely defensive positions in cities or took refuge in fortified buildings. Momentarily, there appeared to be no force capable of crushing insurrection.

Calleja received word of the insurrection on 19 September, three days after the outbreak and much too late to assist. While the Tenth Militia Brigade was better trained and organized than some other militia divisions, they were not prepared to respond to a popular uprising of immense magnitude in the Bajío provinces. Indeed, neither Calleja nor any other senior commander had anticipated a civil war in which their Mexican forces would be fighting a large segment of the population.

Notwithstanding the perils and his own doubts about the loyalty of the population, Calleja moved quickly to mobilize the resources of the north. He assessed the military situation, met with his unit commanders, harnessed the civil bureaucracy to enlist men from towns and haciendas, and halted shipments of minted silver from the mining districts to Mexico City that might fall into the hands of the insurgents.[28] From the outset of his preparations, Calleja encountered severe shortages that were to make war difficult in Mexico. First, except for the old muskets and pistols already held by the two provincial dragoon regiments in San Luis Potosí, there were few additional firearms available to equip an expanded army. Second, because of the limited technical knowledge of artisans such as blacksmiths, farriers, and other metalworkers in the Mexican north, early efforts to manufacture artillery pieces, musket barrels, and even swords were less than successful. While Calleja recruited 1,500 laborers to form an infantry unit and 2,600 ranchers, stockraisers, and vaqueros from regional haciendas who were excellent horsemen for new cavalry units, he described these forces as poorly mounted, ill-equipped, inadequately armed, and incapable of engaging in immediate combat.[29] Most of the new recruits possessed no weapons other than lances that were comparatively easy to manufacture and the ubiquitous machetes. When these men heard rumors about the implacable nature of the rebels and the size of their multitudes, many lost their appetite for combat and deserted.

As might be expected given the popular appeal of the Hidalgo Revolt, Calleja could not be certain about the loyalty of the northern Mexicans. Overburdened by the weight of decisions and preparations within his jurisdiction, he informed the new viceroy, General Francisco Javier de Venegas: "This is the time to work rather than to write."[30] Hidalgo's forces occupied Guanajuato, took a dangerous if unsuccessful swipe at Mexico City in the Battle of Las Cruces near Toluca, and before long captured the major cities of Valladolid (Morelia) and Guadalajara. Revolutionary agents propagated messages that proliferated new centers of rebellion and spawned regional guerrilla bands that occupied their home districts and disrupted commerce and communications. At the same time, however, the crisis permitted Calleja to free his growing army of civilian interference and to conceive a program that would militarize his province and, later, the country.

Calleja's career as an innovative wartime commander commenced in the chaotic months following the organization of the Army of the Center. He assembled a small army of approximately 5,500 troops composed largely of the northern militias reinforced by some regular infantry companies and militia units from the old provincial forces. Brushing aside the normal powers of the urban governments, provincial intendants, and other authorities who represented local civilian interests and the central regime, Calleja established special wartime taxes to support his army and even risked a rupture with the Church when he ordered the confiscation of a portion of the tithes.[31] Unlike most other brigade commanders, he possessed the network of connections and skills to mobilize manpower and to organize an effective system of logistical support. Each town, village, or hacienda contracted to provide draft animals, flour, wool, livestock, and other supplies needed to maintain the army.[32] Ordered by Viceroy Venegas to march his brigade to Querétaro with other loyal units concentrating there from Puebla, Calleja tactfully refused until his army was prepared. The recruitment of Indian lancers and bowmen, instruction for his forces, and the mobilization of artisans to manufacture lances that were the most basic weapon of the royalist forces required additional time. If there had been a momentary opportunity for the royalist armies to crush the insurgency in its formative stages, neither Calleja's hastily recruited army nor any other units of the provincial forces were able to act decisively. By October, Calleja's advance guards on the roads south of San Luis Potosí reported sighting enormous insurgent formations—estimated to number as many as 40,000 to 50,000 men. After seeing them loaded with booty pillaged from towns and haciendas, Calleja described them as swarming like ants to incite the country to rebellion.[33]

Disregarding the psychological effect of the enormous imbalance in numbers, Calleja concentrated upon logistics and planning that allowed him to engage and disperse much larger rebel formations with negligible casualties. He was a careful commander and the only senior officer in Mexico to conceive a strategy designed to confront an insurrection that spread from one region to another threatening cities, mining districts, agriculture, transportation, and communications. The defeat of a rebel force on the battlefield produced little long-term impact. Calleja noted: "It [insurrection] is reborn like the hydra as its heads are cut off."[34] He formulated a comprehensive military system designed to achieve successes with the least possible risk.[35] The Army of the Center advanced southward from San Luis Potosí to disperse the poorly armed and worse led rebel forces at the engagements of Aculco, Guanajuato, and finally on 17 January 1811, at Puente de Calderón outside Guadalajara. Only the latter engagement should be described as a set-piece battle in the normal sense of the term, with the rebels suffering heavy casualties from artillery fire and massed musketry before they fled. The royalists lost a few men at Calderón, but most injuries inflicted by the rebels were contusions and bruises caused by stones thrown by hand and sling rather than by bullets. Of more long-term importance than these battles, Calleja had to deal with the rapid diffusion of insurgency that swept out of the Bajío to ignite new centers of guerrilla warfare in distant Mexican regions. Despite his connections with the Mexican north, by 1812 Calleja had to lead his army on an exhausting campaign to besiege the fortified towns of Zitácauro and even further south of Mexico City against José María Morelos at Cuautla Amilpas.

During each phase of the revolt, Calleja exhibited caution that caused some contemporaries and many historians to characterize his generalship as overly conservative or uninspired. From the beginning, however, he was aware that his army was the only royalist force in Mexico capable of defeating the much larger rebel formations. Although some Spanish officers and a few European expeditionary battalions began to arrive in Mexico in 1812, the Mexican royalists had to bear the major brunt of the fighting. Calleja feared any battle or siege that might result in an inconclusive standoff or a royalist defeat. Approaching the prospect of a siege at Zitácauro in November 1811, without easy access to supplies or munitions, Calleja warned that a royalist failure might cause the provinces to rise up en masse and the rebels to occupy Mexico City in as few as three days. In a postscript to a dispatch to Viceroy Venegas that he deleted later from the finished copy, Calleja noted: "Winning a hundred battles will not secure us, but the one that we may lose could cost us the kingdom forever."[36] Given this understanding, there was no margin of error for impetuous attacks or risky campaigns.

By marching with his soldiers, sharing their chronic dysentery and other hardships of the campaign, Calleja earned both respect and loyalty. Separated for years from their home districts, the northern militiamen soon became professionals who depended upon their commanders for promotions and other rewards. The war severed the old military command structure that had been dependent upon the viceroy-captain general and office of the sub-inspector general, eliminated the role of the urban governments to grant patronage through nominating officer candidates, and eroded the fiscal controls of the intendants and subdelegates of the civil administration over the military. As early as 1812, officers and soldiers who had campaigned with Calleja since the beginning of the rebellion had come to follow him rather than simply to serve the Spanish state.[37]

Beyond achieving victories, Calleja had to formulate policies that would pacify and restore normal controls over the population. The Army of the Center might crush the Bajío insurgents in one sector, but other districts and provinces beyond the military reach rose up to join the revolutionary movement. Bivouacked with his army near Celaya on 20 November 1810, Calleja learned that the rebels had occupied Guadalajara and Valladolid (Morelia), and circled behind royalist forces in the north to capture his hometown of San Luis Potosí. He informed the Viceroy that it was impossible for his army to respond to each new challenge without annihilating itself as a fighting force by being broken down into a multitude of divisions.[38] These concerns hardened Calleja's attitude toward the use of terror as a means to separate the civilian populations from active or passive support for the insurgents. Already smarting at the "insolent and audacious" attitudes exhibited by the people of Salamanca and Irapuato, when someone at Irapuato ripped down one of his proclamations offering amnesty to rebel supporters, Calleja decided to inflict brutal exemplary punishment. He ordered a roundup of forty men found near the scene of the crime; when they could not or would not identify those responsible, he compelled them to draw lots selecting one in ten for execution by firing squad.[39]

Not only did Viceroy Venegas approve Calleja's introduction of decimation, but he authorized the unrestricted use of summary justice under martial law. Prisoners of prominent social and political positions were no longer sent to Mexico City for trials. Such procedures detached too many troops for escort duties and reduced the terrifying impact of exemplary punishments that were to be carried out immediately after sentencing by military courts. Calleja was well aware that the rebels had adopted the policy of executing some Spaniards who supported the royalist cause. Venegas reported the murders of eight *gachupines* (European Spaniards) at Huichapan, 130 at San Felipe, or a total of at least 600 victims since the introduction of their cruel plan to exterminate Europeans. He commanded Calleja "to forget humanity in order to destroy any who have ordered or who have played a role in these atrocities." The Viceroy described the rebels as a cancer that had to be excised, citing as an example the town of Zapotlan el Grande, where the Indians had risen up and put all whites to the knife whether they were Europeans or Mexicans.[40]

To hasten pacification, Calleja experimented with a number of draconian punishments designed to deter insurgency. At Guanajuato on 25 November 1810, he took the Viceroy's orders to heart. First, using denunciations, royalist troops rounded up former rebels including civilian workers of Hidalgo's cannon foundry, civil servants, and employees of the insurgent mint. Calleja reported to Venegas that as he wrote his dispatch, twenty-three executions by firing squad proceeded. The following day, Calleja held a gruesome lottery of jailed rebel prisoners to select eighteen to be hung in the city square. The summary public executions continued for several days and included all rebel officers of the rank of captain or above. By 3 December, a crowd of local people went to Calleja's house to proclaim their loyalty, obedience, and submission. Some protested that their priests had deceived them into supporting the party of Independence.[41] With the populace traumatized by fear of the gallows, Calleja halted the daily executions and published a decree offering amnesty. In 1812, following his victory in the siege of Zitácauro, Calleja punished insurgent sympathizers by razing the entire town and eleven nearby Indian villages.[42] After the even more exhausting siege of Cuautla Amilpas against Morelos, Calleja again burned the town to the ground, leaving only the churches. In subsequent years, however, he altered his views about sacrificing entire towns; and in 1813, as viceroy, he renounced this form of indiscriminate violence that punished the innocent along with the guilty. He informed his commanders: "We do not wish to convert the country into a frightful desert and to increase existing evils and the hatred with which measures of this nature are viewed."[43]

Although Venegas believed that rebel forces succeeded only in isolated regions where there were no organized royalist forces to counter them,[44] Calleja was more pessimistic. Despite his victory at the Battle of Calderón on 17 January 1811, he expressed harsh criticism of his own green troops who "show little or no sign that they are imbued with the principles of honor and martial glory." Only the greater disorder and cowardice on the rebel side made the royalists shine by comparison. Even so, Calleja feared that they were beginning to learn how to fight. At Calderón as the engagement developed, some royalist units along the front line began to waver. Recognizing imminent danger, Calleja rushed to take personal command. During the later stages of the battle, Brigadier Manuel de Flón, Conde de Cadena, was surrounded and cut down as he led an assault on the grand battery of the rebel artillery.[45]

Following this battle, Calleja's forces pursued Hidalgo and the rebel leadership into the Mexican north. At the Hacienda de Bledos, in late February 1811, Calleja was ready to reoccupy San Luis Potosí and march on the frontier town of Matehuala. Although he wanted to chase the rebels as far north as Saltillo or even into the Province of Texas, Viceroy Venegas refused to grant permission for the Army of the Center to move so far from the populated provinces of Mexico. He feared that unpacified districts in the south could stimulate a new uprising.[46] Calleja worried about the danger of intervention from the United States on behalf of the rebels, and he agreed with the Viceroy that new methods had to be found to pacify those districts that produced a succession of guerrilla and bandit gangs. Each new outbreak of violence caused district authorities to request garrisons of troops detached from the Army of the Center. Since it was obvious that this force could not provide troops to look after all incidents, Calleja experimented with the concept of raising new armed militias recruited in towns and rural districts, armed militias that could deter raids, garrison their territories, and track down guerrilla gangs that mixed insurgency with a strong element of more traditional banditry. One of these royalist self-defense companies based at the mining community of Catorce commanded by the town curate, José María Semper, succeeded in defeating the band of the well-known insurgent leader Lego Villerías. Some other local defense companies raised in San Luis Potosí and Río

Verde achieved similar successes and managed to disperse several guerrilla bands.[47]

By June 1811, Calleja's experience with counterinsurgency led him to conclude that without comprehensive new policies, the fragmented insurgency employing guerrilla warfare eventually would exhaust and overwhelm the limited resources of the royalist army. Based upon the minor successes of local self-defense militias, Calleja conceived a new kind of pacification plan that would have been anathema to many European officers. First, for propaganda purposes and to set the scene, he took it upon himself to proclaim an end to the rebellion. Any remaining insurgents now became criminal bandits, thieves, and delinquents who were to be tracked down and eliminated without mercy. Having attacked the legitimacy of the insurgents, Calleja introduced a tiered system of counterinsurgency that devolved much of the responsibility for local defense upon patriotic militia forces recruited and funded in the cities, towns, and rural districts. Through the implementation of a plan called the Military-Political Regulations, Calleja sought to polarize the Mexican population and, if possible, compel most people to support the royalist cause. The new militias were to regain control over vast areas of the countryside; to isolate and marginalize the insurgents; and to harden urban defenses with the construction of block houses, parapets, and ditches so that the lightly armed guerrillas could not attack without artillery and full siege equipment.[48] The plan was designed to create an impenetrable barrier of urban and rural companies throughout the country. As Calleja explained, the operational army could not continue to weaken itself by detaching small forces to chase guerrillas or to garrison every threatened village or hacienda. By presenting a seamless urban-rural front of patriotic militia forces, the main force of army divisions and flying cavalry detachments could concentrate their firepower upon the major remaining centers of insurgency.

Although Calleja's plan was highly effective in parts of the Mexican north, he underestimated the ongoing strength of insurgency in some other regions. Moreover, his counterinsurgency thinking of 1811 failed to comprehend other changes as the major theaters of war shifted further to the south.[49] Engaged in counterinsurgency operations in Guanajuato, Zacatecas, and San Luis Potosí, Calleja did not relish the prospect of having to become the conqueror of the south. Moreover, bilious attacks and chronic dysentery so weakened him that in July 1811 he contemplated having to relinquish command of the Army of the Center.[50]

Although by mid-1811 the severed heads of the rebel commanders Father Hidalgo, Ignacio Allende, Juan de Aldama, and Mariano Jiménez arrived at the Bajío towns to be displayed as grisly object lessons to would-be rebels, Calleja worried more than ever that battlefield victories were meaningless. In the south, José María Morelos raised new forces; and the rebels fortified the town of Zitácauro, driving royalist units from the region and into the refuge of the city of Toluca.[51] Throughout the country, amnestied insurgents took up arms again as soon as they could evade royalist reprisals. Towns and villages that presented an outward appearance of sincere loyalty when the Army of the Center passed nearby, declared again for the rebels when the royalists were out of sight. Calleja's response was to implement the Military-Political Regulations, but even with the introduction of urban and rural militias, the main operational forces eroded by having to detach companies and squadrons to garrison the towns and districts where insurgent activities continued. Calleja's officers feared that there would be insufficient troops to prevent a renewed coalescence of rebel bands that might once again unite massive forces. In addition, military duty in dispersed garrisons away from the watchful eyes of commanders often mixed companies from different battalions and regiments, exposed the soldiers to lack of discipline and even seduction by the rebels, lowered their fighting spirit, and led many men to desert in order to return to their home provinces.[52] Calleja's solution was to supplement the lower tier of the counterinsurgency system based at the local and district levels with a strong European Spanish expeditionary army that could engage the major insurgent bands and besiege their numerous fortifications.

After a year of wartime duty, the Army of the Center showed signs of exhaustion that became more obvious in royalist fighting forces throughout the decade. Ordered to besiege rebel Zitácauro, Calleja expressed reservations about any campaign that would force him to leave the northern provinces undefended. The rainy season made the roads impassable for artillery, and logistics were a nightmare. Morelos and other insurgent leaders recognized that they might overcome insurgent weaknesses in organization and firepower on the conventional battlefield through the adoption of a defensive strategy based upon guerrilla warfare and well-prepared fortifications. By drawing the royalist armies into protracted sieges distant from their main bases, it seemed likely that disease, desertion, and overextended supply lines would pin down the most effective royalist armies and gradually erode their fighting ability. In the meantime, rebel guerrilla bands operating in their home districts could sever the logistical tail of the royalist forces—especially if the insurgent fighters fortified positions of difficult access off the normal transportation routes and in zones of tropical climate where yellow fever, malaria, and other diseases served as their allies against unacclimatized troops.

Concern about protracted sieges renewed Calleja's apprehensions about provoking a watershed royalist defeat that might end the war. At Zitácauro, his objective was to overwhelm the rebels in a sudden *coup de main* rather than tie down his forces in a more gradual strangulation of the enemy fortress. Calleja argued that if protracted sieges could be avoided, the rebels would be confounded and surrounding districts would soon grant support to the royalist side. A prolonged siege would have exactly the opposite effect. In a devastated region, supplies and provisions were difficult to secure. The army would suffer higher losses to disease and desertion over time than from a decisive battle at the outset of the siege. Once the rebels resisted for a day, they would persuade themselves that they could last for another, and other surrounding towns might begin to support them in their success. Of even greater concern, while the royalist forces were pinned down in one siege, other provinces could rise up once more to rejoin the rebellion.[53] Calleja recalled the recent disasters of the French army before Zaragoza and the failure of the British assaults commanded by General Beresford at Buenos Aires. An abortive assault almost inevitably caused a loss of morale and provoked desertions. Moreover, Calleja continued to worry about the fighting ability of his Mexican soldiers, who, he argued, "do not make war against the insurgents as the Spaniards do against the French."[54] These fears of possible insurgent successes strengthened Calleja's resolve to use brutal exemplary punishments designed to terrorize the rebels. At Zitácauro, he stated that it was essential to destroy the "phantasm of insurgent impregnability."[55]

Calleja was correct to fear the protracted sieges that weakened the royalist forces over the decade of war up to their final collapse in 1821. At Cuautla Amilpas in 1812, Calleja led a siege that tested all his skills as a senior commander. When they could not crack the rebel fortifications by rapid assaults, the royalist besiegers encountered major problems with logistics and disease. At the same time, Calleja prevailed eventually when starvation in the besieged fortress drove Morelos to attempt a breakout and escape through the royalist lines. Given the outcome, it is impossible to sustain the conclusions of some recent Mexican historians that Morelos somehow triumphed during the siege and flight from Cuautla.[56] However, having lost the initiative and finding his army bogged down in exactly the kind of siege he wished to avoid, Calleja determined to make a bloody example of the place so that no future insurgents would see value in fortifying themselves in towns.

Morelos had done a thorough job of preparing his defenses—burning forage and wood needed by the royalist army and throwing up parapets so strong that Calleja required large caliber siege guns. In February 1812, the rebel defenders repulsed a royalist assault with effective artillery fire of their own and deployed sharpshooters from the Pacific coast who were excellent marksmen.[57] Gradually, as Calleja predicted, the Army of the Center lost its initiative; many officers contracted debilitating dysentery, and much of the army also suffered from venereal diseases that further damaged morale. Urgent requests for siege mortars, large caliber cannons, and reinforcements from newly arrived expeditionary battalions from Spain could not be met quickly because the insurgents fortified other locations and interdicted transportation routes.[58] When Brigadier Ciriaco de Llano and 1,500 troops of the Army of the South based at Puebla reached Cuautla on 1 March 1812, they possessed few provisions, very little ammunition, and no money to pay the troops. After the difficult journey from Puebla and a failed siege at the rebel-held town of Izúcar, the uniforms of the soldiers were in rags and the gun carriages of their mobile artillery had fallen to pieces.[59]

Fortunately for Calleja, the besieging army outlasted Morelos and his garrison. In the end, the siege was a brutal competition to see which side would face exhaustion first. Shocked by conditions and the lack of leadership exhibited by many officers, Calleja expressed open criticism of the abilities of his infantry commanders and absolute horror at the high levels of disease and hospitalization. By the end of April 1812, more than 800 royalist soldiers were incapacitated by illness and 150 officers suffered chronic dysentery. While Calleja realized from rebel deserters that the Cuautla garrison was even worse off—reduced to eating insects, hides, and anything else vaguely edible, he expressed grudging admiration for their continuing high morale.[60] Finally, on 2 May 1812, in a surprise breakout, Morelos and his garrison dashed through the royalist lines. Calleja ordered the expeditionary Battalion of Asturias to contain the escape and dispatched the Battalion of Guanajuato to enter Cuautla in order to cut off the rebel rearguard and artillery. Ordered to spare no insurgent officer, the royalist cavalry pursued the rebels. The chase, which took place over seven leagues, left the ground strewn with 816 rebel dead.[61] Protected by the heroic tenacity of his personal guards, Morelos escaped to fight another day. Although Calleja had won the battle and begun a process that eventually marginalized the southern insurgents, his opponents overlooked the weakened condition of the royalist besiegers and attacked him for permitting Morelos to get away at all.

Even before he became viceroy in 1813, Calleja's opponents criticized his military conduct and held him personally responsible for failing to terminate Morelos at Cuautla Amilpas. At the same time, the officers and soldiers of the Army of the Center who served him through the campaigns and battles against Hidalgo and then during the sieges of Zitácauro and Cuautla Amilpas defended him tenaciously. Although historians have often identified political bickering between Calleja and Viceroy Venegas, the documents show no signs of major disagreements between them on the strategies required to suppress the insurrection. Calleja's chronic dysentery and other illnesses contracted during the campaign ending with the fall of Cuautla forced him temporarily to resign his command.[62] However, Calleja's high reputation and the knowledge in Spain that the Mexican war was going badly for the royalists convinced the imperial government to name him viceroy.

Having attained the highest political and military office in New Spain, Calleja confronted the depressing realities of an exhausted treasury, an interdicted transportation and communications system, and sagging morale on the royalist side. Throughout much of the country, insurgent forces—often fragmented into bands that fought in their home districts and coalesced if they could outnumber the royalists—paralyzed agriculture, commerce, industry, and especially the silver mines that provided the principal income for the treasury. Against an array of different enemies, Calleja described an army "scattered over the enormous extension of hundreds of leagues and divided into a multitude of small weak divisions."[63] Based in the major cities and towns, many garrisons were surrounded and cut off by insurgent-controlled rural countryside. In many cases, royalist regional commanders lacked effective communications. For example, from July 1812 to February 1813 guerrilla bands in Veracruz province severed all contacts between the capital and the coast. Of potentially greater concern, Morelos recovered after Cuautla to rebuild his shattered forces. With an army of 14,000 to 16,000 troops, he conquered Oaxaca and much of the Mexican south.

From this quite pessimistic beginning, as viceroy, Calleja introduced programs based upon his own experience to unite dispersed royalist forces and to implement his Military-Political Regulations. By 1815, the royalist army had defeated Morelos and dispersed most of the major insurgent forces. In what was a summary state of the war report for his successor, Juan Ruíz de Apodaca, Calleja portrayed a country well on the road to total pacification.[64] He stressed the effective use of force and royal amnesties to insurgents that had reduced insurgency to little more than dispersed banditry. Despite his optimism, however, Calleja's counterinsurgency programs controlled but did not defeat insurgency. Even in the most pacified regions, military dispatches described a continuing conflict that would alert any twentieth-century observer to the existence of a classic guerrilla war. Wherever necessary, royalist forces could gain the initiative in most regions through the concentration of units and the use of superior firepower. At the same time, the royalists failed to hold the villages and rural countryside that were essential for agriculture and stockraising. Despite the tiered levels of counterinsurgency introduced by Calleja's Military-Political Regulations designed to mobilize the population, many regions remained unorganized and required permanent garrisons of regular troops. Calleja's wish to degrade all insurgents as "bandits, thieves, and common delinquents"[65] simply did not square with the realities. His military strategies produced numerous victories but failed to eradicate the political or social roots of rebellion. When pressed, the insurgents simply abandoned their positions to superior conventional forces and returned later to re-establish their occupation. In isolated regions and in provinces such as Veracruz, Calleja failed to grasp the full significance of guerrilla war. Forgetting his own experiences as a field commander in 1810 to 1812, he bragged about meaningless victories against guerrilla bands and published lists of amnestied insurgents as absolute proof of royalist successes. He missed the fact that temporary surrender under amnesties allowed guerrillas simply one more means to prolong the war. Over the decade, some insurgents surrendered with amnesties as many as eight or ten times. Nevertheless, Calleja achieved as much as was possible from a counterinsurgency program implemented by an unpopular colonial regime. He departed Mexico with his career intact, leaving a strategic plan and programs that survived for almost six years until Mexican independence.

Many of the northern officers who served under Calleja in the Army of the Center went on to become major figures during and after the Independence War. Gabriel Armijo became Comandante General of the Provincia del Sur; Matías de Aguirre of the Dragoon Regiment of San Luis attained high army rank; and Francisco de Orrantía was commander of the Cavalry of Nuevo Santander. Between 1830 and 1840, Anastasio Bustamante, Luis Miguel Barragón, and Manuel Gómez Pedraza, who served with Calleja as junior officers, became presidents of Mexico. In many respects, Calleja created a northern dynasty similar to the one that dominated the nation following the twentieth-century Mexican Revolution. While his victories on the losing side of the Independence War have been criticized often by generations of Mexican nationalist historians, Calleja set the tone for the decade of counterinsurgency struggle. He raised an army capable of defeating the rebels on the battlefield and in the numerous sieges of isolated mountain peaks, islands, and other rebel strongholds that continued unabated until 1821. Calleja's Military-Political Regulations served to compel Mexicans to choose between the insurgency and royalist causes. He raised an effective army, militarized the population, and provided the framework to extend counterinsurgency to its point of exhaustion. Through his adoption of unorthodox military policies, Calleja prolonged Spanish rule in Mexico. Despite his successes as a general and as a strategist, however, Calleja offered few solutions to the political, social, and economic problems that underlay the mass insurgency directed against Spanish rule. Over the short term, Calleja's policies simply neutralized the Mexican rebels. The problem was that the insurgents were willing to persevere indefinitely to erode the will of the royalist forces. In 1821, to terminate the debilitating war, the officers trained by Calleja saw their salvation in changing sides to embrace the concept of national independence.

NOTES

1. Lucas Alamán, *Historia de México desde los primeros movimientos que preparon su independencia en el año de 1808 hasta la época presente*, Vol. IV (México, 1851), 477.
2. Carlos María de Bustamante, *Cuadro histórico de la revolución mexicana*, Vol. I (México, 1961), 45.
3. Ibid., 398.
4. Julio Zárate, "La guerra de independencia," in Vicente Riva Palacio, ed., *México a través de los siglos*, Vol. II (México, 1967), 520. The original publication date was 1888–1889.
5. Xavier Tavera Alfaro, "Calleja, represor de la insurgencia," in Carlos Herrejón Peredo, ed., *Repaso de la Independencia* (Zamora, 1985), 89.
6. See Christon I. Archer, "The Royalist Army of New Spain: Militarism, Praetorianism, or Protection of Interests?" *Armed Forces and Society*, 17 (1990), 99.
7. See Zárate, "La guerra de independencia," 522. For recent repetitions of Alamán's comment on Calleja playing the role of a modern Hernan Cortés, see, for example, Doris M. Ladd, *The Mexican Nobility at Independence, 1780–1826* (Austin, 1976), 117; and Timothy E. Anna, *The Fall of the Royal Government in Mexico City* (Lincoln, NB, 1978), 181.
8. Zárate, "La guerra de independencia," 522.
9. Aláman, *Historia de México*, 475.
10. Ibid., 476.
11. Representación del Comandante y Sub-Inspector Félix Calleja de la 10 Brigada y Provincias Internas dependientes del virreinato, 14 May 1802, Archivo General de las Indias, Sevilla, Sección de México (cited hereafter as AGI, Mexico), leg. 1465. For some published documentation on Calleja, see "Don Félix María Calleja del Rey: Actividades anteriores a la guerra de independence," *Boletín del Archivo General de La Nación* (cited

hereafter as AGN), I (segunda serie, no. 1, 1960), 57–86; (no. 2), 253–97; and (no. 4), 553–81.

12. Viceroy Conde de Revillagigedo to Antonio Valdés, no. 515 reservada, AGI, Mexico, leg. 1532.

13. Viceroy Marqués de Branciforte to Manuel Alvarez, no. 908 reservada, 30 October 1797, AGI, Mexico, leg. 1445.

14. Branciforte to Alvarez, no. 911 reservada, 30 October 1797, AGN, Correspondencia de los Virreyes, series 2, vol. 34.

15. The king issued the royal commission appointing Calleja to this command on 20 September 1800; see Patentes de comandantes y ayudantes veteranos de las brigadas de milicias, Madrid, AGI, Mexico, leg. 2424.

16. José de J. Nuñez y Domínguez, *La virreina mexicana: Doña María Francisca de la Gándara de Calleja* (México, 1950), 59–75.

17. Viceroy Miguel José de Azanza to Antonio Cornel, no. 685, 27 March 1800, AGI, Mexico, leg. 1452; and Viceroy Félix Berenguer de Marquina to José Antonio Caballero, no. 796, 26 September 1802, AGI, Mexico, leg. 1465. The other outstanding officer was Lieutenant Colonel Pedro de Alonso.

18. José de Iturrigaray to Caballero, no. 1022, 27 May 1806, AGN, Correspondencia de los Virreyes, series 1, vol. 230.

19. Revillagigedo to the Marqués de Campo de Alange, no. 486, 1 August 1792, Archivo General de Simancas, Guerra Moderna, leg. 6964.

20. Azanza to Cornel, no. 685, 27 March 1800, AGI, Mexico, leg. 1452.

21. Marquina to Caballero, no. 796, 26 September 1802, AGI, Mexico, leg. 1465.

22. Fernando Villanueva to Viceroy Miguel José de Azanza, Colotlán, 10 January 1799, AGN, Indiferente, vol. 157-B.

23. See Christon I. Archer, *The Army in Bourbon Mexico, 1760–1810* (Albuquerque, NM, 1977), 199–201.

24. Representación del Comandante de la décima Brigada de Milicias de la Nueva España, Don Félix Calleja, 27 December 1802, AGI, Mexico, leg. 1465.

25. Calleja to Viceroy José de Iturrigaray, 6 September 1805, AGN, IG, vol. 315-A.

26. Report of the Auditor de Guerra, Miguel Bataller, 9 February 1806, and of Viceroy José de Iturrigaray, 11 February 1806, AGN, IG, vol. 315-A.

27. García Revollo had served in the army for forty-nine years. He first arrived in Mexico with Lieutenant-General Juan de Villalba, commissioned to raise a Mexican army.

28. Calleja to Viceroy Francisco Javier de Venegas, San Luis Potosí, no. 2196, AGN: Operaciones de Guerra (cited hereafter as OG), vol. 169. Also see Alamán, *Historia de México*, I, 452–55.

29. Calleja to Venegas, Campo de Pila, 15 October 1810, AGN:OG, vol. 169; and Calleja to Conde de la Cadena (Manuel Flón), San Luis Potosí, 2 October 1810, AGN:OG, vol. 94A.

30. Calleja to Venegas, no. 2197, 28 September 1810, AGN:OG, vol. 169.

31. Calleja to Venegas, 19 August 1811, AGN:OG, vol. 199.

32. Francisco Ignacio Gómez to Calleja, Cienega, 21 September 1810, AGN:OG, vol. 180.

33. Calleja to Venegas, Campo de Pila, 9 October 1810, AGN:OG, vol. 169.

34. Calleja to Venegas, 20 August 1811, AGN: OG, vol. 140.

35. Calleja to Venegas, 26 January 1811, AGN:OG, vol. 187.

36. Calleja to Venegas, Acambaro, 27 November 1811, AGN: OG, vol. 195.

37. Petition of captains, Army of the Center, 1 February 1811, AGN:OG, vol. 165.

38. Calleja to Venegas, Campo de Molina de Saravia, 20 November 1810, AGN:OG, vol. 170.
39. Calleja to Venegas, Hacienda de Burras, 23 November 1810, AGN:OG, vol. 170.
40. Venegas to Calleja, 27 November 1810; and 8 December 1810, AGN:OG, vol. 170.
41. Calleja to Venegas, Guanajuato, 26 November 1810; 27 November 1810; 28 November 1810; and 3 December 1810, AGN:OG, vol. 170. See also Alamán, *Historia de México*, II, 56-60.
42. Calleja to Venegas, 20 January 1812, AGN:OG, vol. 201.
43. Calleja to Governor of Veracruz José de Quevedo, 2 May 1813, AGN:OG, vol. 692.
44. Venegas to Calleja, 23 November 1810, AGN:OG, vol. 170.
45. Calleja to Venegas, 18 January 1811, AGN:OG, vol. 171.
46. Calleja to Venegas, Campo de Pila, 4 March 1811; and Venegas to Calleja, 11 March 1811; and Calleja to Venegas, San Luis Potosí, 11 March 1811, AGN:OG, vol. 181.
47. Calleja to Venegas, Aguascalientes, 21 May 1811, AGN:OG, vol. 185.
48. Reglamento político militar que deberón observar bajo las penas que seóala los pueblos, haciendas, y ranchos ... Aguascalientes, 8 June 1811, AGN:OG, vol. 186.
49. Calleja to Venegas, León, 13 July 1811, AGN:OG, vol. 188. For a discussion of the counterinsurgency program, see Christon I. Archer, "The Counterinsurgency Army and the Ten Year's War," in Jaime E. Rodríguez, ed., *The Independence of Mexico and the Creation of the New Nation* (Los Angeles, 1989), 85-108.
50. Calleja to Venegas, León, 17 July 1811, AGN:OG, vol. 188.
51. Calleja to Venegas, 21 July 1811, and Calleja to Nemesio Salcedo, Guanajuato, 24 July 1811, AGN:OG, vol. 188.
52. Calleja to Venegas, 14 August 1811, AGN:OG, vol. 190.
53. Calleja to Venegas, 30 November 1811, AGN:OG, vol. 195.
54. Calleja to Venegas, Cuautla Amilpas, 18 April 1812, AGN:OG, vol. 200.
55. Venegas to Calleja, 17 November 1811, AGN:OG, vol. 195.
56. Ernesto Lemoine Villicaña, *Morelos: su vida revolucionaria a travós de sus escritos y de otros testimonios de la época* (México, 1965), 59.
57. Calleja to Venegas, 12 April 1812, AGN:OG, vol. 200.
58. Calleja to Venegas, Campo de Cuatlisco near Cuautla Amilpas, 20 February 1812, and Venegas to Calleja, 21 February 1812, AGN:OG, vol. 198.
59. Calleja to Venegas, 1 March 1812, AGN:OG, vol. 200.
60. Calleja to Venegas, 24 April 1812, AGN:OG, vol. 200.
61. Calleja to Venegas, 4 May 1812, AGN:OG, vol. 198.
62. Petition of officers, Toluca, 30 January 1812; Venegas to Calleja, 31 January 1812; and Petition of Captains of the Army of the Center, February, 1812, AGN:OG, vol. 165. For material on Calleja's illnesses and his temporary replacement by naval Brigadier Santiago Yrisarri, see Venegas to Calleja, 2 February 1812, AGN:OG, vol. 198.
63. Calleja to the Minister of War, 15 March 1813, Archivo General de Indias (cited hereafter as AGI), Mexico, leg. 1322.
64. Calleja to the Marqués de Campo Sagrado, no. 11 reservado, 6 September 1816, AGI, Mexico, leg. 1322.
65. Reglamento Político Militar, AGN:OG, vol. 186.

3

From Genius to Intellect: Unorthodox Union Officers in the American Civil War

Carol Reardon

It was April 1863, the third April in what Northern optimists had once dismissed as "a three-month war." The enthusiastic ninety-day recruits of 1861 who prayed they would not miss their chance to fight wondered now if they would live to see the war's end. The editors of the *Army and Navy Gazette*, a new Northern paper devoted to war news, tried to explain why the fighting continued with no end in sight:

The Iron Duke and Lord Nelson of England, Washington, General Scott and Decatur, with a few more lights of lesser brilliancy . . . are, perhaps, the only names which represent the military genius of the Anglo-Saxon race, during a period of a thousand years. What the present gigantic struggle may bring forth, it is difficult with the limited prescience of mortals to foretell. In all the battles of the war thus far, though on many a bloody field we are proud to refer to such names as Rosecrans, Hooker, and others, who have done credit to the military talent of America, we have not yet had that man who could step forward, with a mind sufficiently comprehensive to grasp the contest in detail, and to lead a noble, intelligent, patriotic and enthusiastic army to complete and unconditional success.

With fresh memories of the great defeat at Fredericksburg and the great bloodletting at Stone's River the previous December, Northern readers were warned that success would come only when their armies were "held in perfect mastery by the controlling mind" of "an extraordinary man." Time, the editors concluded, was "the great sifter" that would "bring out from a nation of twenty millions the right man, and . . . place him in his appropriate position."[1]

So spring passed into summer, bringing decisive Union victories at Gettysburg and Vicksburg in the first week of July 1863. Had that genius appeared? Apparently not. "With all due respect for the generals to whom the country now looks for succor and support, we cannot detect in them any but a mere conventional military talent," the editors wrote after those battles. "McClellan, Fremont, Halleck, Burnside, Hooker, Pope, and other major generals and brigadier generals in the United States Army are simply men of fine military talent, and would suit well to carry out to the letter the mandate of some commanding genius," but "[t]hey cannot create. They cannot avail themselves of those hidden secrets of success through which Napoleon would force victory almost in the very teeth of impossibility." When that military savior "does appear at the head of our armies, we shall know the fact at once. . . . He will boast not of what he intends doing, but do what he intends."[2]

As the editors' comments suggest, the Civil War generation's concept of "genius"—or "brilliancy"—carried very precise meaning. Genius was a natural endowment. It revealed itself in powerful creativity and originality that defied analysis or explanation. It could lie dormant until freed by inspiration or intuition, and it might express itself in unpredictable and spectacular ways. Genius could not be acquired in a classroom, by mastering technique, or by sheer hard work. It was much the superior of mere talent, which could be cultivated by intensive study and application but only within the limited range of one's intellect. And, unfortunately, genius was a dangerously obsolete fragment of eighteenth-century military thinking still being applied uncritically to generals in this nineteenth-century war.[3]

The frustrating search for a military genius among Union commanders during the Civil War lay the groundwork for a revolution in and a long-term redefinition of the prerequisites for responsible and successful generalship. Traditional measures of a man's ability to command would not fall easily. Even so well informed a man as the editor of the *New York Tribune*, Horace Greeley, could write with complete confidence that: "The atmosphere, the fume of the bivouac, was much more likely to produce military genius than the textbooks of West Point."[4] Unending bloodletting, however, convinced more and more soldiers in the U.S. Army to embrace a new vision of leadership that cautioned against—sometimes even dismissed as careless and dangerous—a reliance on the emergence of the individual genius. Instead, they promoted an increased attention to the military education of *all* officers as a surer guarantee of victory. Those who articulated arguments to end "the search for genius" to promote "the military education and intellectual improvement of all"—and we cannot even identify many of them or their converts by name—were some of the more unheralded heretics of the American Civil War.

Mobilizing the North for war raised many questions for the Lincoln administration, and for many reasons the commissioning of general officers was a particularly thorny one. If the U.S. Army could have provided an intact command structure capable of expanding to meet the war emergency, Lincoln might have been able to sidestep the issue. In 1861, however, the U.S. Army faced an acute leadership crisis. Its most senior generals, such as Winfield Scott, were too old to lead armies in the field. Some likely successors—including Robert E. Lee and Joseph E. Johnston—had resigned to join the Confederacy. Many of the remaining loyal officers would be needed in ordnance or quartermaster or some other staff duty essential to building a new U.S. Army. Lincoln could not fill all his command slots with professional soldiers.

Additionally, the President could not afford to dismiss a deeply felt popular conviction dating back to colonial times that the concentration of power in a standing army was a threat to the liberties of the people. In 1861, the U.S. Military Academy seemed to show evidence of that precise concern. Long a target of critics who condemned it as a bastion of militarism and elitism, West Point now came under attack as a breeding ground of traitors. So many graduates and faculty had defected to the new Confederacy that the loyalty of all West Pointers was now somehow suspect. With bluntly stated distrust of Military Academy graduates and a cockiness borne of inexperience in martial matters, Senator Lyman Trumbull of Illinois demanded that Lincoln "dismiss from the army every man who knows how to build a fortification and let the men of the north with their strong arms and indomitable spirit, move down upon the rebels and I tell you they will grind them to powder."[5]

For both practical and emotional reasons, then, there would be no quick fix for Lincoln's military leadership quandary. The complexities of the problem soon became apparent. What qualities should Lincoln demand of the many candidates seeking general's stars? Although militia experience or Mexican War service would be useful, it could not be the only consideration. The patriotism and generosity of the lawyer and businessman James Wadsworth, a military neophyte who recruited and then equipped whole regiments of New York troops, could not be overlooked. Nor could the need to forge a spirit of national unity and purpose be ignored. With some Democrats already condemning "Mr. Lincoln's War" or the "Black Republican War," the President had to win over key constituencies previously cool to his party's actions; making generals of the German-born Franz Sigel, the pro-war Democrat John McClernand, and the Irish emigré Michael Corcoran became part of Lincoln's national (or grand) strategy to rally support for the war and help recruit from these key ethnic and political groups. For many reasons, then, in apportioning what T. Harry Williams has called Lincoln's "military patronage," nonmilitary concerns easily could outweigh a man's military qualifications for general's stars.[6]

Reduced to its most simplified form early in the war, when patriotism was at high pitch—and professional soldiers in short supply and not entirely trusted—evidence of commitment to the Union and a strong personal character stood highest among the requirements for high rank. This seemed justified—and not naive—when even some of the best known military writers of the day, if selectively quoted and superficially read, seemed to back the notion that the keys to successful generalship could be found in a man's character, no matter what his life's calling. Jomini, for one, wrote:

The most essential qualities for a general will always be as follows: First, *a high moral courage, capable of great resolutions* [emphasis added]; Secondly, *a physical courage which takes no account of danger* [emphasis added]. His scientific or military acquirements are secondary to the above-mentioned characteristics, though if great they will be valuable auxiliaries. It is not necessary that he should be a man of vast erudition. [7]

Jomini said much more on the subject, including a blunt statement that a general "should be perfectly grounded in the principles at the base of the art of war;" but, in 1861, it was difficult to convince patriotic military amateurs of the importance of intellectual preparation for leading troops into battle. Even as late as mid-1863, at the mere suggestion that generals could actually learn about the art of command in war, one critic swore that "A great soldier like a deadshot and an honest lawyer are *born* [emphasis added] and not made," a sentiment that, with colorful variations, surfaced repeatedly for years.[8] It was too easy to invoke the memories of a legion of American military heroes—such as Andrew Jackson, Francis Marion, and Daniel Morgan—whose reliance on courage and character, and not their intellectual attainments, had secured their places in national history as great men and victors in war. The cult of genius would not surrender without a fight. One convert wrote:

In the beginning, it was the fashion to sneer at those who had made the profession of arms their study, and an experience in Congress was apparently regarded as a more essential qualification to command, than a course of study at West Point. Indeed, there seemed to be in some quarters a half suspicion that the possession of military knowledge and conscientious regard for the essential principles of military science, were in some way a disqualification for the public service.[9]

As a result, a veteran later recalled, the Union's first command structure included "ward managers, heads of fire-companies, bosses of mining gangs, heroes of the prize-ring, professional gamblers, popular bar-keepers" in addition to hordes of politicians and a few West Pointers.[10] Any one of these men might be the long-sought military genius who would save the Union.

Taking a cue from Jomini, as so many Civil War soldiers did, a commander's need for physical courage seemed straightforward enough. Early on, so long as Northern soldiers viewed the conflict as the crucible in which their own manhood would be tested, courage in the face of the enemy—what historian Gerald F. Linderman has described as "heroic action undertaken without fear"—seemed to offer sufficient evidence of a man's capacity to command at any rank.[11] Lieutenant Rush Cady of the 97th New York Infantry conferred what he no doubt considered the ultimate compliment on Major Charles Northup after the battle of Antietam in 1862: "as to 'standing fire,' judging from the testimony of eye witnesses, and from the bullet holes which his clothes afterwards exhibited, the decision must be made that he stood it like a Major."[12] For generals, the standards were higher. After the battle at Fair Oaks, Virginia, in June 1862, an artilleryman confided to his diary that while General Erasmus Keyes was "much more engaged in looking after his personal effects . . . than his command . . . Old [General Silas] Casey himself was brave as a lion, and remained while his men would stand; he lost everything but the clothes he stood in."[13] The need to display one's personal bravery was so strong that one officer felt compelled to explain to his family that in leading an attack at the head of his troops, a "mounted officer is as likely to be hit in the back, and more likely to be hit in the side, than in the front, and don't ever do an officer the injustice to think ill of him for such a wound."[14]

As essential as physical courage, as Jomini argued, was another kind: moral courage. Jomini had written: "A man who is gallant, just, firm, upright, capable of esteeming merit in others instead of being jealous of it, and skilful in making this merit conduce to his own glory, will always be a good general, and may even pass for a great man."[15] A responsible general must be able to channel all these traits toward one goal: performing his military obligations in good faith and to the best of his ability. This was the basis of his military character. Early in the war, while the search for genius continued, failure to win battles or fulfill duties within one's capacity and authority solely from a lack of military knowledge was deplored, but since, as many believed, a winning general had to be "an extraordinary man"—a genius—and most men were not, losing a battle was "no particular ground for self-deprecation."[16] But if an army's reverses could be traced directly to some personal weakness in the commander, he should be forced to give up his position.

But were courage and character enough? A stark realization set in by 1863 that a Washington, a Napoleon, or a Wellington might not emerge from the repeatedly defeated set of morally and physically brave Union generals when the Union needed him most. Prudence, frustration, and a growing sense of impatience all dictated that the complexities of this war—the emergence of mass armies of green troops, the size of the battlefields on which they fought, and the rapidly changing technology of war—required a reassessment of how it was fought. Observers in and out of uniform agreed that their generals still needed such timeless qualities as physical courage and strength of character. By 1863, however, impatient Northerners, tired of waiting for the yet-to-emerge military genius, added and gave dramatically increased attention to a third qualification: competence in military art and science; they argued that "the correct employment of reason is the essentiality of . . . genius."[17] No matter how many officers have "noble hearts, unquestioned courage, [and] unfaltering patriotism," one commentator observed, military leadership with "no intellectual culture" at its foundation worked against the nation's best interest.[18]

Champions of the new orthodoxy soon stepped forward. One in the forefront was General Silas Casey, the man who stood "brave as a lion" at Fair Oaks and the author of a widely used tactics manual consulted by both volunteer and regular officers. By 1863, he was an active member of the selection board choosing officers for newly raised regiments of United States Colored Troops. Casey repeatedly attempted to make clear that "to have good and efficient troops it is indispensable that we should have good officers." Northern volunteers "deserve to have officers to command them who have been educated to the military profession." Casey warned that "*zeal alone* [emphasis added] is not sufficient," and "what we require for a good officer is zeal, combined with knowledge." Casey demanded that mastery of military knowledge be one test for appointment and advancement, and he warned that when a political leader places in command an incompetent officer who does not meet this standard, "he is guilty of *manslaughter* [emphasis added]."[19] At fifty-six years of age, Casey was not pushing for changes that would promote his own career. A combat veteran himself, he strongly believed that courage and character, even backed by experience, were not enough. He made those ideas stick when he could, and after the war he took pride in the officers whom his board had selected, noting that "as a body they were superior to [officers in white regiments], physically, mentally, and morally."[20]

The new formula seemed straightforward enough: officers who were proficient in military studies saved soldiers' lives. But it seemed to take several years of war for the new realities to sink in. Waste "is the grand characteristic of this war," wrote one Union officer at the beginning of the spring campaign of 1864. "We waste arms, clothing, ammunition, and subsistence; but, above all, men . . . because we have no military or social caste to make officers from." Realizing that the United States was not likely to develop a class system to make up for this deficiency, he noted that it could be made up in another way. Units "that have been officered by gentlemen of education" have invariably performed better than those who were not.[21]

While this soldier stopped short of a specific endorsement of military education, many others did not. One officer appealed to his brother volunteers to accept a moral obligation not to "regard the Army as only a temporary profession and make no attempt to become proficient at it"; he encouraged them "to create for themselves a higher standard of professional knowledge" through "some judicious course of reading" to improve their ability to carry out their duties.[22] Still others called for institutional efforts to improve the military competence of army officers: "That there should be some systematic training for the education of every calling in life, would seem to be the universal opinion among men," one man wrote, wondering why no such accommodation had been made for the two professions that demanded in particular "men of the most superior intellectual attainment and force of character. These two are Statesmanship and Generalship." Military education must be intensive, extensive, and as some would point out, ongoing, even into peacetime. As challenging as the current times were, the responsibilities facing those officers who made the army their career would grow even more after the war. No time should be lost in preparing officers for the future because experience had shown that "no man [should] gain a position until he shows that he has both capacity and acquirements equal to the demands of the position"; and in years ahead, "whatever may be our desires, whatever our apprehensions of large standing armies, we cannot conceal from ourselves that, probably, for all future time, a much larger military establishment than was ever before contemplated must be maintained by us."[23]

Intellectual and literary debates helped change minds in headquarters tents and in Washington; however, in the field, it took only the personal experience of years of indecisive fighting to convince soldiers of the urgency of improving the military competence of their leaders. Their standards for what made a "good" officer changed. By 1863, an officer's personal courage, if unaccompanied by a deep commitment to life-conserving competence, won few plaudits from combat veterans of any rank—each lesson on the road to this realization had cost lives. After a series of assaults against Confederate entrenchments at Cold Harbor, one Union staff officer explained that "the good pluck in generals" that had won high praise in 1861 meant little now. He complained about civilians who say, "'Oh, everyone is brave enough; it is the head that is needed.' ... but I can tell you that there are *not* [emphasis added] many officers who of their own choice and impulse will dash in on formidable positions. They will go anywhere they are *ordered* [emphasis added] and anywhere they believe it is their *duty* [emphasis added] to go," but now "it requires a peculiar disposition to 'go in gaily,' as old Kearny would say."[24] Or more properly, "would have said": General Philip Kearny was long dead, killed at Chantilly in 1862 in front of his men when he tempted death one time too often. Kearny had then been the very model of bravery, and the army had mourned his loss. Two years later, the survivors of Kearny's old division would not be so forgiving of an officer's displays of personal bravado, especially if it might cost them their lives. At Petersburg, one veteran, after a brief skirmish in which death "filled the air like snowflakes in a winter storm," blasted General Francis C. Barlow's tactics: "The most stupid private, and we have legions of them, would know better than to push a column out in this way, no connection right or left and both flanks in the air."[25] Courage combined with competence replaced courage alone as a soldierly ideal. The soldiers implicitly understood what General Casey meant when he equated manslaughter with the assignment of untrained officers to troop command.

Character, like courage, and even in combination with courage, also proved insufficient as a measure of a general's qualification for command as the war went on. The relationship between enlisted men and officers, said one volunteer, is "something so different in kind from anything which civil life has to offer, that it has proved almost impossible to transfer methods or maxims from the one to the other." It required a respect for authority to a degree civilians did not understand and with which they could not easily comply. "Implicit obedience must be still admitted to be a rare commodity in our army," wrote one officer late in the war.[26]

But early in the war, a general's strong character was supposed to help him build an effective military force from these free-willed men. As General Joseph Hooker had said, "it is the commander that gives tone and character" to his men.[27] So long as soldiers accepted the role as their general's "chisel" and believed they might give "perfect and successful expression" to "the military genius" of their commander, the force of character triumphed.[28] But experience, and especially a series of defeats, sooner or later bred disillusionment in most soldiers. In their reassessment of what was needed in their generals, character—like courage—was no longer a satisfactory measure of a man's suitability to command.

Perhaps no general found himself caught so completely in the changing relationship between character and generalship as did Joe Hooker. His men had idolized him on early battlefields where his personal leadership won him the nickname of "Fighting Joe." When General Carl Schurz heard of Hooker's accession to command of the Army of the Potomac early in 1863, he was sure victory would soon follow. General Hooker "has what all commanders of this army who preceded him lacked, the first element of military success—self confidence."[29] None could deny Hooker's confidence, even if they did not care for the arrogance that accompanied it: "With his habitual modesty, he has remarked that with a certain force he could 'drive the Rebels to Hell or anywhere else.' The administration's plan doesn't involve so extensive a campaign, only that we go as far as Richmond," one of his soldiers commented sourly.[30] But most of his soldiers mirrored Hooker's own confidence; he was, as one of his corps commanders said, "a great favorite," and the men "were enthusiastically devoted to him."[31]

At the battle of Chancellorsville in early May 1863, after a characteristically confident start, Hooker inexplicably halted and surrendered the initiative to the Confederates. His men did not understand why. Then, after Stonewall Jackson's flank attack routed the Union XI Corps and Hooker himself was stunned by a cannonball that struck his headquarters, responsible command gave way to chaos and confusion. Reserves went unsummoned. Plans were made for a withdrawal. But—and this quickly became clear when the Union line stabilized after Jackson's attack—only the high command seemed at the point of collapse. The rank and file of Hooker's army had not lost their will to fight.

After the battle, and as the story unfolded, many soldiers began to feel quite differently about "Fighting Joe." It was not just that Hooker had lost a battle—all his predecessors had done that, and some, such as George McClellan, were still great favorites of the army. It was not that Hooker had failed to show his usual bravery in the face of the enemy. He had personally tried to rally the fleeing soldiers of the XI Corps when Jackson hit them. But he had also revealed personal weaknesses his men had not seen before, weaknesses that undermined their faith both in him and in his ability to carry out his command obligations in a responsible way. His sudden indecision was bad enough, and the rumors of his drinking to insensibility did not sit well with his men. Worse than all this, however, he had tried to shift the blame for the defeat away from himself and onto the shoulders of his men, soldiers who he later said "appear to be unwilling to go into a fight." Indeed, Hooker had said, "in my judgment, there are not many who really like to fight."[32] If, as Hooker had said earlier, the commander set the character of his men, the soldiers of the Army of the Potomac no longer agreed with him. During the march into Pennsylvania in June, when false rumors swept through the marching columns that Hooker was relieved and McClellan restored to command, the soldiers cheered with joy.

Growing disaffection with generalship was not limited to the soldiers of the Army of the Potomac. Nor was Joseph Hooker the only target. Survivors of Ambrose Burnside's disastrous Fredericksburg campaign in December 1862 revealed it plainly. Private R. B. Goodyear of the 27th Connecticut spoke for thousands of his comrades when he wrote in early 1863:

I must not enumerate the humbugs and impositions practiced upon the army and from which we suffer repeated disasters and defeats. The soldier of today has a keen perception. He . . . is not slow to detect the real character of the war as it is conducted. Abused, humbugged, imposed upon and frequently half-starved and sick, he sees himself. . . . Led on to slaughter and defeat by drunken and incompetent officers, he has become disheartened, discouraged, demoralized.[33]

Such soldiers could only feel misused and betrayed. After two years of war, they had indeed grown wiser in the ways of war, but they wondered if their generals had. After Chancellorsville, one private from Ohio showed considerable insight in his critique of Hooker's generalship: "It is quite a different thing to fight when ordered, from saying *when* and *where* [emphasis added] to fight. Strategy and tactics differ from individual heroism."[34] In the minds of the men whose very lives depended on responsible generalship, courage and character without competence no longer sufficed as qualifications for their generals.

To a congressional committee investigating the conduct of the war, General Daniel Butterfield, Hooker's chief of staff, tried to explain the pitfalls of commanding the armies of a republic at war. After an early defeat, General Irvin McDowell had been charged "with drunkenness when it was well known he never touched liquor of any kind. . . . McDowell, [John] Pope, McClellan, Burnside, have all heard their share of this kind of attack; some have been called drunkards, some cowards, some fools. It is the nature of our people; the arduous duties and responsibilities of commanders is not fully appreciated by all."[35] But soldiers of all ranks, from generals to privates, appreciated more than Butterfield knew. As one officer wrote of veterans of his acquaintance, they will always be ready "to comply with a reasonable order, not because it is an order, but because it is reasonable."[36] A "reasonable" order reflected a commander's competence and was not primarily a reflection on his character. The most courageous general in the army would not win back the confidence of these men if he did not show sufficient military competence to use them to good result. In their own way, they too had grown impatient with the nation's and administration's search for genius.

Early in the war, the dimensions of the war emergency and the political exigencies of forging a sense of national unity had undercut the importance of military education as a qualification for a commission. Still, despite much bluster to the contrary from soldiers and politicians alike, possession of military knowledge had never been discarded as useless. Effective on 22 July 1861, the day after the debacle of First Bull Run, military commissioning boards grilled new regimental and battery officers to test their knowledge of drill manuals and service regulations or assessed their potential for mastering it. The process was necessary. Company officers—and sometimes regimental officers—in state units were elected by a popular ballot of the soldiers. It was not unusual to find captains such as one from Pennsylvania "whose last command had been a pair of draft horses" and who ordered his men around a pit in the road with "the stentorian command to 'Gee round that hole.'"[37] General George G. Meade was not optimistic of improvement until the officer selection policy was changed:

The men are good material, and with good officers might readily be moulded into soldiers; but the officers, as a rule, with but very few exceptions, are ignorant, inefficient and worthless. They have not control or command over the men, and if they had, they do not know what to do with them. We have been weeding out some of the worst, but owing to the vicious system of electing successors which prevails, those who take their places are no better.[38]

But for commissioning into the highest ranks, where the stakes were considerably higher and the challenges as yet unknown, there were no such boards. Simply put, no one would have known how to measure a man's capacity for generalship.

Much responsible dialogue on the question fell victim to the unique vulnerability of West Point graduates at the beginning of the war. In addition to fighting allegations of treasonous activities at the school on the Hudson, West Pointers were effectively denied any authoritative voice in such important questions as the selection of general officers. After all, as critics observed, they were no more experienced at generalship than green recruits. Indeed, for thirty years before the war, the West Point curriculum included only a single course that remotely touched on questions of grand strategy, and no one could predict how—or even if—Professor Dennis Hart Mahan's class on the art of war would have a lasting impact on any soldier's military mind years later.[39] In fact, the entire West Point curriculum underwent an extensive and widely publicized congressional evaluation in 1860, and criticism had prevailed over praise. Especially of concern were officers' own assessments of their education in subjects most important to future generals. As Lieutenant R. J. Dodge commented, "The time given to strategy is . . . entirely too little. The subject is one of the gravest importance; and in no other branch of the military art is 'a little learning' so dangerous a thing."[40] Captain George W. Cullum agreed completely: "The great object of the education at the Military Academy, which is to form accomplished officers, cannot be fully attained . . . without a more thorough knowledge of the science of war. Now, it is made subordinate to almost every branch of instruction at the Academy, and even 'veterinary science' is made the rival in importance to the 'science of war.' "[41]

Equally unsettling, antebellum army officers—regardless of the source of their commission—were not known to continue their studies of the art of war once on active duty. Lieutenant J. B. Holabird explained there were many reasons for this: "one, the absence of all stimulus; also, the nature of their duties, the jealousy and sneers of old and incapable officers, etc."[42] Lieutenant A. M. McCook added that he and his fellow officers were "usually scattered by single companies, and if concentrated are in the field on campaigns in pursuit of Indians, and in consequence, cannot have recourse to books."[43] The problems were so pervasive that at the start of the war, Northerners learned to their dismay that the search for generals who understood the intricacies of military strategy was like "calling for sailors among Mongol Tartars who had never seen the sea."[44]

So what did Civil War generals—West Pointers and ex-civilians alike—have to learn to make and execute strategic designs, and how were they to learn it? Early in the war, the "how" seemed simple enough. The body of military literature written in or translated into English that discussed the theory of the art of war on the generals' level was sufficiently small for any commander to grasp basic principles without excessive mental application. Reprints of Jomini's *Art of War* and Napoleon's maxims were readily available. But even the most respected of these works could not have prepared generals for the scope and nature of the war they faced. On a more practical level, tactics manuals abounded, but only Casey's and one or two others gave even the slightest attention to maneuvers of units larger than a regiment. Even then, those manuals read more like "how-to" books that were very useful when it was time to execute a maneuver, but not very insightful on how to decide when or if to order that movement. An early 1864 description of generalship verified the centrality of decision making to high command that few aspirants for general's stars appreciated early in the war: "A battle between armies of a hundred thousand or more men, consists of a series of part-actions, distinct in time and space. The principal duty of a commander is to combine these actions into a whole, to form and use properly his reserves, and thus secure final success."[45] Courage and character, and even superficial familiarity with military books, were simply not enough.

Perhaps the fullest description of the art of Civil War generalship comes from P. G. T. Beauregard, a Southerner and a West Pointer, who gave the matter considerable thought in large part to justify many of his own actions: "The great principles of war are truths, and the same to-day as in the time of Caesar or Napoleon . . . their applications being but intensified by the scientific discoveries affecting transportation and communication of intelligence. These principles are few and simple, however various their deductions and application." Generalship, he continued, consists of

seeing through the intricacies of the whole situation, and bringing into proper combination forces and influences, though seemingly unrelated, so as to apply those principles, and with boldness of decision and execution appearing with the utmost force, and, if possible, superior odds, before the enemy at some strategic, that is, decisive point. And although a sound military plan may not be always so readily conceived, yet any plan that offers decisive results, if it agrees with the principles of war, is as plain and intelligible as those principles themselves, and no more to be rejected than they.[46]

Beauregard's strategic vision clearly required intensive intellectual effort to master the principles of war and their applications in various combinations. This was beyond the capacity of a general who is merely a brave man or a good man. He must also be an intelligent man well versed in military knowledge.

Why was this not obvious early on? The recent curricular evaluation suggested that West Point graduates held no monopoly on esoteric military knowledge. Numerous complaints about the declining intellectual abilities of recent incoming classes seemed verified when former superintendent Colonel Richard Delafield argued against raising graduation standards too high, stating that: "The demands of our service do not require it."[47] Indeed, early battles suggested to the Northern public that the one-time cadets who had remained loyal to the Union had not benefited much from their military classes. In two early battles in Virginia—major ones by 1861 standards only—Union generals Irvin McDowell and Charles P. Stone, both of whom had graduated from West Point, were thrashed soundly by Confederate opponents. In a third, a Confederate West Pointer had inflicted a serious defeat on a considerably larger Union force. A poem summed up some of the North's frustration after three defeats:

> Big Bethel, Bull Run, and Ball's Bluff
> Oh, alliteration of blunders!
> Of blunders more than enough
> In a time full of blunders and wonders
> History, shut up your books
> Or blot from your record the story,
> Nor honor such scenes with a look,
> Where the shame eclipses the glory
> Two thousand men against six
> Led as the blind lead the blind
> Two thousand men hemmed in by six
> And the rushing river behind
> For no one's to blame, and yet,
> who issued the order?
> We men may forgive and forget,
> but not the Eternal Recorder.[48]

If the U.S. Army's professionals could not win victories, then it should not be so surprising that military education remained low among the qualifications for high command for so long. Political considerations aside, a series of beaten West Pointers made it easy to open the door to military amateurs, at least partly on the notion that if they could not do any better, they could not possibly do any worse. Their lack of formal military education did not matter anyway, one Northerner argued, since "the theory or the principles of war repose upon common sense, and . . . he who is possessed of the strongest share of common sense will most readily acquire knowledge of the principles of war, and will be at the same time less hampered by them in actual practice."[49] The inspiration and creativity to which he alluded was the heart of genius, of course, and genius could not be taught—at West Point or anywhere else. Indeed, Senator Benjamin Wade of Ohio proclaimed that "if the war continues . . . you will have men of genius enough, educated in the field, and infinitely better educated than they possibly could be" at West Point.[50]

Until the emergence of Grant and Meade in mid-1863, few West Point–trained Union generals had a record of battlefield success that could be used to fight against this impression. Political generals—men such as Robert Milroy, Franz Sigel, and John C. Fremont, among others—went from defeat to defeat, and while their failures were bad for Northern morale, similar results from West Point graduates McClellan, Pope, Don Carlos Buell, Burnside, and Hooker did nothing to restore the reputation of professional military education. Their countrymen wondered aloud how their generals, some of whom did claim to have read widely on modern warfare, could repeatedly demonstrate that they "had gained but little practical knowledge from all their reading." The generals might have studied war on maps and fought battles on paper, but "how little do they think of . . . the generalship that move the puppet masses on the mimic field."[51] They had shown neither creativity nor inspiration—no genius—and they had lost and lost again.

Career army officers had special reason to be concerned about this national obsession for genius. Most West Point graduates—with the obvious exception of McClellan, who peppered his letters to his wife with phrases like "again I have been called upon to save the country"—did not claim the mantle of genius and did not like the implications of such a search for the future of their profession or its impact on the war effort.

General Meade despaired of the popular misconceptions about generalship under which he and his brother officers labored. He wrote that "the wise public" and the press "are under the delusion" that generals are supposed to be "omnipotent, and that it is only necessary to go ahead to achieve unheard-of success. Of course, under such circumstances, neither Caesar, Napoleon nor any other mighty genius could fail to meet with condemnation, never mind what he did," if it were short of decisive victory. Meade had seen what happened to unsuccessful claimants for the crown of genius. The Northern press and people showered a general with "undue and exaggerated praise before he does anything,"—he may well have been thinking of the press nicknaming George McClellan "the Young Napoleon"—then they displayed "a total absence of reason and intelligence in the discussion of his acts when he does attempt anything." They then deny him "even ordinary military qualifications unless he achieves impossibilities."[52] The *Springfield Republican* hailed "Little Mac" as a military genius in 1861 but had changed its tune by April 1862: "Is McClellan a greater man than Napoleon, or a monster humbug?"[53] Meade himself undoubtedly cringed if he read the *New York Times* a few days after his victory at Gettysburg: "Through the brief campaign Gen. Meade's genius has shown resplendent. . . . he has, within four days of that on which he assumed command, achieved [this great victory]. It is the work of eminent military genius—of genius such as has not heretofore been displayed in this war."[54] A week later, the same papers called him timid for allowing Lee's army to escape across the Potomac River to the safety of Virginia.

Tradition dies hard, but with the war two years old and no genius in sight, some Northerners finally dared to suggest that "A great general, like true greatness in any sphere, is the product of a long series of events in any particular country. It would be folly for us to expect from the thin soil of a past, such as that which America presents, a Shakespeare, a Milton, a Burke, a Schiller, or a Napoleon."[55] The stakes were too high to place so much faith on such a slender hope. Something had to be done to bring out the best in the officers at hand. A better-educated officer corps—and some system to continue raising the standards for a professional knowledge of the laws of war and their application—was an option worth exploring. So far, one commentator observed, a "single retrospective glance will show that from [1861 on] we have been educating such generals in the only school where they can learn . . . the vicissitude of success and disaster—glory and danger," the battlefield. "How many generals have been eliminated in this schooling process!" he wondered.[56] He might have added, "and at the cost of how many lives?"

Making the mastery of military knowledge an important part of a man's qualifications for command was a natural outgrowth of all these concerns. But it brought no immediate and dramatic changes. Indeed, the education impulse did not rise to the level of an organized "movement" until the postwar years, and it often won over its Civil War–era converts one by one. It was tied to no special interest group, although West Point graduates tended to embrace it first, some from a sense of genuine professionalism and others only for self-validation. But not all West Pointers rallied to the cause, and perceptive volunteer officers came to understand the benefits of a military education before some of their professional colleagues. In mid-1864, a volunteer colonel concluded that his three years of active duty had taught him that in the education of officers, "the total value of the professional training has proved far greater, and that of the [previous] general [educational] preparation far less than many intelligent observers predicted. . . . Nothing but great personal qualities can give a man by nature what is easily acquired by . . . men of very average ability who are systematically trained to command."[57]

The new emphasis on military competence changed the Union army in a number of important ways. The Civil War generation spoke of the ability to put together successful combinations—an antecedent of the modern concept of "strategic vision"—by executing movements according to skillful applications of well-understood principles of war. Familiarity with these concepts made successful strategic and tactical combinations far more likely. In March 1864, when General Ulysses S. Grant took command of all the Union armies, he planned the most sweeping strategic combination that any American general had attempted to date. General Philip Sheridan, one of Grant's most useful implements in making his plans succeed, explained why it worked: Grant gave "systematic direction . . . to our armies in every section of the vast territory over which active operations were being prosecuted, and further . . . this coherence, this harmony of plan, was the one thing needed to end the war, for in the three preceding years there had been illustrated most lamentable effects of the absence of system." With the "manifold resources of his well-ordered military mind," Grant "guided every subordinate then, and in the last days of the rebellion, with a fund of common sense and superiority of intellect," he ended the war decisively.[58] This was a man who could oversee part-actions and combine them for victory. By his own admission, Grant was not a devoted student of the art of war in the usual sense—he told visitors that the only military books he owned were his West Point texts[59]— but like many other successful generals, he had the foundation of military knowledge on which to build, and to a remarkable degree he was able to make use of it.

General William T. Sherman agreed entirely with Sheridan's assessment of the commanding general. When Grant took charge of all the armies, Sherman admitted that he had questions about Grant's "knowledge of grand strategy and of books of science and history," but he soon discovered that Grant's ability to use what he did know erased any fears.[60] Grant's special talents inspired an insightful comparison from Sherman: General John McClernand, a political appointee with

an intense selfishness and lust of notoriety . . . could not let his mind get beyond the limits of his vision, and therefore all was brilliant about him and dark and suspicious beyond. My style is the reverse. I am somewhat blind to what occurs near me, but have a clear perception of things and events remote. Grant possesses a happy medium and it is for this reason I admire him. I have a much quicker perception of things than he; but he balances the present and remote so evenly that results follow in natural course.[61]

Sherman—who understood the concept of genius—did not give that title to Grant when rendering professional assessments of his generalship.

By 1864, the Union's most experienced and successful senior commanders had come to appreciate and demand the assistance of similarly competent subordinates who could carry out complex maneuvers. Grant and Sherman showed in their selection of generals and in the replacement of unsatisfactory officers that they would accept nothing less. Not a month into the 1864 Virginia campaign, Grant dismissed a number of his generals on the grounds that they had performed their military duties poorly. Relieving generals was always a thorny business, but Grant escaped the usual storms of criticism because he showed "a uniform system in the matter, and . . . the long complained of capriciousness and vacillation in regard to removals and reinstatement, as well as in regard to appointment no longer exists." Noting with pleasure that not all of the relieved officers were volunteers and not all of the replacements were fellow West Pointers, the *Army and Navy Journal* concluded that "Grant will pay little attention to the incident of his subordinates being 'Abolitionists' or 'Conservatives,' or 'Germans' or 'Irishmen,' but will only see to it that they are *soldiers* [emphasis added]" who had mastered their art.[62]

Sherman confronted the issue directly when General James McPherson, one of his army commanders, was killed near Atlanta in July 1864. Sherman's criterion for McPherson's replacement was not seniority, as tradition dictated, but proven competence. To find the right man, he passed over two volunteer officers with commendable combat records and picked a career soldier with a West Point education. In explanation, Sherman wrote: "It was all-important that there should exist a perfect understanding among the army commanders," a common ground that could only come from the standard foundation of an education in the military art. "I wanted to succeed in taking Atlanta, and needed commanders who were purely and technically soldiers, men who would obey orders and execute them properly and on time; for I knew that we would have to execute some most delicate manoeuvers, requiring the utmost skill, nicety, and precision."[63] He did not pass over more senior officers simply because they were not West Pointers, as they charged. He had also passed over Joseph Hooker, who "seemed jealous of all the army commanders, because in years, former rank, and experience, he thought he was our superior."[64] As he had throughout the war, Sherman followed a consistent pattern of giving top consideration for promotion only to men who had shown a willingness to master military knowledge, West Pointer or not. He endorsed the generalcy of Stephen Hurlbut, a lawyer, because "I found him far above the average in the knowledge of regimental and brigade drill." Similarly, he urged that William K. Strong, a wool merchant, be promoted because he was a "good, kind-hearted gentleman, boiling over with patriotism and zeal" who sincerely evinced a desire to learn his new profession. "I advised him what to read and study," Sherman added.[65] He was so committed to responsible leadership that he was quick to respond to critics of his famous march to the sea. To those who thought it either risky or an exercise in personal glory hunting, he explained its intellectual justification:

Every movement I have made in this war has been based on sound military principle, and the result proves the assertion. At Atlanta I was not to be decoyed from the fruits of my summer's work, by Hood's chasing to the left. . . . Nor was I rash in cutting loose from a base and relying on the country for forage and provisions. I had wagons enough loaded with essentials, and beef cattle enough to feed on for more than a month, and had the Census statistics showing the produce of every county through which I designed to pass. No military expedition was ever based on sounder or surer data.[66]

In the end, it seems that the much maligned Hooker had gotten one thing right: a commander could set the tone and character for his men. Under Grant and Sherman, and other enlightened commanders such as George Thomas, it became increasingly important to introduce, maintain, and then improve military competence throughout the ranks.

The quality of staff officers was one area of clear improvement. These men had become extensions of the commander on the huge battlefields of the Civil War and had to communicate his orders and ensure that they were carried out expeditiously. A Union general's staff was not an operational staff as it is understood today; initially, many Civil War staff officers were merely military dilettantes who found the lure of officer's rank and association with the high command irresistible. They often were not even good messenger boys. George McClellan, despite his delusions of perfection, admitted that he learned early on to entrust important staff matters to Regulars and to a few "educated soldiers" from foreign countries. Of his staff volunteers, he wrote: "The most useless thing imaginable is one of these 'highly educated' civilians. . . . it takes them a long time to learn the fact that they know nothing. . . . I would not for the world have any new ones."[67]

As the war continued, staff officers came to understand the part they played in a well-run army, and they resented those who did not respect their new-found professionalism. A member of Meade's staff in 1864 wrote that

it is a crying mistake to think, as many do, that an aide is a sort of mounted messenger—an orderly in shoulder-straps. An aide *should* be a first-rate military man; and, at least, a man of more than average intelligence and education. It is very difficult, particularly in this kind of country, to deliver an order verbally, in a proper and intelligent way; then you must be able to report positions and relative directions, also roads, etc.; and in these matters you at once see how deficient some men are, and how others have a natural turn for them. To be a good officer requires a good man.[68]

The press for military competence even filtered down to the enlisted ranks, if their officers had the initiative to maintain solid training programs. The time had gone when privates could brag, as one young Pennsylvanian had in the fall of 1862, that "It does not require a well drilled soldier to fight well. . . . All that is needed is plenty of courage, a good gun, and ammunition for it and I will insure the fight."[69] Despite the private's bragging, the drilling of new recruits was normal procedure, so the true test of commitment to military competence came later, when soldiers were tired and jaded combat veterans. It was easy to pick out the converts. In March 1863, Colonel Robert McAllister of the 11th New Jersey wrote: "I am examining some officers & sergeants in tactics and have been at it most all day. I will not promote anyone until I examine them thoroughly. . . . I have our Sergeant on hand now. I suppose I have asked him four hundred questions and am not more than one half through. He answers very well. I think he is worthy of promotion. He is a real student."[70] Even after victory at Vicksburg, in addition to regular drills for enlisted men, Sherman reminded his officers through a general order that:

Every officer who accepts a commission in the army, accepts a high trust. He is bound to study his profession, and not only acquaint himself with the drill which is merely the machinery of his trade, and the regulations, which enable him to feed, clothe, and provide for his men. . . . If he sits down in ignorance and idleness, drawing his pay and consuming the resources of his country without an adequate return of labor and service, he is guilty not only of a high misdemeanor, but a breach of trust.[71]

Officers and men attuned to the new intellectualism of their leaders—even if they were not quite aware of it—made a far more efficient and reliable army in the field.

If, as new military historians assert, an army reflects the society that produces it, the army's turn of military education as a central element of generalship should have come as no great shock. In the Northern states, the public school movement had thrived for nearly a generation. Education was well on its way to becoming a measure of a man's worth in the civilian world; why should not this cultural baggage carry over into the army? Not all soldiers understood this, but Grant appreciated the kind of men that made up his forces:

The armies of Europe are machines; the men are brave and the officers capable; but the majority of the soldiers in most of the nations of Europe are taken from a class of people who are not very intelligent. . . . Our armies were composed of men who were able to read, men who knew what they were fighting for, and could not be induced to serve as soldiers, except in an emergency when the safety of the nation was involved, and so necessarily must have been more than equal to men who fought merely because they were brave and because they were thoroughly drilled and inured to hardships.[72]

He was not alone in understanding his men. "A democratic people can perhaps carry on a war longer and better than any other; because no other can so well comprehend the object, raise the means, or bear the sacrifices," wrote Colonel Thomas Higginson, a volunteer officer. But to win, "[p]ersonal independence in the soldier, like personal liberty in the civilian, must be waived for the preservation of the nation." The army "is an aristocracy, on a three-year's lease," he wrote.[73] Another volunteer took up the theme, adding an important qualification: if the "perfect army is the perfection of aristocracy . . . the *aristocracy of education* would be my criterion. Education, in our country, inspires respect and gives power to command," and is the best ensurer of victory.[74]

Why is all this important? Acknowledgment that generalship had an intellectual component fully as important as character and courage first surfaced in the United States during the Civil War. This generation's rejection of genius and their embrace of intellect was the first shot in a long war to redefine the art of responsible command on all levels of a modern military establishment, with greater emphasis on the higher ranks where the stakes were the highest. In the postwar years, Civil War veterans took the lead in pushing the cause of military education for the army's officer corps. No one pushed harder than Colonel Emory Upton, who rewrote the infantry, cavalry, and artillery regulations in light of his Civil War experience within a few years of the conflict's end. A harsh critic of many of his own brother officers' command decisions—especially Grant's frontal assaults in Virginia in 1864—Upton in the 1870s revamped the curriculum of Artillery School to combine practical education in gunnery and ordnance with theoretical instruction in strategy and tactics. He wrote with pride to a West Point classmate: "You know how ignorant our generals were, during the war, of all the principles of generalship. Here, I think, we can correct that defect and form a corps of officers who in any future contest may prove the chief reliance of the Government."[75]

Upton's sponsor, another advocate of education, was Sherman, who built on Upton's success at the Artillery School and ordered the opening of the Infantry and Cavalry School at Fort Leavenworth in 1881. With the Army War College as the capstone, over thirty educational establishments for officers and enlisted men would be in operation by 1914. Within those schools, remarkable men of the next generation, such as Captains Arthur L. Wagner, Eben Swift, Arthur L. Conger, and more, followed Upton's and Sherman's path, using theoretical, history-based instruction to teach an entire command philosophy called "safe leadership" based on cooperation, coordination, and teamwork.[76] The Civil War, once the front line in the war for educated officers, now became one giant laboratory in generalship.

Resistance to the work of Upton, Sherman, and others who had rejected genius also endured. "Only war teaches war" was a popular refrain of critics of military intellectualism well into the twentieth century. A man "cannot be educated into a commander of men any more than he can into a poet, or an artist, or a Christian," argued one artilleryman in the 1890s.[77] Some officers resented the idea of grown men having to spend time in classrooms like schoolboys. "We are all too old to have wisdom crammed down our throats like food down the necks of Strasburg geese," one disgruntled colonel complained.[78] Still others endorsed practical, immediately useful military training but drew the line at education in the art of war; so few would ever use it that it seemed like an expensive luxury. Just a few years before World War I, Enoch Crowder, the U.S. Army's Judge Advocate General, wrote with entire confidence to a retired comrade who had been active in the military education movement through his entire career: "Character outweighs attainment in our profession and this is a fact to be kept in the foreground in selecting generals."[79] As late as 1914, students at the Army War College had to be warned explicitly that their course of study was not designed to promote "genius or brilliancy," which "may be discouraging to an officer who imagines that the daring and unerring combinations of a Napoleon are as possible as ever."[80] The persistence of outmoded forms of evaluating command potential show in clear relief just how heretical some Civil War officers had been.

The Civil War generation's proponents of military education, many of them lost to history, were ahead of their time. The pages of history largely remain silent about their quest; most studies of American military intellectualism begin in the 1880s. Still, it is clear that Sherman would not have been alone in asserting that "To be at the head of a strong column of troops, in the execution of some task that requires brain, is the highest pleasure of war."[81]

NOTES

1. "Great Generals," *Army and Navy Gazette*, 1 (4 April 1863), 77.
2. "Able Generalship," *Army and Navy Gazette*, 1 (11 July 1863), 250.
3. For a discussion of this idea, see Penelope Murray, ed., *Genius: The History of an Idea* (New York, 1989), 1–8. For this concept applied to generalship, see Samuel P. Huntington, *The Soldier and the State* (Cambridge, MA, 1956), 28–30.
4. "Political Attacks on West Point," *Blue and Gray Magazine*, 9 (December 1991), 51.
5. Ibid.
6. T. Harry Williams, *Lincoln and His Generals* (New York, 1952), 3–14.
7. Baron Jomini, *The Art of War,* trans. Capt. G. H. Mendell and Lt. W. P. Craighill (Philadelphia, 1862), 50.
8. "Answers to Correspondence," *Army and Navy Gazette*, 1 (6 June 1863), 191.
9. "Popular Appreciation of Military Education," *Army and Navy Gazette*, 1 (21 November 1863), 200.
10. "Our Military Past and Future," *Atlantic Monthly*, 44 (November 1879), 568.
11. Gerald F. Linderman, *Embattled Courage: The Experience of Combat in the American Civil War* (New York, 1987), 17.
12. "Antietam Impressions," *Blue and Gray Magazine*, 3 (November 1985), 13.
13. Allan Nevins, ed., *A Diary of Battle: The Personal Journals of Colonel Charles S. Wainwright, 1861–1865* (New York, 1962), 79.
14. John Burnham to his family, 4 October 1862, in Annette Tapert, ed., *The Brothers' War* (New York, 1988), 97.
15. Jomini, *The Art of War*, 50.
16. "Great Generals," 77.
17. "The Central Principle," *Army and Navy Gazette*, 1 (4 April 1863), 81.
18. "Volunteer Officers," *Army and Navy Journal*, 2 (4 September 1864), 69.
19. "The Competency of Our Officers," *Army and Navy Journal*, 1 (10 October 1863), 99.
20. Joseph T. Glatthaar, *Forged in Battle: The Civil War Alliance of Black Soldiers and White Officers* (New York, 1990), 59.
21. Theodore Lyman, *Meade's Headquarters, 1863–1865: Letters of Colonel Theodore Lyman*, ed. George R. Agassiz (Boston, 1922), 203.
22. "Volunteer Officers," 69.
23. Unsigned editorial, *Army and Navy Journal*, 1 (14 November 1863), 178.
24. Lyman, *Meade's Headquarters*, 139.

25. Ruth L. Silliker, ed., *The Rebel Yell and the Yankee Hurrah: The Civil War Journal of a Maine Volunteer* (Camden, ME, 1985), 175.
26. Thomas W. Higginson, "Regular and Volunteer Officers," *Atlantic Monthly*, 14 (September 1864), 348.
27. "Army of the Potomac—General Hooker," *Report of the Joint Committee on the Conduct of the War* (Washington, 1865), 149.
28. "Great Generals," 77.
29. Carl Schurz to family, 26 March 1863, in Joseph Schafer, ed. and trans., *The Intimate Letters of Carl Schurz, 1841–1869* (Madison, WI, 1928), 280.
30. Silliker, *Rebel Yell and Yankee Hurrah*, 71.
31. "Army of the Potomac—General Sickles," ibid., 14.
32. "Army of the Potomac—General Hooker," ibid., 149.
33. R. B. Goodyear to Sarah, 14 February 1863, in Tapert, *The Brothers' War*, 132.
34. Robert Hoffsommer, ed., "The Rise and Survival of Private Mesnard," *Civil War Times Illustrated*, 24 (January 1986), 25.
35. "Army of the Potomac—General Butterfield," *Report of the Joint Committee*, 84.
36. Higginson, "Regular and Volunteer Officers," 349.
37. Charles Carleton Coffin, *The Boys of '61; or, Four Years of Fighting* (Boston, 1881), 3. A good description of the action of these boards can be found in Nevins, *A Diary of Battle*, 4–5.
38. George Meade, Jr., ed., *The Life and Letters of George Gordon Meade* (New York, 1913), 231.
39. For the most recent assessment of the antebellum curriculum at West Point, see James L. Morrison, Jr., *"The Best School in the World": West Point, the Pre–Civil War Years, 1833–1866* (Kent, OH, 1986), 53, 227 n.36.
40. "Report of the Committee, Appointed . . . to Examine into the organization, system of discipline, and course of instruction of the United States Military Academy at West Point," Senate Miscellaneous Document No. 3, 36th Congress, 2nd Session, p. 183.
41. Ibid., 324.
42. Ibid., 86.
43. Ibid.
44. "The Education of Generals," *Army and Navy Journal*, 1 (5 September 1863), 26.
45. "Battles between Officers," *Army and Navy Journal*, 1 (16 April 1864), 564.
46. G. T. Beauregard, "The First Battle of Bull Run," in *Battles and Leaders of the Civil War*, Vol. I, eds. C.C. Buel and Robert U. Underwood (New York, 1888), 223.
47. "Report of the Committee, Appointed . . . to Examine into the organization, system of discipline, and course of instruction of the United States Military Academy," 148.
48. "Ball's Bluff," in *The Rebellion Record*, ed. Frank Moore, Vol. III (New York, 1864), 32.
49. "The Central Principle," 81.
50. "Political Attacks on West Point," 51.
51. "The Education of Generals," 26.
52. Meade, *Life and Letters*, 352.
53. *Springfield Republican* (MA), quoted in Charleston (SC) *Mercury*, 26 April 1862.
54. *New York Times*, 6 July 1863.
55. "Able Generalship," 250.
56. "The Education of Generals," 26.
57. Higginson, "Regular and Volunteer Officers," 348.

58. Philip H. Sheridan, *Civil War Memoirs of Philip H. Sheridan* (New York, 1991), 352–53.
59. John M. Schofield, *Forty-Six Years in the Army* (New York, 1897), 523–24.
60. William T. Sherman, *The Memoirs of General W. T. Sherman*, Vol. I (New York, 1875), 401.
61. M. A. DeWolfe Howe, ed., *The Home Letters of General Sherman* (New York, 1905), 272.
62. "The Removal of Generals," *Army and Navy Journal*, 1 (28 May 1864), 664.
63. Sherman, *Memoirs*, Vol. II, 86.
64. Ibid., 59.
65. Ibid., Vol. I, 219.
66. Howe, *Home Letters of General Sherman*, 321.
67. Stephen W. Sears, *George B. McClellan: The Young Napoleon* (New York, 1988), 237–38.
68. Lyman, *Meade's Headquarters*, 121.
69. William Gilfillan Gavin, ed., *Infantryman Pettit: The Civil War Letters of Corporal Frederick Pettit* (New York, 1990), 22.
70. James I. Robertson, ed., *The Civil War Letters of General Robert McAllister* (New Brunswick, NJ, 1965), 270. The sergeant was promoted to second lieutenant.
71. General Order No. 65, 9 August 1863, copy in William T. Sherman Papers (U.S. Army Military History Institute, Carlisle Barracks, PA).
72. Ulysses S. Grant, *The Personal Memoirs of Ulysses S. Grant*, Vol. II (New York, 1885), 531.
73. Higginson, "Regular and Volunteer Officers," 348.
74. "Volunteer Officers," 69.
75. Peter Smith Michie, ed., *The Life and Letters of Emory Upton* (New York, 1885), 418.
76. Carol Reardon, *Soldiers and Scholars: The U.S. Army and the Study of Military History, 1865–1920* (Lawrence, KS, 1990), Chapter 1.
77. Capt. James Chester, "Military Misconceptions and Absurdities," *Journal of the Military Service Institution of the United States*, 14 (1893), 503.
78. Col. George S. Anderson, "Practical Military Instruction," *Journal of the Military Service Institution of the United States*, 47 (1910), 331.
79. Gen. Enoch Crowder to Maj. (ret.) Matthew Forney Steele, 8 September 1912, Box 13, Matthew Forney Steele Papers (U.S. Army Military History Institute, Carlisle Barracks, PA). I would like to thank Dr. Richard J. Sommers for bringing this item to my attention.
80. "Introduction to the course of study," Army War College Curricular Files, 1913–1914 (U.S. Army Military History Institute, Carlisle Barracks, PA).
81. Sherman, *Memoirs*, Vol. II, 407.

4

Alfred von Tirpitz's Heretical Orthodoxy

Ivo Lambi

This chapter will concentrate on the place of Admiral Alfred von Tirpitz in German defense and foreign policy before World War I; it will ignore his role during the war and his activity as a right-wing politician. It will also play down his role in German internal politics before 1914 and the extent to which the construction of the fleet served in the stabilization of the imperial regime so fully discussed by Volker Berghahn. To paraphrase Berghahn, the emphasis will be on the construction of the fleet against England, rather than against the Reichstag.

"Although clear proof is lacking," writes Berghahn, "there is every indication that at the turn of the year 1899–1900 the final decision was reached to make the army the main victim of financial pressure."[1] The beneficiary of this decision was Tirpitz's navy. It was a fateful decision for Germany's waging of World War I during which the German army carried the brunt of the war effort and Tirpitz's vaunted High Seas Fleet confronted its British opponent in only one major engagement, the battle of Jutland, from 31 May to 1 June 1916. After the battle the Chief of the High Seas Fleet, Admiral Reinhard Scheer, informed Kaiser Wilhelm II that "there can be no doubt that even the most successful fleet action in this war will not force England to make peace." In support of this conclusion Scheer referred to Germany's "disadvantageous military-geographic position" and to Britain's "great material superiority."[2] These comments tersely point to the inherent weaknesses of the Tirpitz plan.

In his memoirs Tirpitz remarks about the development of his naval doctrine: "While we found out these things empirically in the small exercise area before the Kiel Bay, the American Admiral [sic] Mahan simultaneously developed them theoretically from history."[3] Tirpitz's naval doctrine received its clearest definition in the *Dienstschrift Nr. IX* (Service Manual No. IX), "General experiences drawn from the maneuvers of the autumn exercise fleet," dated June 1894, when he was Chief of Staff in the High Command.[4] In this memorandum Tirpitz drew explicitly on his experiences and implicitly on naval history, including the writings of Mahan. He regarded the fleet as an offensive weapon, seeking to establish command of the sea. Only command of the sea made available the means to force the enemy to conclude peace—including blockades, coastal devastations, and landings with army support, cutting off trade, and damaging colonies: "A state which has sea interests or—what is equivalent—world interests must be able to represent them and to make its power felt beyond territorial waters. National world trade, world industry, and to a certain extent high-seas fisheries, world transportation, and colonies are impossible without a fleet [capable of taking] the offensive." The Holy Roman Empire and Holland had declined along with their sea power, whereas growing American world interests were pressing for the construction of an offensive fleet. In any case, only a fleet capable of taking offensive action enhanced a power's value as an ally and exerted influence on neutrals.

"The entire endeavour of the strategic fleet offensive," wrote Tirpitz, "will . . . in principle be aimed at coming to a battle as soon as possible." To be successful against an enemy who might want to avoid battle, a one-third supremacy was necessary. Refuting the claims of the *jeune école*, Tirpitz asserted

that no event in recent times [*Neuzeit*] justified the assumption that an offensive with big squadrons will present greater difficulties than in bygone days. But since it is the best and in many cases indeed the only means of naval warfare which is capable of having a positive effect on the enemy, it will also in the future be as correct and necessary as naval warfare itself.

Cruiser warfare, as recommended by the *jeune école*, although correct in some circumstances, could never be decisive in gaining control of the sea. "It is, rather, the last and only means of the vanquished or originally impotent naval power."

Within the High Command, Tirpitz was the key figure in the struggle against the Imperial Naval Office, which continued to stress cruiser warfare and make unsuccessful piecemeal demands to the Reichstag. Until the outbreak of World War I, Tirpitz was to push singlehandedly for the construction of ships of the line. As an auditor of the ultranationalist historian Heinrich von Treitschke, as a Social Darwinist, and as an imperialist, Tirpitz had already written in December 1895: "Germany sinks in the next century quickly from her position as a great power unless she now systematically and without waste of time advances her general sea interests."[5] He made the case more elaborately to Wilhelm at the time of reporting over the second navy bill:

The statement of Salisbury: great states become greater and stronger and small states become smaller and weaker, [is] also my view. . . . Since Germany has remained particularly backward in respect to sea power, it is a vital question for Germany as a world power and civilized state [*Kulturstaat*] to catch up with what has been missed. . . . Germany must keep her population German and develop herself further as an industrial and commercial world power. . . . In the case of such commercial and industrial development, points of contact and conflict with other nations increase. Naval power is essential if Germany does not want to go under.[6]

It was understandable that Great Britain would be one of the nations with which conflict would become possible. As Tirpitz remarked in December 1899, "we must undoubtedly in the next century get into a conflict with England at some point on the globe, be it from economic rivalry or as a result of colonial friction."[7] Tirpitz stated to Wilhelm in the memorandum in support of his first navy bill: "For Germany the most dangerous naval enemy at present is England. It is also the enemy which we most urgently require a certain measure of naval force as a political power factor."[8]

At the same time, according to previous German building and operations plans, the navy was expected to serve as a weapon in the traditional scenario of a war of Germany and its allies against France and Russia and be able to direct its offensive thrusts "as far as Brest and Cherbourg and . . . as far as Kronstadt." With Britain specifically in mind, Tirpitz maintained that "[o]ur fleet must be so constructed that it can unfold its greatest military potential between Heligoland and the Thames. . . . The military situation against Britain demands battleships in as great a number as possible."[9] The great imbalance of overseas bases in Britain's favor condemned to futility any commerce raiding and transoceanic activity on Germany's part.

In order to achieve his aim, Tirpitz was to demonstrate great persistence after becoming Secretary of State of the Imperial Naval Office [*Reichsmarineamt*]. In 1897 he turned on his former superior in the High Command of the Navy, Admiral Eduard von Knorr, and brought about the fragmentation of that agency, making the Imperial Naval Office in 1899 the *primus inter pares* of the several naval agencies directly responsible to the Emperor, managing to maintain its primacy until the outbreak of the war, dismissing and suppressing such supporters of different strategic doctrines as Curt Maltzahn and Victor Valois, who emphasized the importance of cruiser warfare, and silencing such advocates of submarine warfare as Lieutenant-Commander Franz Rust, the retired Vice-Admiral Karl Galster, Captain Lothar Persius, and Vice-Admiral von Schleinitz.[10] The man whose career started in the highly experimental torpedo section was to prove highly suspicious of any experimentation and of weaponry that would detract from his emphasis on ships of the line. Reluctant to experiment with submarines to begin with, before the outbreak of World War I he made "no secret that he saw the U-boat only as a possible auxiliary to the battleship."[11]

He saw uniformity in naval opinion as essential to secure the support of the Emperor (according to Wilhelm Deist—at heart, a supporter of cruiser warfare), the civilian leadership, the Reichstag, and the public for his naval program. Tirpitz proved to be an excellent manager of parliamentary affairs and public relations and a successful manipulator of the political leadership and of the Emperor. Instead of piecemeal requests, he presented the Reichstag coherent building plans and tried to establish an automatic replacement tempo of three large ships per year (replacement age in 1908 was set at twenty years), which would have deprived the Reichstag of substantial control of the naval budget, for it could not any more unilaterally change the legal commitment for ship replacements than it could unilaterally abolish individual troop units.[12] But none of Tirpitz's five new navy laws gave him a perpetual building rate of three large ships per year. "Until this was done—and as long as the German fleet lacked adequate strength against Britain—Tirpitz continued to depend on the Reichstag."[13]

It is clear that in Tirpitz's opinion fleet construction was a long-term operation. He did not have to convince the Reichstag that unlike his predecessor Admiral Friedrich Hollman, he was not demanding a "boundless navy [*uferlose flotte*]," but he had to take into consideration financial resources, availability of steel, armor and armaments, the capacity of the dockyards, and the shortage of officers, noncommissioned officers, and technical personnel.[14] He wrote to Prince Heinrich of Prussia in 1905: "One can indeed raise armies out of the ground as Scharnhorst and Gambetta did; but to build up a fleet with necessary bases and reserves requires the life span of a generation."[15]

Although Tirpitz made some statements to the effect that the naval strength provided by the first naval bill of 1898 served as a power factor against Britain, according to an estimate of the Admiralty Staff of January

1900 it would not have sufficed to break a British blockade of the German coast. But Tirpitz admitted in his memoirs: "It was always clear to me . . . that the First Navy Law did not create the ultimate fleet." In the summer of 1898 he was considering introducing a further increase before 1905 and proposed to Wilhelm on 28 November 1898 that one be undertaken in 1902. Ten months later he presented to him the draft of a naval bill to be introduced in 1901 or 1902 that would provide for forty-five ships of the line, forty for the home fleet, five for Asia, eight large cruisers for the home fleet, one for Asia, two or three for America, twenty-four small cruisers and ninety-six torpedo boats for the home fleet, and an assorted number of small ships for transoceanic service. In 1920, when the goal would have been reached,

Your Majesty has an effective strength of forty-five ships of the line along with complete accessories—so powerful . . . that only England [will be] superior. But also against England we undoubtedly have good chance through geographical position, military system, torpedo boats, tactical training, planned organizational development and leadership united by the monarch.

Apart *from* our by no means hopeless conditions of fighting, England will have lost [any] political or economic . . . inclination to attack us and will as a result concede to Your Majesty sufficient naval presence [*Seegeltung*] for the conduct of a grand policy overseas [*eine grosse uberseeische Politik zu fuhren*].[16]

According to the calculations of the Imperial Naval Office, the following were already available in 1899 to confront the German strength initially proposed by Tirpitz for 1920: fifty-three British ships of the line and sixty armored or large cruisers; forty-five ships of the line and twelve large cruisers; or actually envisaged by the Second Navy Law, thirty-eight ships of the line and fourteen large cruisers. In addition, the French possessed thirty-two ships of the line and nineteen armored or large cruisers, and the Russians had twenty-three ships of the line and fifteen armored or large cruisers.[17] This materiel would merely have to be replaced so as to maintain a lead over Germany.

How could Germany challenge such a superiority? Tirpitz, the head of the Budget Department of the Imperial Naval Office, Eduard von Capelle, the naval attaché in London, Carl Coerper, Grapow of the Admiralty Staff, and Kaiser Wilhelm himself claimed that the British would run out of trained manpower and money to maintain their superiority over the German fleet.[18] In 1903 in their calculations for the construction of a third double squadron of ships of the line, which would give Germany in 1930 fifty-seven or sixty such ships, Capelle and his assistant, Harald Dahnhardt, seriously doubted if Britain could secure the manpower to maintain the current 2:1 ratio in large ships against Germany.[19]

According to Tirpitz: "The lever of our *Weltpolitik* was the North Sea: it worked indeed over the whole globe without us needing to deploy anything directly anywhere else."[20] "Expressed bluntly," writes Paul Kennedy, "Tirpitz saw his battlefleet in the form of a sharp knife, held gleaming and ready, only a few inches from the jugular vein of Germany's most likely enemy."[21] He assumed that Britain would continue to disperse ships to defend its imperial interests around the world. As stated in the preamble of the Second Navy Bill, "it is not necessary that the battle fleet at home is equal to that of the greatest naval power. In general this naval power would not be in a position to concentrate its entire force against us."[22]

This calculation was based on the assumption that antagonism between Britain on the one hand and France and Russia on the other would continue, an assumption shared until 1904 by the German political leadership. This antagonism would, according to Tirpitz, compel Britain to disperse its fleet around the world, particularly in the Mediterranean and the Far East.

But, as Paul Kennedy says: "The choice lay between areas where *potential* threats existed to British interests, such as in the Far East, and a region (the North Sea) where British *national security*—given the supposition that an Anglo-German conflict was imminent—was involved, and there could be no doubt that to the British the latter was most important."[23] The British Admiralty was perfectly aware of the need to maintain a sufficient force in the home waters to ensure command over them even before recognizing Germany as a naval threat.[24] But in October 1906 the First Sea Lord, "Jackie" Fisher, wrote to the Prince of Wales: "Our only probable enemy is Germany. Germany keeps her whole fleet always concentrated a few hours of England. We must therefore keep a fleet twice as powerful of that of Germany concentrated within a few hours of Germany."[25] Many German operational planners were aware of the obvious fact that Britain would never declare war on Germany before it could confront Germany with an overwhelming superiority. It was therefore extremely unrealistic on Tirpitz's part to assume that the British would not respond effectively to the obvious German threat to control its home waters.

The risk theory, which was also based on continuing friction between Britain and other naval powers, particularly France and Russia, was another of Tirpitz's explanations why Germany did not need a fleet as large as the British. According to the risk theory, the German fleet might indeed be defeated by the Royal Navy, but the latter would suffer such losses as to be vulnerable to Russian and French naval forces. Britain's own position as a world power would thus be brought into question.[26] This was the deterrent function of the German navy.

The illusory nature of the risk theory, however, became clear after the conclusion of the *entente cordiale* between Britain and France and the Russian involvement in the war with Japan in 1904. With its Russian ally substantially weakened and the Russian navy engaged with Japan and eventually destroyed altogether, it was unlikely that France would subsequently attempt to benefit from the weakening of the navy of its new British friend through a war with Germany. On October 31 and November 1, 1904, Tirpitz himself rejected a defensive alliance with Russia, for in a war against Britain as Russia's ally "we could . . . with our as yet under-developed navy pay the price with our foreign trade and colonies."[27] At the same time Felix von Bendemann, Chief of the North Sea Station in Wilhelmshaven, described Germany's position in case of a British preemptive attack against it as nearly hopeless on both military and political grounds: Britain's naval preponderance over Germany was immense; France was friendly to it; Russian naval power in Europe was nonexistent; and Austria-Hungary and Italy did not count as naval powers.[28] Waldenmar Vollerthun, head of the Information and Intelligence (N[Naval]) Department of the Imperial Naval Office, now also stated that since Russia was useless as a potential German ally and since France was a probable British ally, a war with Britain had become an impossibility for Germany. Showing full appreciation of Mahan, Vollerthun stated: "Our continental position, ground between the upper and the lower millstone on the one hand [and] the need for overseas development on the other hand have led to a politically untenable situation."[29]

Before the German navy reached the strength constituting a risk to Britain and serving as a deterrent, Germany, according to Tirpitz, would have to pass through a danger zone, a time when its navy would be recognized as a threat by the British and could be destroyed by them with impunity. As clearly demonstrated by recent historiography, it was Bernhard von Bulow's task as Secretary of State of the Foreign Office and as Chancellor to guide Germany through this difficult period.[30]

As of 1909 the emphasis on the risk theory and alliance value of the German navy came to be replaced by Tirpitz and his subordinates by an acceptable relationship between the British and German navies; either two German capital ships to three British capital ships, or less frequently, three German to four British capital ships. Such ratios would protect Germany from a British attack and serve as a guarantee to Britain against a German attack.

It appears, however, that Tirpitz himself was not entirely clear about the length of the danger zone; if he was, he did not want others to be aware of it. Nor could he be clear. As his calculations that Britain would not reinforce its fleet in European waters, that the risk theory would prevail, and that Britain would falter in an armaments race were proven incorrect, and as new complications arose—such as the need to widen the Kaiser Wilhelm Canal from Kiel to the Elbe to make its passage by German dreadnoughts possible—the danger period would be lengthened, justifying the younger Helmuth von Moltke's comment at the so-called war council meeting of 8 December 1912 that the navy would never be ready.[31] On 28 September 1899 Tirpitz had suggested to Wilhelm that the danger zone would last until 1920.[32] Wilhelm himself stated in 1899 that he did not expect the navy to become an effective force in *Weltpolitik* for another twenty years; and according to the Austro-Hungarian ambassador Count Ladislaus Szogyeny's reports a year later, Wilhelm, along with other leading German statesmen, saw Germany as an heir to the British Empire but did not expect this to happen in his lifetime.[33] At other times Wilhelm envisaged shorter periods of risk: in May 1898 he stated that in terms of naval power, peace with Britain would only have to be preserved until 1901; at the end of 1904 he said that it was only necessary until 1906, and in that year he remarked that German naval power would never meet the Royal Navy with any chance of success.[34] According to Bulow's memoirs, Tirpitz told him in the beginning of his chancellorship that 1904 to 1905 would be the most critical point of the danger zone: "After this foreseeably most critical moment the danger of an English attack would decrease further and further. The English would then realize that action against us would also expose them to excessive risk."[35] In February 1905, however, Tirpitz noted that the next five years would be the most serious danger zone for Germany.[36]

The decision of the Imperial Naval Office on 22 September 1905 to build ships of the line with twelve 28-cm guns and 18,000 tons displacement, two of which were launched in 1908, made it necessary to widen the Kaiser Wilhelm Canal (opened in 1895 and expected by some to double the effectiveness of the German fleet) to make it passable to the new ships. The widening of the canal was not to be completed before June 1914. In January 1909 Tirpitz replied negatively to Bulow's inquiry whether Germany could resist a British attack. At the same time he himself admitted the bankruptcy of his theory that the fleet could increase Germany's alliance value when he maintained that France and Russia would join Britain if it were to declare war on Germany.[37] At a high-level conference of political and military leaders on 3 June 1909, Tirpitz gave his opinion that "the danger zone in our relationship with England would be overcome in five to six years, thus approximately by 1915, after the enlargement of the Kaiser Wilhelm Canal and the preparation of the Heligoland position. Already in two years it would be considerably less."[38] At the time of the Agadir crisis in 1911, Tirpitz noted: "As for naval war the time is as unfavourable as possible. Each subsequent year brings a much more favourable situation. Heligoland, Canal, Dreadnoughts, U-boats, etc."[39] At the so-called war council meeting of 8 December 1912, Tirpitz pleaded for an additional year or year and one-half before war was to be started for the completion of the canal and the fortifications of Heligoland.[40] And in May 1914, Tirpitz told Admiral von Muller that six to eight years would be required for the fleet to be able to face Britain.[41]

In spite of the prolongation of the danger zone, Tirpitz's main concern remained with the construction of ships for the future, not with the fighting at present. By necessity he neglected many wishes of the so-called Front: the Admiralty Staff, the Baltic Sea and the North Sea Stations Commands, the Chief of the First Squadron, and as of June 1903 his successor, the Chief of the Fleet, whose concern was with fighting a war now, as political tension increased. According to Tirpitz it was not possible to have quantity—numbers of battleships—and quality—fighting efficiency—at the same time. His emphasis was on quantity, that of the Front was on quality.[42] As he reported to Wilhelm in 1898, as a result of increased construction "a number of wishes and requests of the front would have to be dropped, particularly coastal fortification."[43]

Following the Dogger Bank incident, pressure for improved war preparedness continued, and Tirpitz himself gave in on improving the defenses of Heligoland; if well fortified, the island would improve both the offensive and defensive position of the fleet in the German Bight.[44] But in response to advocates of defense through submarines, torpedo boats, and better coastal fortifications, now supported by Bulow himself, Tirpitz retorted on 4 January 1909: "We can double and triple our torpedo-boats and submarines, we can spike our entire coast with cannon, but this part of our naval power can in no way have a pacific influence. Without a battle fleet we would be exposed to every insolence on the part of England."[45] Between 1906 and 1909, Tirpitz was criticized by the Kaiser's brother Prince Heinrich, Chief of the High Seas Fleet, for neglecting the war preparedness of the fleet, which came to be supported in 1909 by the Chief of the Admiralty Staff, Count Friedrich von Baudissin. With the help of the Chief of the Naval Cabinet, Admiral Georg Alexander von Muller, Tirpitz prevailed and both Heinrich and Baudissin were dismissed.[46] Between August 1910 and February 1912, Tirpitz sided with the Admiralty Staff against the Chief of the High Seas Fleet, Admiral Henning von Holtzendorff, in favor of deploying the fleet in the North Sea rather than the Baltic.[47]

Following the Agadir crisis of 1911, there was increased pressure from the "Front" to make the navy more effective: to introduce cannons of greater caliber, improve the engagement of recruits, and speed up trial periods for new ships. In the summer of 1912 Tirpitz came to be criticized by Wilhelm for allowing Germany to fall behind other states in the quality of naval construction and for being too removed from the needs of the "Front."[48] On 8 December Wilhelm ordered the navy to make various preparations for a war against England, which, however, were not assigned a particularly high priority by the naval agencies.

But how could a German navy that according to Tirpitz's official statements would at best constitute only three-fourths of the strength of the British in capital ships successfully fight against the British? Paul Kennedy maintains that Tirpitz expected to fight a defensive battle against a close British blockade of the German North Sea coast. But it is not clear that this was Tirpitz's intention. In his early writings, there is constant emphasis on offensive naval warfare and an imminent decisive naval battle. Tirpitz's first notions about operations against an overwhelmingly superior British fleet in 1894 to 1896 envisaged a "death-ride" of the entire fleet into the Thames at the outset of hostilities.[49] But Tirpitz never envisaged that a temporary establishment of command over the sea should be followed by an invasion of the British isles.[50]

Throughout his tenure as Secretary of State of the Imperial Naval Office, Tirpitz was aware of the possibility of the distant blockade of the German North Sea coast. Kennedy himself quotes Tirpitz's criticism in 1897 of the High Command's plan for a strategic defensive against France in the Baltic and North Sea: "One wants to await the enemy and to defeat him here. The purpose is to keep open our imports. But I believe now that the enemy will not come at once and that we will then wait with our large fleet while France without much loss cuts off two-thirds to three-quarters of our imports in the Channel and North of England."[51] In April 1907, he maintained that in a few years Britain would not be able to enforce a close blockade of the German coast: "She would limit herself then to the closing to us of the passage north and south of England and stand with her bulk in the North Sea, leaning on England. Such an extended blockade would have pretty much the effect of a close coastal blockade. In the long run we would not be able to survive it economically."[52] Germany would, however, be able to attack the British coast. In January 1909, Tirpitz wrote to Bulow that only light British forces could carry on the blockade of the German coast, whereas the bulk would be located "behind the Dogger Bank in the proximity of England."[53] Early in 1912, while working on the naval bill that was to be introduced later in the year, the Imperial Naval Office considered the need for additional cruisers for the purpose of supporting sorties of torpedo boats and submarines against a distant blockade.[54]

Within the context of planning for an offensive strategy against Britain as initiated in January 1908 by the new Chief of the Admiralty Staff, von Baudissin, Wilhelm Taegert, who as A4 was in charge of operational planning against Britain, took into consideration a distant blockade against Germany. Although it was contrary to the offensive naval traditions of the Royal Navy, such a blockade appeared to have been examined by the British Admiralty.[55] In subsequent operational planning against Britain by the Admiralty Staff and other naval agencies, a distant British blockade of the North Sea was taken into full consideration.[56]

By the fall of 1913 British naval maneuvers of 1912 and 1913 and French naval maneuvers of 1913 had made it clear to the Admiralty Staff that in case of war Germany would be faced with a distant blockade against which long-range sorties of the High Seas Fleet or submarines and light forces were necessary, as had been advocated by Baudissin and by his successor Max von Fischel.[57] But such long-distance advances had been limited by their successor August von Heeringen's directive of 24 October 1911 to offensive operations seeking battle with the enemy as soon as possible in German waters, that is, the southern part of the North Sea and the Skaggerak.[58] On 3 December 1912, Wilhelm approved an even more restrictive directive to the Chief of the Fleet:

1. The War is to be carried out from the German Bight.
2. The chief war task should be to damage the blockading forces of the enemy as far as possible through numerous and repeated tasks day and night, and under *favourable circumstances* to give battle with all the forces at your disposal.[59]

The war game that the Admiralty Staff played to test action against the distant blockade resulted in the leader of the German side, Paul Behncke, losing twice in undertaking sorties with the High Seas Fleet against the British coast.[60] The report of the war game to Wilhelm was dated 5 May 1914 but was not presented to him before 26 May. The new Chief of the Admiralty Staff, Hugo von Pohl, reported that the existing power relationship did not permit such fleet sorties as undertaken in the war game; they could only be undertaken by submarines and mine layers, and the bulk would be kept back "for an energetic ceaseless struggle against the forces guarding the German Bight"—which might not be there! Pohl noted that Wilhelm thoroughly agreed with the conclusions drawn from the war game and added: "In all defensive plans . . . the offensive idea is not to be dropped," attributing great importance to the cooperation of submarines with the fleet.[61] Unable to find a suitable strategy against the distant blockade, the Admiralty Staff at the outbreak of World War I, allegedly much to Tirpitz's disapproval, chose the defensive strategy against the most improbable close blockade.[62]

At the time that the Admiralty Staff concentrated on the offensive thrust against Britain, the Imperial Navy Office, in May 1909, prepared a defensive operations plan against Britain that Tirpitz acknowledged with interest, but he pointed out that its underlying assumption, the maintenance of the fleet *in being*, was not part of current operational preparations.[63] How this defensive plan originated is unknown. Tirpitz's comment regarding it could be taken to mean that he preferred a defensive strategy.[64] On the other hand, in August 1910 he approved of a memorandum by Admiral Fischel, intended to be submitted to Wilhelm and to be distributed to the commanding Admirals, favoring offensive operations against Britain from the North Sea, as opposed to Holtzendorff's defensive concentration in the Baltic. In this memorandum Fischel justified the offensive North Sea Strategy as follows:

In the final analysis we are fighting for access to the Ocean whose entrances on both sides of the North Sea are in England's hands. However the war is fought, we are essentially the attacker, who wants to challenge the enemy's property. The naval law takes this into consideration by laying the stress of our naval power on ships of the line. Thus we are equally directed by our waging of war and the particular nature of our naval development to seeking a decision in the open sea.[65]

But Tirpitz recommended that both Holtzendorff's and Fischel's strategies be tested by war games.[66] It is therefore difficult to conclude with certainty that Tirpitz was opposed to an offensive strategy against Britain.

What was necessary for a successful offensive against Britain if it would concentrate naval power in home waters and the risk theory no longer had any validity, as was the case after 1905, when accepting Fisher's challenge Tirpitz entered an arms race with Britain? As Paul Kennedy points out, the problem of Tirpitz's fleet having to wrest command of the sea from Great Britain makes more sense if, indeed, he tried to outbuild its fleet. At no point did Tirpitz maintain that any of his navy laws provided for his maximum aims; he allegedly told Ambassador Count Anton von Monts in 1897 and Chancellor zu Hohenlohe-Shillingsfurst in 1898 and wrote to Admiral Wilhelm von Lens in 1914 that his aim was to have a fleet as great as Britain's.[67]

While German naval officers referred to the American naval historian and strategist Alfred Thayer Mahan as St. Mahan,[68] and Wilhelm II was purporting to learn *The Influence of Sea Power upon History 1660–1873* (1890) by heart, it is doubtful whether Mahan was really understood by the advocates of German naval power, including Tirpitz himself. Mahan writes:

The principal conditions affecting the sea power of nations may be enumerated as follows: I. Geographical Position. II. Physical Conformation, including, as connected therewith, natural productions and climate. III. Extent of Territory. IV. Number of Population. V. Character of the People. VI. Character of the Government, including therein the national institutions.[69]

In particular, Germany fell short of Condition I: Geographical Position. According to Mahan:

It may be pointed out, in the first place, that if a nation be so situated that it is neither forced to defend itself by land nor induced to seek extension of its territory by way of land, it has, by the very unity of its aim directed upon the sea, an advantage as compared with a people one of whose boundaries is continental. This has been a great advantage to England over both France and Holland as a sea power. The strength of the latter was early exhausted by keeping up a large army and carrying on expensive wars to preserve her independence; while the policy of France was constantly diverted, sometimes wisely and sometimes foolishly, from the sea to projects of continental extension. These military efforts expended wealth; whereas a wiser and consistent use of her geographical position would have added to it.[70]

Germany's geographical position in Europe, with extensive land frontiers toward an unreconciled France in the West, an increasingly hostile Russia in the East, and a doubtful friend, Austria-Hungary, in the South had provided Otto von Bismarck with his *cauchemars des coalitions* at the time that he considered Germany to be a saturated power and made it appear as such to others. Since Bismarck's dismissal, France and Russia had allied against Germany. Germany's geography, its continental opponents, the effect that its world and navy policy had on its continental position, and the limitation of its financial resources, made Germany according to

Mahan's criteria a less successful candidate as a sea power than either France or Holland. Although at the turn of the twentieth century the navy appears to have been given priority over the army in the armament program, by 1912 political and financial considerations were to force the German leadership to assign higher priority to the build-up of the army than of the navy. On 1 January 1912 the Kaiser declared in his New Year's message to the commanding generals: "The navy leaves the major part of the financial means available to the army."[71]

Particularly unsuitable for Germany's geopolitical position and resources was Tirpitz's decision to build a navy against Britain. According to Mahan the attacking naval force required a superiority of thirty-three percent over its opponent, as Tirpitz himself recognized in *Dienstschrift Nr. IX*. Moreover, as Mahan wrote in 1902, Germany's geographical position against Britain was particularly weak:

Great Britain . . . lies to Germany as Ireland does to Great Britain, flanking both routes to the Atlantic. . . . Sea defence for Germany, in case of a war with France or England, means established naval predominance at least in the North Sea; nor can it be considered complete unless extended through the Channel and as far as Great Britain will have to project hers into the Atlantic. This is Germany's initial disadvantage of position to be overcome only by adequate supremacy in numbers.[72]

As indicated, Fischel and Tirpitz had both recognized the problem. To wrest the command of the sea from Britain and to obtain access to the Atlantic, Germany needed a substantial naval superiority over Britain—if Britain did not leave its naval forces dispersed around the globe, if the risk theory was proven invalid, if Germany did not find allies that would strengthen its naval position against Britain, and if it did not (as in World War II) gain control of the French and Norwegian coastlines, which would eliminate a distant blockade. Unless, perchance, Britain might somehow flounder in the course of the armaments race.

Not conforming to Mahan's requirements of naval power, particularly in relationship to Great Britain, Tirpitz's battleship doctrine became a heresy both with respect to Mahan as well as to Germany's defense requirements. As a heresy, however, it became an orthodoxy propagated and enforced by Tirpitz before 1914, and it subsequently re-emerged in Admiral Erich Raeder's naval plans before World War II.

NOTES

1. Volker R. Berghahn, *Der Tirpitz-Plan. Genesis und Verfall einer innenpolitischen Krisenstrategie unter Wilhelm II* (Dusseldorf, 1971), 250.
2. Holger H. Herwig, *Luxury Fleet: The Imperial German Navy 1888–1918* (London, 1980), 190.
3. Alfred von Tirpitz, *Erinnerungen* (Leipzig, 1919), 47.
4. Bundesarchiv-Militararchiv, Freiburg (cited hereafter as BA-MA), N 253 (Nachlass Tirpitz)/34, "Dienstschrift Nr. IX., Allgemeine Erfahrungen aus den Manovern der Herbstubungsflotte," 16 June 1894.
5. Ulrich von Hassell, *Tirpitz. Sein Leben und sein Wirken mit Berucksichtigung seiner Beziehungen zu Albrecht von Stosch* (Stuttgart, 1920), 103.
6. BA-MA, F 2044, PG 66074, "Vortrag. Rominten, 28 September 1899." A corrected version appears in Tirpitz, *Erinnerungen*, 107. For a later statement by Tirpitz, see ibid., 57–58. See also Tirpitz's letter to his daughter Blanca on 18 July 1897, quoted in Michael Salewski, *Tirpitz Aufstieg—Macht—Scheitern* (Gottingen, Zurich, Frankfurt, 1979), 52.
7. Volker R. Berghahn, "Zu den Zielen des deutschen Flottenbaus unter Wilhelm II," *Historische Zeitschrift*, 210, no. 1 (1970), 68.
8. Jonathan Steinberg, *Yesterday's Deterrent. Tirpitz and the Birth of the German Battle Fleet* (London, 1965), 209.
9. Ibid.
10. Herwig, *Luxury Fleet*, 38–39.
11. See Gary E. Weir, "Tirpitz, Technology, and Building U-boats, 1897–1916," *The International History Review*, 6 (1984), 174–90. The quotation is from 181.
12. Berghahn, *Tirpitz-Plan*, 111.
13. Ivo Nikolai Lambi, *The Navy and German Power Politics, 1862–1914* (Boston, London, and Sydney, 1984), 150; Berghahn admits this in "Zu den Zielen," 58.
14. American Historical Association, Captured German Documents, Project II, 8, Nachlass Eisendecher, Tirpitz to Eisendecher, 31 August 1897.
15. Berghahn, *Tirpitz-Plan*, 183.
16. Lambi, *The Navy*, 146.
17. Ibid.
18. According to Grapow, if this did not happen, "history of naval warfare proves that the effectiveness of the greater fleet ceases at a certain level." This, according to Grapow, was also confirmed by recent British maneuvers. "Keeping a large fleet together always led to difficulties which offered the weaker opponent a chance to bring a superior force to bear here or there." Ibid., 147–48. See also Berghahn, *Tirpitz-Plan*, 206.
19. Lambi, *The Navy*, 146.
20. Alfred von Tirpitz, *Politische Dokumente*, Vol. 1. *Der Aufbauer deutschen Weltmacht* (Stuttgart: Cotta, 1924), 346.
21. Paul M. Kennedy, "Tirpitz, England and the Second Navy Law of 1900: A Strategical Critique," *Militargeschichtliche Mitteilungen*, 2 (1970), 38.
22. Paul M. Kennedy, "Strategic Aspects of the Anglo-German Naval Race," in *Strategy and Diplomacy 1870–1945. Eight Studies* (London, 1984), 129–160, first published as "Maritime Strategieprobleme der deutsch-englischen Flottenrivalitat," in Herbert

Schottelius und Wilhelm Deist, eds., *Marine und Marinepolitik im Kaiserlichen Deutschland 1871-1914* (Dusseldorf, 1972), 178-210.

23. Ibid., 148.
24. Ibid., 140-42.
25. Ibid., 142.
26. Kennedy, "Tirpitz, England," 35; and Herwig, *Luxury Fleet*, 36.
27. Lambi, *The Navy*, 246.
28. BA-MA, F 2044, PG 66077, Bendemann, "Gedanken uber die augenblickliche kritische Lage," 3 December 1904.
29. Ibid., Vollerthun, "Politische und militarische Betrachtungen uber einen englisch-deutschen Krieg," 27 November 1904, copy.
30. Bernhard von Bulow, *Denkwurdigkeiten*, Vol. 1 (Berlin, 1930), 411-12. For the relevant literature, see Berghahn, *Tirpitz-Plan*, esp. 380-415; Peter Winzen, *Bulow Weltmachtkonzept. Untersuchungen zur Fruhphase seiner Aussenpolitik 1897-1901* (Boppard am Rhein, 1977), esp. 86-108; Paul M. Kennedy, "German World Policy and the Alliance Negotiations with England," *Journal of Modern History*, 40 (1973), 605-25; Paul M. Kennedy, *The Rise of Anglo-German Antagonism. 1860-1914* (London, Boston and Sydney, 1980), 223-88; Lambi, *The Navy*, 155-60, 174-81; and Lamar Cecil, *Wilhelm II. Prince and Emperor, 1859-1900* (Chapel Hill and London, 1990), 329-36.
31. Lambi, *The Navy*, 382-83. For a summary of the debate on the so-called war council, see ibid., 382-84.
32. Tirpitz to Wilhelm, 28 September 1899; see Herwig, *Luxury Fleet*.
33. Lambi, *The Navy*, 155.
34. Ibid., 155-56.
35. Bulow, *Denkwurdigkeiten*. Vol. 1, 413.
36. Tirpitz, *Aufbau*, 17.
37. Lambi, *The Navy*, 298.
38. Johannes Lepsius, Albrecht Mendelssohn Bartholdy, and Friedrich Thimme, *Die Grosse Politik der Europaischen Kabinette 1871-1914, Sammlung Diplomatischen Akten des Auswartigen Amtes. Im Auftrage des Auswartigen Amtes herausgegeben* (Berlin, 1924-1927) 40 volumes in 54 (cited hereafter as *GP*), Vol. 28, No. 10306, Protokoll siner Besprechung im Reichskanzlerpalais am 3. Juni 1909 uber die Frage einer Verstandigung mit England (pr. 3 Juni 1909), 176.
39. Tirpitz, *Aufbau*, Tirpitz to Capelle, 12 August 1911, 205.
40. Lambi, *The Navy*, 382-83.
41. J. C. G. Rohl, "Admiral Muller and the Approach to War, 1911-14," *Historical Journal*, 3 (1969), 667.
42. BA-MA, N 253/4, "Notizen zum Immediatvortrag—indiensthaltunsplan bis 1903," 20 February 1899.
43. Ibid., F 2044, PG 66075, "Notizen . . . ," 28 November 1898.
44. Ibid., 277-78.
45. *GP*, Vol. 28, No. 10247, Tirpitz to Bulow, 4 January 1909, 55.
46. Lambi, *The Navy*, 278-79.
47. Ibid., 351-52, 391-92.
48. Ibid., 373-75.
49. See BA-MA, N 253/34, "Dienstschrift Nr. IX, Allgemeine Erfahrungen aus den Manovern der Herbstubungsflotte," Berlin, 16 June 1894; Tirpitz, *Erinnerungen*, 53-54, Tirpitz to Stosch, 12 February 1896; Hassell, *Tirpitz*, 105-106, misdating Stosch's letter

to 2 February; it was probably at Tirpitz's advice that his disciple, August von Heeringen, three weeks later completed the first official operational study against Britain, BA-MA, F 5597, III, i-10, Vol. 1, "Gesichtspunkte fur einen Operationsplan der heimischen Streitkrafte bei einem Kriege Deutschland allein gegen England allein," 5 March 1896. In "The Development of German Naval Operations against Britain, 1896-1914," *English Historical Review*, 89 (1974), 50-51, the first thorough examination, Paul M. Kennedy mistakenly attributes this document to the Chief of Staff, Otto von Diederichs.

50. On 23 October 1898, he agreed with the position of Alfred von Schlieffen, Chief of the Great General Staff, that the invasion of England was an impossibility: "Even if we should succeed in landing two army corps in England, that would be of no avail, for these corps would not be strong enough to maintain their position without support from home." Approximately a year later he criticized the reference to Napoleon's need for naval mastery of the English Channel only for so long as to transport his army to England: "This was Napoleon's error. If he had really succeeded in getting across, then he and his army would have been lost as in Egypt." See Lambi, *The Navy,* 129; and Kennedy, "The Development," 55.

51. Kennedy, "Strategic Aspects," 148-49; quoted in Lambi, *The Navy,* 143.

52. GP, XXIII, ii, No. 8006, Tirpitz to Bulow, 20 April 1907, enclosure, Uber doe Bedeitimg des Seebeuterechts, 20 April 1907, 364-65.

53. Ibid., Vol. XXVIII, No. 10247, Tirpitz to Bulow, 4 January 1909, 54.

54. BA-MA, F 2041, PG 66062, Novellen-Rede," draft. There is a comment on the margin: the "Reinkonzept" has been given to C, E, and DI.

55. BA-MA, F 5589, III, i-10n., Vol. 2, A4 Taegert, "Denkschrift zum OP/08: Wie wird der Fein versussichtlich handeln?"

56. Lambi, *The Navy,* 343-47.

57. Ibid., 338-55.

58. Ibid., 392.

59. BA-MA, F 2020, PG 65975, "Zum immediatvortrag. Entwurf zum Operationsbefehl fur den Krieg gegen England," 28 November 1912, initialed A4, approved by Wilhelm on 3 December 1912. Quoted in Kennedy, "The Development," 69.

60. See Lambi, *The Navy,* 403-4.

61. BA-MA, F 2021, PG 65977, Pohl, "Denkschrift zum Immediatvortrag uber das strategische Kriegsspiel des Admiralstabes Winter 1913/14, 5 May 1914.

62. Lambi, *The Navy,* 422-23.

63. BA-MA, F 2045, PG 66081, Memorandum by von Usslar, von Bulow, and Vollerthun, 17 May 1909, presented by Paschen, 17 June 1909.

64. See Lambi, *The Navy,* 351.

65. Quoted by Carl-Axel Gemzell, *Organization, Conflict, and Innovation. A Study of German Naval Strategic Planning, 1880-1940* (Lund, 1973), 79-80. Herwig is in error when he states that Tirpitz chose not to reply; see "The Failure," 80.

66. BA-MA, F 5589, III, 1-10b, Vol. 3, "Ostesse oder Nordsee als Kriegschauplatz," 12 August 1910; ibid., N 253/24, Tirpitz to Fischel, 16 August 1910.

67. Kennedy, "Strategic Aspects," 159-60.

68. BA-MA, F 5588, III, 1-10a, Vol. 1, Zu A 2533 IV, statement of B, 8 October 1902.

69. Alfred Thayer Mahan, *The Influence of Sea Power upon History 1660-1783* (London, n.d.), 28-29.

70. Ibid., 29. For German naval power according to Mahan, see in particular Kennedy, "Strategic Aspects," 140; and Holger H. Herwig, "The Failure of German Sea Power, 1914–1945: Mahan, Tirpitz, and Raeder Reconsidered," *The International History Review,* 10 (1988), 68–105.

71. Quoted in Lambi, *The Navy,* 370.

72. Alfred Thayer Mahan, *Retrospect and Prospect: Studies in International Relations Naval and Political* (London, 1902), 165–66. See also Herwig, "The Failure," 79; Kennedy, "Strategic Aspects," 157; and Kennedy, *The Rise,* 422.

5

The Youth of General A. A. Brusilov: The Making of an Unconventional, Conventional Professional

David R. Jones

The day of inspection by the new divisional commander had arrived. He had a reputation for being a martinet where horsemanship was concerned. On this occasion, he had ordered the Horse Grenadier Guards to demonstrate their skills in a steeplechase. As the officers prepared, they nervously eyed one of their fellows. This obese gentleman's figure was evidence of too much time spent in local restaurants, and he himself was doubtful and despondent about the coming test. And as his fellows expected, his first jump proved a disaster. This could have led to the unfortunate captain's forced retirement. But the general was in a forgiving mood and generously offered the regiment a second chance, in a month's time, to save their comrade. Yet despite his best efforts, the oversized officer could not surmount the hurdles. Then his fellows conceived a bold plan to pass the inspection. Working swiftly, they skillfully graded the track so that at the far end, where the "bear" would have to jump, the hurdle was considerably lower than normal. Praying that this device was not evident from the reviewing stand, they then staged their ride-past—and this time passed muster without a hitch. But later, those involved could never swear that they had in fact fooled the general, or that, rather, he had not winked at their device out of respect for the imaginative and innovative manner in which the regimental family had protected one of its own.[1]

The general in question was Aleksei Alekseevich Brusilov. A tough and respected cavalryman who expected his men to be more at home in the saddle than in a restaurant or taproom, he served in a branch with a reputation, perhaps not wholly deserved, for its conservatism and adherence to tradition. But as this story suggests, he could be more tolerant of imaginative solutions to even the smallest military problems than many of his colleagues, despite their superior technical or professional educations in the Engineer, Artillery, or General Staff Academies. It was precisely this quality that was to win him a reputation as an unconventional innovator during World War I, as well as that of a political heretic in the eyes of many of his colleagues in the aftermath of the Bolsheviks' October Revolution of 1917.

Most Western students of military affairs associate Brusilov with the stunningly successful Russian offensive on the Southwest Front in 1916. This is usually considered the bright spot in an otherwise unremittingly gray chronicle of defeats that preceded the overthrow of the tsar in February 1917, a sort of exception that proves the rule of general tsarist military incompetence. For the few that recall that he also commanded the aborted "Kerenskii offensives" a year later, this impression is stronger still. This aside, very few now remember that the illustrious commander of 1916, the man who held the rank of General-Adjutant to the Tsar, ended his life as director of the Red Army's stud farms, a fact that earned him the title of traitor in the eyes of the majority of White emigrés. But as even this brief review of the last years of his career illustrates, even a superficial recounting of the best known facts of Brusilov's life mark him as one of those fascinating figures sometimes met with in history: an eminently conventional fellow who ends by being one of the most unconventional of his peers.

In light of these facts, it is surprising that the general's life has attracted so little attention from biographers. Surely, one would think, a man whose career was as replete with seeming contradictions as was Brusilov's must be of interest to those so often fascinated by even lesser quirks of human nature. This is particularly noticeable when one considers that the 1916 campaign has been extensively studied within the former Soviet Union, and that his memoirs have appeared in at least seven Russian and two English editions as well as in French. Yet to the best of my knowledge, there have only been two serious attempts at biographies: I. I. Rostunov's historical study of 1964 and Sergei Semanov's "documentary-tale" of 1986.[2]

Of course, historians can never hope to uncover satisfactorily all the wellsprings of their subjects' motives and behavior. If this is true even in full-scale psycho-historical biographical studies based on an ample supply of primary documentary and personal materials, it is obviously even truer of briefer discussions. Further, even with full access to the relevant archives, it seems likely that accounts of the formative years and, indeed, the bulk of Brusilov's life, from 1853 to 1906, must remain sketchy and largely concerned with his professional service. As he himself noted, he kept no diary and there is apparently little left in the way of personal correspondence for the decades before 1905. So while we may properly assume, for example, that the death of his only son was an event of considerable significance, we are left without any direct evidence that clearly indicates its impact on his subsequent actions.[3]

Although discussion of Brusilov's youth must remain largely speculative, to look at aspects of his personality and crucial events in his early life may explain how a cavalryman from the conventional background of Imperial Russia's military gentry became one of the leading military innovators of World War I and, later, died in the service of a revolutionary regime built on the ruins of the dynasty his family had served so faithfully for over two centuries. As I. I. Rostunov put it, Brusilov was first and foremost "a representative of the privileged stratum of the old regime," and his service in the ranks of the Red Army, therefore, could only represent a dramatic break "with the traditions of his milieu."[4]

The truth of Rostunov's remark is abundantly clear from even a superficial review of Brusilov's family background. The Brusilovs were a gentry family from Orel province with a strong tradition of military service. Aleksei Alekseevich's great-grandfather had served Peter the Great, his grandfather Catherine the Great, and his father Alexander I, Nicholas I, and Alexander II. So it is not surprising that he, as well as his second brother, Boris, entered the army. Indeed, at this stage the family rebel seems to have been his third and youngest brother, Lev. Breaking with family traditions, Lev Alekseevich chose to serve with the navy, in which he eventually commanded a cruiser during 1904 and 1905 and, before retiring due to bad health in 1908, became the first Chief of the Naval General Staff.

At the same time, we should note that the military milieu and traditions surrounding these youths were not just those of the tsarist army, but those of the Caucasian Army. This distinction is an important one. The troops serving in the Caucasus under the direct command of the tsar's viceroy in Tiflis constituted what we might call a frontier army. Having emerged victorious from a long, exhausting struggle with Muslim mountaineers in August 1859, it still had to fulfill the interrelated tasks of keeping the remaining mountain tribesmen cowed in the interior while defending a long, difficult frontier against possible Turkish attempts to recover lost territories. For these reasons troops of the Caucasian Army, unlike those in European Russia, had little time before 1878 to rusticate in the deadening peacetime atmosphere of the provinces. Rather, tempered by decades of continual conflict, they were considered by many to be the best and most experienced of Russia's soldiers, from the ranks of which emerged the line of great Caucasian commanders. Officers thirsting for a real experience of war, as well as a highroad to decorations and rapid promotion, sought service with this army, which also absorbed the misfits from units elsewhere. As a result, its traditions were its own and celebrated a multitude of the heroic feats of arms so common along frontiers of almost continual conflict. Equally important, these same traditions also represented a rich mixture of the spirit of adventure and romanticism that was chronicled so vividly by Lermontov and Tolstoy, as well as a respect for the unorthodox that is so necessary in the conduct of irregular or guerrilla warfare.[5]

In retrospect, it seems hard to deny that all this had a strong influence upon the young Aleksei. Born in Tiflis on 31 August 1853, he was the son of Aleksei Nikolaevich Brusilov, a sixty-six-year-old major-general who had become a cavalry officer in 1807, fought Napoleon from 1812 to 1814, and served in the Caucasus since 1839. His mother, Maria-Louise, was only twenty-seven or twenty-eight years of age. Polish by nationality, she was the daughter of a civilian bureaucrat who may have arrived in the Caucasus as an exile after the Polish rising of 1830.[6] Whatever the case, the family was apparently a close one. Despite their differences in age, the Brusilovs seem to have gotten along well together and quickly had two other sons, Boris and Lev, separated by another, Aleksandr, who died shortly after birth. Undoubtedly, the household in which young Aleksei spent his first six years was dominated by military concerns. This was, after all, the period of the Crimean War, which added considerably to the problems facing the Caucasian troops as the Turks actively intervened to support their co-religionist mountaineers. That Aleksei senior, who now served in the military-judicial branch of the army, was involved in these events is obvious: in 1856 he was promoted to the rank of lieutenant-general. He evidently intended his eldest son to follow in his footsteps: on 8 August 1857, he registered the boy for entry into the Corps of Pages, the elite civil and military school that was attached to the Imperial Court in St. Petersburg. In 1859, the three Brusilov boys suffered a double loss. First, their father died of croupous pneumonia, then their mother, a few months later, of consumption. To a large extent, the blow was cushioned by the prompt action of their aunt, Genrietta Antonova Gagemeister, who immediately took the three boys to her home in Kutaisi. Being childless, she and "Karl Maksimovich, her husband, loved us very much," Brusilov later recalled, "and they both took the place of our mother and father in the full sense of the terms."[7] Despite his later laconic recounting of these events, they cannot help but have left their mark on both the six year old and his four-year-old brother, Boris. Indeed, it is perhaps not fanciful to ascribe their teenage problems in the Corps of Pages, from which Boris eventually "dropped out," to a delayed reaction to their parents' death. If this remains conjecture, it does seem that the stoicism and cool head that Aleksei displayed once he had overcome his vague, adolescent "nervous" condition in the school can in part be explained by his having to set an example, as the oldest brother, at an early age in a family gripped by tragedy.

The same event may also have left him determined to fulfill his late father's wishes and follow him into an army career in the cavalry. Meanwhile, the military atmosphere was not absent from the Gagemeister house either. Karl Maksimovich was a military engineer, and the home had frequent military visitors. So although his aunt's musical and literary tastes broadened his horizons, the "deepest influences of my youth," Brusilov later wrote, "were undoubtedly the tales of the heroes of the Caucasian wars. Many of them were still living and visited my family."[8] As a result, he continued to imbibe the romantic traditions of the Caucasian Army while living surrounded by the high mountains and southern, semitropical climate in which the same legends had been forged. Small wonder that when he returned as a young lieutenant of dragoons, he emulated the vices of any number of literary models in gambling and dueling, and when the time came, the military virtues of the Caucasian heroes of his youth.

His aunt and uncle, Brusilov tells us, "spared no cost in educating us."[9] As so often is the case with wealthier members of Russia's provincial gentry, the Brusilov children received their initial lessons from private tutors at home. Unlike many of his later colleagues, the young Aleksei was fortunate in receiving an excellent grounding in French, Russian, and German. Although he proved to be without musical talents, Brusilov at this time began developing a love of literature. His taste would be expanded subsequently by his time with influential relatives, the Stemboks of St. Petersburg, and he reportedly remained a passionate reader of both fiction and nonfiction for the rest of his life. Overall, the strengths and weaknesses of the program of home study are reflected in his scores in the entrance exams to the Corps of Pages: "excellent" in foreign languages, but only "satisfactory" in all other subjects.

When Brusilov reached age fourteen, Karl Maksimovich took him to St. Petersburg. There, on 9 July 1867, he began his new life in the Corps of Pages. After passing the qualifying exams, he was placed in the third form on 14 November of that year. As already noted, the "corps" was in fact a school for the sons of the social, bureaucratic, and military elite of the empire. Founded by the Empress Elizabeth in October 1759, this institution initially had existed as a court school for sons of nobility who were destined for civil or military service. In October 1802, however, Alexander I had transformed it into a specialized military school to train officers for the Imperial Guards. Brusilov entered the corps at a time when Alexander II's great War Minister, D. A. Miliutin, was reorganizing and "modernizing" Russian military education. The Corps of Pages then comprised seven classes or forms: five providing an all-round general education, followed by two devoted specifically to military training. The first five forms were the equivalent of the upper five in a cadet corps or, under Miliutin, a military gymnasium. In their day, education in these later institutions was much more progressive than that found in their civilian counterparts, the courses of which were closely tied to a narrow study of the ancient classics.

Students passing out of the fifth form then entered the specialized classes. These were taught in accord with a curriculum similar to the two-year program of the regular military schools that trained future commanders in the infantry, cavalry, or artillery. The subjects included such basic military disciplines as tactics, fortification, artillery, topography, and military sketching (for instance, maps, fortifications, and artillery lines of fire), as well as the content of the existing military statutes and basics of military administration. In the summer, pages in these forms also participated in practical exercises and maneuvers with units of their chosen branch of service at an annual camp at nearby Krasnoe Selo and, during the winter, continued their specialized training in the appropriate facilities in St. Petersburg. Thus Brusilov, for example, would have learned the elements of caring for horses, as well as riding and cavalry drill, in the stables and riding hall attached to the court, and in summer attached to the Nikolai Cavalry School. Apart from the quality of instruction, a graduating page had the right of entering his regiment of choice. If he left after the sixth year, he normally would enter a line unit, but if he had the grades and resources, he could enter the elite Guards on passing out of the seventh and last form.[10]

Brusilov's tenure as a page deserves careful scrutiny both because of the insights it provides into the development of his character, and because his performance there was later used as a means of denigrating his military reputation. Take, for example, the somewhat dismissive comments of the snobbish British general, Sir Alfred Knox: Brusilov had been educated at the Corps of Pages, but, passing out low, had only obtained a commission in the Cavalry of the Line.[11] When this view of his schooling was coupled with Knox's later allegation that "he suffered from the lack of higher military education,"[12] it explained how young staff officers could dismiss Brusilov, even after his success of 1916, as "uneducated."[13] This, in the eyes of his critics of 1917, meant that in spite of his recognized "character and common sense" as a commander-in-chief, he represented "a positive danger, as he would give way in everything to the politicians."[14]

These comments raise two issues: the first concerns the nature of his military education; the second, the extent to which he could be talked into actions he might otherwise have avoided. In describing this period, Brusilov himself is of little help with regard to its details. Given his early background, we might expect that the broad-ranging general educational program of the pages would have suited him well. Even so, he later admitted that he had "studied in a peculiar manner: those subjects which I liked, I mastered very quickly and well; others, which I found to be alien to me, I studied with reluctance and only did enough to pass on to the next class—my pride would not permit me to repeat a year."[15] Even this determination, he tells us, was not enough to get him through the fifth and last of the general educational forms. Faced with the humiliation of being kept behind his comrades, he "preferred to take a year's leave and to go home to uncle and aunt in the Caucasus."[16]

This brief account seems quite straightforward. Nonetheless, his most recent biographer suggests that Brusilov may have been downplaying, if not concealing, an emotional crisis that occurred at what "undoubtedly was a dangerous, not to say critical point in his coming to age."[17] The evidence for this, as for so much else in the general's early life, is fragmentary. Nonetheless, a review of the reports of his class instructors suggests that something was afoot, although interpretations as to its exact nature must remain at best suppositions. At the very least, the same reports allow us a glimpse of the outstanding traits of his character as observed by the adults who had most contact with him during the years from 1867 to 1870.

In the first place, it seems that the transition from the cherished (not to say pampered) home in Kutaisi to life in a military school cannot have been easy. Even so, the initial transition seems to have been made easily enough. If young Aleksei, the Caucasian provincial, was intimidated by the sons of the upper levels of the sophisticated aristocracy of the Russian empire, the exalted position of his own relations in the capital must have provided a certain security. These were the family of an uncle on his father's side, Iulii Ivanovich Stembok, the Director of the Department of State Lands and a leading figure in the St. Petersburg bureaucracy. Again, his relationship with the Stemboks, with whom he spent his first two school vacations, were apparently cordial enough to help cushion him from charges of being an outsider or country bumpkin.

Within the Corps of Pages, Brusilov seems to have been well liked and to have settled in satisfactorily, from the assessment of his first teacher, Staff Captain S. V. Peskov.[18] According to his report of May 1868, when Aleksei left the third form, he was "of a playful and even mischievous, but sound and straightforward character." Apparently good-natured and open, he "never hides his bad sides and does not brag about his merits." If it was true that the youth "is sometimes coarse and sharp in conversations," he nonetheless had "a pure heart, . . . has proper respect for his own and others belongings, and in his dress is always neat and not gaudy." Overall, Peskov concluded that his student had considerable ability, was developing well enough, "but enjoys lazing about and therefore his academic progress is only fair."

In retrospect, the first sign of more serious problems appeared when Brusilov returned to the school after vacationing with the Stemboks. Writing on 1 September 1868, Peskov noted that his charge "has become somewhat reserved in conversation."[19] But this still was only a minor cloud on the horizon, and little else seems to have changed while he was in the fourth term. The final report of another instructor, Major N. S. Pokrovskii, reiterated the remarks of Peskov. In conduct the youth remained "direct and self-confident," as well as "reasonable and therefore compliant." When one "reproaches him for his faults, he is difficult to bully, but easy to convince."[20] Overall, the major regarded Brusilov as being basically "sound," noting that he "pardons injuries, is helpful to others" and, perhaps significantly, "has few false impressions about his relationships with his comrades." As for his school work, however, Pokrovskii like Peskov was less positive. True, he admitted, as a student Aleksei had "well developed abilities," but his progress could hardly be judged to be satisfactory. Rather, the major concluded, "he is not interested in work. Everything bores him for no reason."

Obviously, then, the school's program was not sufficiently interesting, or Brusilov had other things on his mind, or both. In any case, he now vacationed for another summer with the Stemboks, and in late August returned to enter the fifth and final form before seriously undertaking military subjects. Again he immediately began to slip and the assessment at that time noted tersely: "Works very little."[21] Matters quickly went from bad to worse by the end of that school year, and in May 1870, the assessment presented a very different picture from that of a year earlier. Now his instructor noted that young Aleksei was "considerably behind" in his work both because "he continues to be lazy" and because he is "very frequently in the hospital." Apart from the suspicion that his student was malingering, the teacher added: "Is smoking and has made friends with a circle of trouble-makers." Finally, and perhaps most indicative of the change in behavior, he charged that now Brusilov's once winning "frankness has come to be used as a means of obtaining a pardon after some offense."[22] Against this background, his failure to pass into the sixth form was to be expected, and his instructors must have greeted his subsequent return to the Caucasus with considerable relief.

What are we to make of this episode when considering Brusilov's life as a whole? On the surface, it seems simple enough to dismiss it as a typical case of adolescent rebelliousness, a phenomenon with which most parents are familiar. But we should also ask whether or not Semanov is correct in seeing this crisis as something other than normal, and in ascribing the apparent boredom and malingering to some deeper distress.[23] If he is correct, the factors involved might well include a delayed reaction to his parents' deaths, brought on by a certain homesickness for the Caucasus of his youth, and the need to once again please a new group of friends and relatives. This last, for example, commonly develops in children: a desire to please, to appear pliable, and an ability to manipulate those who have charge of their lives. Similarly, a desire to win the approval and respect of peers frequently leads youngsters to join the radical fringe of their equals, who in turn are dismissed by their elders as "trouble-makers" or here, more precisely, "dare-devils." Again, given Brusilov's love of literature, his penchant for identifying with literary heroes, the nature of his reading during vacations with the Stemboks (which included Dostoevsky and other contemporary writers), his behavior at this time may well have been in part that of the romantic poseur. In any case, it does seem obvious that from the point of view of his studies, vacations with his relatives were more a hindrance than a help.

In addition to all this, another element may have been present. After all, it is not impossible that given his wide-ranging tastes, experiences in the more civilian environment of the Stemboks, and his imminent entry into serious military studies in the sixth form of the pages, young Aleksei may have begun to doubt the desirability of a military career. If so, this surely would have created feelings of guilt vis-à-vis his late father, feelings that would have increased in intensity as the moment of decision approached. Whatever the case, it is reasonable to see this as a period of uncertainty for young Aleksei and, if so, to assert that a year in the bracing mountain air and formative environment of Kutaisi was sufficient to restore his determination. A year later he returned as a new man to the

Corps of Pages, passed the entrance examination for the sixth and specialized form, and began his studies as a cavalryman with a diligence not evident in his earlier years. As a result, he graduated from the sixth form on 29 June 1872; and, with his fellows, Alexander II personally awarded him the rank of ensign.

While this seems to confirm the charge that Brusilov could be overly accommodating, we should note that he himself was capable of manipulating others. Although he was open to the arguments of others, there is no reason to conclude that as an adult he was overly pliant. Indeed, it was this same willingness to entertain the ideas of others that served him so well in 1916 by permitting him to see beyond the orthodoxies of his fellow front commanders. Further, the young Aleksei seemingly emerged from personal crises with increased reserves of self-control and reliance, qualities that would stand him in good stead throughout his later career and often tragic personal life. Against this background, General Knox's description of the "lithe and active" sixty-two-year-old of 1916 has the ring of accuracy. Noting his kind reception, the British envoy wrote that "Brusilov gives one the impression of cunning, with small, deep-set eyes and thin lips, but he is intelligent and self-reliant—not a man to lose his head in a tight place.[24]

Leaving questions of character aside, what can we say about Brusilov's early education, or Knox's charge that his poor marks prevented him from entering the Guards? It is true that failure to pass out of the seventh (or second purely military) form of the Pages with excellent marks generally precluded entry into these elite regiments. Yet there is no reason to assume that had he so wished, the reformed Aleksei could not have met this test. But at the same time, he seems to have felt unable to cope with a second, more informal but nonetheless indispensable requirement: that of independent wealth. A Guardsman's life, especially in the cavalry, was anything but cheap, and the financial demands it made far exceeded his official salary. Conscious of this fact, and of the need to husband resources for educating his two brothers, the young Brusilov accepted that this life was beyond his means. Another factor in his decision was a desire to serve in his native Caucasus, a course of action urged on him by the Gagemeisters. He resolved, therefore, to forego the seventh form and instead took advantage of the free choice of regiment allowed graduating pages to select the 15th (later the 43rd) Tver Dragoons, stationed near Tiflis. If this regiment lacked the luster of the Guards, it was still one of the most glorious and renowned in the Imperial Army.

In the long run, this decision was of major significance for Brusilov's later career. In the first place, any bitterness it may have occasioned would have been salved by his promotion to the rank of colonel in the Guards cavalry in the late summer of 1892. In the meantime, he had received the chance to develop his view of military life in the Caucasian Army where, the romanticism of the frontier apart, military skills were highly valued and encouraged. Service in the Guards, on the other hand, would likely have developed his more social side, would probably have involved him in the intrigues for which Petersburg society was justly famous, and would have forced him to pay more attention to the military form of the parade square than the practice of war. This decision, as well as his own native intelligence and early developed sense of autonomy, was a major factor behind both the mature Brusilov's professional dedication and his apparent aloofness from the capital's social whirl.

The same decision also helps explain his attitude toward the revolutions of 1917. Young Guards officers had their loyalty to the person of the monarch continually reinforced by daily personal military and social contacts with the Emperor and other members of the dynasty. For their colleagues in the Caucasian Army, however, the tsar was much more distant and hence could become a symbol of the state, rather than the individual, to whom they owed loyalty. This tended to promote an equation of "Tsar" with "Fatherland," in which the latter could easily become dominant. At least that was the case with Brusilov, who seems only to have met the monarch once during his first decade of service, on the occasion of his graduation from the Pages in 1872. His full expression of this attitude, of course, only came much later. Thus he told confused young colleagues in the dark days following the Bolshevik coup of 1917 that while governments came and went, Russia remained. Therefore their only honorable course, this quintessential professional insisted, was to remain aloof from civil strife and wait for the day when they would again be needed to battle Russia's external enemies.[25]

Otherwise, the slur that Brusilov was "uneducated" has ramifications quite apart from the period under consideration. Its import, in fact, is that the commander of 1916 to 1917 had never attended the Academy of the General Staff, a qualification that many (especially all those who had done so) considered to be absolutely indispensable for those holding the highest positions. As an ensign-cavalryman, Brusilov had the basic military education provided junior officers and, despite his problems, had a general educational background that was superior to that received by the majority of his army fellows. Even so, in this period his greatest military interest seems to have been the care and training of cavalry mounts, and horses would remain a lifelong passion, as did literature and the theater. His well-developed linguistic skills and reading habits undoubtedly enabled him to educate himself militarily later in life.[26] But the young officer was still a long way from the front commander of 1916.

Indeed, in 1872 Brusilov still retained a romantic view of military life presented in song and story. This is clear from his own account of his trip home to the Caucasus. "I was ecstatic with my rank," he noted dryly, "and thanks to this was led into great stupidity" that ended by being swindled out of all his cash by gamblers.[27] Further, like contemporary officers such as Pushkin, Lermontov, and Tolstoy, who encased their military and barrack experiences in novels, Brusilov and his fellows took affairs of honor seriously. As a result, duels were not uncommon. On one occasion, he himself acted as second, for which he received a sentence of four months confinement (later reduced to two) in the Main Guard-House in Tiflis. Although this forced the postponement of his appointment as regimental adjutant, at the time it seems to have had little impact upon the young officer. It was only later, when he had to perform the adjutant's duties in wartime conditions, that his early romanticism seems to have dissipated.

With his usual modesty, Brusilov later downplayed his military interests during his initial period of service. Having described the artistic and theatrical diversions of nearby Tiflis, along with the succession of duels and other "scandals," he concludes with some unflattering comments on the professional attitudes of himself and his fellows. "We were not shining examples," he wrote, "neither with regard to our military knowledge, nor our love of study. We did not involve ourselves in efforts at self-education. The exceptions among us in this regard were few, although the Caucasian War had drawn to the Caucasus many people of superior education and talents." In general, he discerned "a sharp line between those officers with little education and, opposite them, people with higher educations who had dropped into their midst." In addition, there were also the "adventurers," including an Italian who told the most "uncommon tales," as well as an officer who had invented "an electric device for hunting bears."[28]

Despite his participation in the duel, Ensign Brusilov obviously impressed his superiors with his competence. If he showed no more interest in furthering his military knowledge than did his fellows, he nonetheless adapted readily and fully to the routines of service life (the drills, the hunts, the reviews, and more). On 14 April 1874, he became a full lieutenant and, on 26 July 1875, received his delayed appointment as regimental adjutant.[29] As this position demanded that the young officer display considerable tact, as well as expertise and responsibility to carry out a wide range of administrative activities, it was not one for which candidates were selected lightly. In fact, Brusilov had been carrying out these duties on an unofficial basis since February 1873. Even so, his final formal appointment came at a fortuitous point in his career, for it placed him in a post of enhanced responsibility throughout the course of the ensuing Russo-Turkish war of 1876 to 1878.

Brusilov's experiences during this conflict mark another turning point in his life. He entered upon his first campaign as a feckless military youth who thirsted for adventure and glory, both of which he got in full measure. In his first action, for example, he captured a Turkish brigade commander by a daring surprise maneuver. During the subsequent Caucasian battles of 1877, he distinguished himself repeatedly: first, during the storm of Ardagan on 16 to 17 May 1877, then in the battles of late August, and, finally, during the assault of the fortress of Kars on the night of 18 November. His feats on these occasions brought both promotion and decorations. On 10 November 1877, he became a Staff-Captain, and in 1878 received his first three combat decorations. Meanwhile, his immediate superiors obviously had followed this progress, and on 19 October had demonstrated their trust in the young officer by placing him in charge of the Tver Regiment's training command.

This brief account gives little indication of the real impact of the war on the young lieutenant. True, like his comrades he welcomed the break in the dull routine of peacetime soldiering, and he later asserted "that there was not a single man in the regiment who did not welcome with all his heart the onset of war."[30] But although few gave serious thought to the possibility they might die, he mused later, none of them—officers and soldiers alike—really understood why they were fighting. Similarly, while he valued Orthodox religious rituals as part of the Imperial Army's traditions, he paid little serious attention either to their darker implications for men about to enter battle or to claims that this was a struggle to free brother (usually Orthodox) Slavs from the tyranny of infidel despots. Rather, at this time he accepted such justifications as given and marched off convinced that his chiefs knew what they were about, and that his duty was to carry out their orders.

One can doubt the extent to which this lack of "moral" preparation bothered him at the time. This is especially the case when we consider that he himself later admitted having little interest or knowledge of the international situation or politics that led to the conflict. Besides, he had little time for such concerns, being immersed in the other, more practical problems that demanded his attention as regimental adjutant: the total unpreparedness of the regimental supply column; the difficulty that many of the regimental mounts had in sustaining the initial 120-kilometer march required of them; the damage they sustained due to the troops' lack of training in loading their horses properly for such marches; and, above all else, the immense difficulty of making good such deficiencies at the last moment.[31]

When Brusilov had to deal with the numerous practical and bureaucratic problems of mobilizing the Tver Dragoons and readying them for battle, this went beyond problems of administration. In his memoirs, in which he dealt with these problems at some length, Brusilov explained "that this immediately revealed the extent to which the incorrect training of riders and their mounts in peacetime, pursued with the goal of achieving beauty and glitter, damages conduct of the business of war."[32] The fault, he concluded, lay not with the Caucasian veterans, who well understood the training required by real combat. Rather, the flaws he had to make good resulted from "requirements from on high," where those in charge had become besotted with the beauty of parade ground drill. "The results of our peacetime training, as I saw it," he wrote, "amounted to this: that we were forced to reap the many fruits of our peacetime training and then, having already gone to war, to learn and teach old skills that had been cast aside by regulations, but which again were in demand now that we had collided with military reality." He concluded on another occasion in his memoirs:

here once again was glaringly evident the truth of what had been said and written by so many, the necessity for which nonetheless is in danger of being forgotten: In peacetime one must demand of the troops, continually and exclusively, precisely what they will find to be necessary in wartime. Subsequently this neglected truth reasserted itself again and again and we often cursed our peacetime methods of training.

Recognition of this military truth is crucial to the rest of Brusilov's career. Others he absorbed as the conflict developed. Of these, two stand out. The first is that the young officer became convinced that any future combat commander, or *polkovodets*, could only command after having withstood the test of fire. In the battles of 1877, his own self-confidence and sense of mission in his chosen career had been tempered and strengthened under fire. That he responded well to the test of combat is clear from his accounts of the actions in which he was engaged. Thus he can describe the cavalry advance on the Turkish fortress of Kars "strolling down the boulevard," admit that "in all honesty . . . we found this 'boulevard' frankly dull," and later calmly tell of saving a General Staff major's life by coolly advising him to duck behind a stone.[33] Furthermore, if modesty apparently restrained him from making the point explicit in his memoirs for this period, Brusilov's comments on training make it clear that

Semanov is correct in ascribing to Brusilov the conviction that battle was the true school of combat.[34]

In addition, the events of 1877, and especially those surrounding the Russians' first attempt to capture Kars, also helped open the young officers' eyes to the fact that graduates of the Staff College, and even battle-tested veterans of past wars, on occasion could demonstrate incompetence. This is evident from his account of the treatment of a journalist, Stemborskii, from the St. Petersburg journal, *Novaia vremenia* (the *New Times*). According to Brusilov, this gentleman was "an accurate and talented" correspondent, who had "joined the Caucasian Army inspired by the best motives" and won everybody's respect by his reporting. But, unfortunately, Stemborskii also possessed a satirical wit and the ability to extemporize in verse. After the Russians' repulse at Zevin, for instance, he produced a set of stanzas entitled "The Baker's Dozen" (*Chertova diuzhina*):

> With trumpets' call, with cymbals' clash,
> THIRTEEN generals,
> And as many thousand soldiers,
> Went into battle, as on parade.
>
> The day was the THIRTEENTH of June,
> The Turks' response was far from feeble,
> Like beasts, the soldiers were slaughtered,
> THIRTEEN times our staff lied.
>
> With trumpets' call, with cymbals' clash,
> With faces blazing . . . Backwards,
> Came THIRTEEN generals,
> But . . . with many fewer soldiers.

Other verses followed, driving the overall point home and, in particular, attacking the conduct of General Geiman. These lines, Brusilov tells us, passed quickly from mouth to mouth through the troops. Needless to say, the high command staff were furious and "rained thunder and lightning down upon the poor Stemborskii." This finished his wartime writing career in the Caucasus; it resulted in his being "expelled from the ranks of the Caucasian Army" by the military authorities.[35]

Brusilov himself was kinder to Geiman, pointing out that for a converted Jew to rise to such a rank, "he must have been an exceptionally talented and wise fellow."[36] Even so, these experiences, along with his conviction that the only real school of war was war itself, naturally produced in him a suspicion of the practical abilities of colleagues whose education had been largely theoretical in nature, or whose peacetime practical training had never undergone the test of battle. Where else, after all, would they learn the value of even such an elementary precaution as the need to duck behind a boulder when under enemy rifle fire? So if young staff officers, like those quoted by Knox, called him uneducated and lamented his apparent lack of formal higher military education, Brusilov would have little time for the views of those *Genshtabisty* who, "happily few in number, were narrow-minded and even brainless, but still consumed by conceit."[37]

In the general's later view, youngsters who graduated from the Academy, which, with service in the Guards, was the highroad to promotion in the Imperial Army, all too frequently seemed to suffer from this defect and to flatter themselves "with the belief that two and one-half years in Staff College had transformed them into stars of the greatest magnitude in the military firmament, and that good generals could not be found anywhere outside of their ranks." So although he credited the majority of staff officers with being intelligent "well up to their work," he still recorded with relish the officer of engineers who once asked which famous commander from Alexander the Great through Suvorov to Napoleon had attended such an academy. On the other hand, that officer noted the success of general graduates of the Staff College—those generals of the "Kuropatkin school"—in the war with Japan of 1904 to 1905, many of whom still held high positions and became Brusilov's colleagues from 1914 to 1917.[38]

Second, Brusilov's experiences in these campaigns emphasized the extent to which "soldiers and officers suffered as one" during wartime. On the battlefield they depended upon one another, and fought and died together. On other occasions they shared the same privations. At the end of the summer of 1877, for example, his brigade found itself "without a supply column while the majority of us had only the shirts on our backs. In the terrible heat which is common in summer in the region," he recalled, "this situation was terrible." Worse still, the "rations were awful." The Russian army of that day, he tells us, lacked field kitchens. This meant that whenever the "troops found themselves on the move or without a supply train, such as was the case with us, then food was passed out by hand and each prepared it as best he could."[39] Given his later repeated instructions on the need for officers to get to know their troops and to take care of their basic necessities, we conclude that these initial experiences left an indelible mark on a man who in effect saw himself as a "soldiers' general."

In other words, Brusilov emerged from the Turkish war as a convert to the principles of the so-called Russian school of war that drew its inspiration from the example of A. V. Suvorov, and which in Brusilov's own day found its foremost practical expression in the tactical precepts of M. I. Dragomirov. True, neither are prominently mentioned in Brusilov's later memoirs. But like his illustrious mentors, he now understood well the need to train troops for war in peacetime since, as Suvorov had put it, "what is difficult in training, is easy in war," and vice versa. Apart from demands for realistic training, there are also striking parallels between Brusilov's later practical conduct and these teachers' precepts on the "moral" factor in warfare, the concomitant need for commanders to know and deserve the trust of their men, and the need for the same commanders to act speedily, offensively, and decisively. Indeed, in this regard Brusilov seems a veritable twin of the most prominent Russian naval leader to emerge from the same conflict—Admiral S. O. Makarov. He, too, understood the true message of Suvorov and Dragomirov, which he summed up in his slogan that in peacetime, one must always *"Pomni vinyl"* ("Remember war").[40]

Despite his increased responsibilities, the young Brusilov found it difficult to return to peace and the almost operetta-like regimental life he had enjoyed before 1876. Arriving at the Tver Regiment's home quarters in September 1879, he spent a restless winter in what he called "extraordinary tedium."[41] To some extent his boredom was alleviated by frequent visits to Tiflis. There he became a regular guest in the home of the late A. M. Fadeev, who had been a member of the council of the Main Administration of the Caucasian Viceroy. A talented family, the Fadeevs included among their ranks the noted military theorist and historian, Rostislav Andreevich Fadeev, and the well-known writer of children's books, Vera Petrovna Zhelikhovskaia. The latter's daughter, Nadezhda, later became Brusilov's second wife and may well have been a romantic interest at the time. Even so, it seems probable that the erudite Rostislav—an influential exponent of the "Russian" or "national" school of war that revered Suvorov as a prime exemplar—would have made the greatest impression on a young officer seeking perspective on his recent experiences. As a result, many of the conclusions that Brusilov himself was already reaching must have received authoritative confirmation in this intellectual milieu.[42]

Unfortunately, his relations with the Fadeevs were severed for one reason or another—in his memoirs Brusilov simply ascribes the rupture to an "intrigue of Vsevolod Sergeevich Solov'Eva."[43] Whether as a result of a broken courtship with Nadezhda or simply because of his frustration with the routine of peacetime soldiering, in the summer of 1880 Brusilov sought an escape into further action. He himself recalls that "up to 1881 I continued to bear my burden in the regiment, the peacetime life of which, with its daily gossip and squabbles, was in the end of very little interest."[44] Only an occasional hunting expedition still enlivened this existence, so he jumped at a chance to volunteer for service with the troops being organized under another "soldiers' general," M. D. Skobelev, to capture the strategic oasis of Akhil-Teke. By this time his health was failing and he was on leave to "take the waters" at the Caucasian spa of Essentuka and Kislovodsk. Despite a personal plea to his divisional commander for permission to join Skobelev's expedition, the restless young soldier found himself forced to watch from the sidelines as Russian arms spread the empire's boundaries still further into the vastness of Central Asia.

In spite of this disappointment, the leave quickly restored Brusilov's health. Not surprisingly, however, he still sought greater challenges and in 1881 applied for a transfer to a unit of Caucasian mountaineers, the Kutaisi Irregular Mounted Regiment. Instead, his commander suggested he join the provisional teaching staff of the reorganized Officers' Cavalry School in St. Petersburg. Seeking an outlet to put his views on training into practice, Brusilov readily accepted, fully expecting to return to his regiment after a short term. But once again his arrival that October in Peter's city on the Neva was to mark another turning point in his life. This time his farewell to the scenes of his youth was to be no mere *au revoir*. Instead, in 1881 he traveled north to begin a new life that would eventually bring glory not only to his own name but also to the nation and empire he would so faithfully serve. Clearly, the Brusilov who emerged from the Turkish War was a very different man from the romantic young lieutenant who had cheerfully set off with his regiment in 1876. Two years later, he had emerged from the conflict a restless veteran who understood fully that war was no mere adventure, but a very serious business indeed. Henceforth he would value the virtues of the military professional in peace as well. Having cut his teeth in combat, he had also come to appreciate the many magnificent qualities of the men for whom he, the commander, bore responsibility. But while he would treat both them and his colleagues with the charm and forbearance he had developed as a youth, behind this lay the stoicism of his childhood, now combined with the calculating mind of a professional who was determined to fight and win.

Similarly, although Brusilov never fully abandoned his earlier artistic and literary tastes, he was now determined that the "lessons learned" so painfully should become integrated in the peacetime training in his arm of the service. As a result, the professional military literature of his day became a large, if not predominant, part of his reading matter. As matters turned out, Brusilov was to receive the opportunity to implement his ideas—thanks to his time with the Officers' Cavalry School, and then as commander of the Guards Cavalry Division. Subsequently, in 1909, when he advanced to assume command of combined-arms units, he sought to familiarize both himself and his men with the appropriate "military verities" as well as with the latest technological advances. To this end, he obviously read widely in the European military literature of his day and frequently visited abroad to observe and study the practices of other armies. As his later attitudes toward aviation and the future of his beloved cavalry demonstrate, he was fully aware of the implications of technology and the need to adapt to its changing requirements.[45]

Nonetheless, for the seasoned if youthful veteran who had emerged in 1878, technology might complicate an issue but would not make it insoluble. The solution would lie in identifying the problem, deciding on the appropriate course of action, preparing one's men accordingly, and then boldly conducting war with the opponent in the spirit of the great Suvorov. He shared this attitude with the young Makarov, which explains their subsequent willingness to break with routine and the precepts of conventional wisdom and seek innovative methods of combat. Unlike his unfortunate naval colleague who perished before Port Arthur in 1904 at the very moment he was about to test his theories and convictions in the stern school of war, Brusilov was to have the opportunity to implement his method on the battlefield. But if the brilliant victory of 1916 is the most conspicuous success of his long career, it seems clear that by 1878, his feet were already planted firmly on the road that would bring him success in the bloody trenches of Galicia. While the majority of his Russian and Western colleagues, despairing of breaking the deadlock of trench warfare, hopelessly continued to throw thousands of new victims into seemingly endless battles of attrition, the one-time cavalryman and his subordinates pioneered methods that eventually would restore mobility to Europe's battlefields.

ACKNOWLEDGMENT

This foray into what some may call "psycho-history" assumes the acceptance of no particular psychological or psycho-analytical "school." Rather, it is based on the proposition put forth by my father, the late Dr. Robert O. Jones, founder of the Department of Psychiatry at Dalhousie University, that "psychiatry is an art, not a science." Without the insights I learned from him into "the ways people respond and work," this chapter would not have been possible, but all conclusions drawn remain my own, and, hence, largely subjective.

NOTES

1. This incident was described to me by Colonel "Billy" Oliferoff, a veteran of the Horse Grenadier Guards, in an interview in San Francisco in June 1968.
2. I. I. Rostunov, *General Brusilov* (Moscow, 1964); and Sergei Semanov, *General Brusilov. Documental'Noel povestovanie* (Moscow, 1986). The latest Soviet edition (the 6th) of his memoirs is A. A. Brusilov, *Moi vospominaniia* (Moscow, 1983), to which all references refer unless otherwise noted. Other Soviet editions appeared in 1929, 1941, 1943, 1946, and 1963, and a separate emigré Russian edition was published in Riga in 1929. The bibliography in Rostunov, *Brusilov*, 239–44, is the fullest listing of his own works, works about him, and studies and document collections of his 1916 campaign. However, it ignores the occasional emigré studies and articles on these matters, some of which include: the English edition of his memoirs entitled *A Soldier's Note-Book. 1914–1918* (London, 1930; reprinted Westport, CT, 1971); the French language *Memoires du General Broussilov. Guerre 1914–1918* (Paris, 1929); and the very few non-Russian studies of the successful campaign of 1916. Of these later books, the best are Norman Stone, *The Eastern Front, 1914–1917* (London, 1975), 232–63; N. N. Golovin's brief essay, "The Brusilov Offensive, 1916," *Slavonic and East European Review*; and the gossip account in General Alfred W. F. Knox, *With the Russian Army, 1914–1917*, Vol. II (London, 1921), 427–82.
3. Brusilov himself opened his memoirs with the statement: "I never kept a diary and preserved only reports, a mass of telegrams and the comments on maps explaining the positions of our own and the enemy's troops in each of the operations carried out"; see Brusilov, *Moi vospominaniia*, 13. The best guide to the sources extant is Rostunov, *Brusilov*, 3–14, and although Semanov seems to use a little additional material, the literary and undocumented nature of his work means that it must be used with caution.
4. Rostunov, *Brusilov*, 3.
5. On the exploits and history of Russia's troops on the Caucasian frontier, see W. E. D. Allen and Paul Muratoff, *Caucasian Battlefields: A History of the Wars on the Turco-Caucasian Border 1828–1921* (Cambridge, 1953).
6. Rostunov, *Brusilov*, 16. The dates used in this article are Western ones, from the Gregorian calendar.
7. Brusilov, *Vospominaniia*, 14.
8. Ibid., 15.
9. Ibid., 14.
10. On the Corps of Pages, see Rostunov, *Brusilov*, 17–18; and Dominic Lieven, *Russia's Rulers under the Old Regime* (New Haven, CT, 1989), 52–56, 98–100.
11. Knox, *Russian Army*, 436.
12. Ibid., 628.
13. Ibid., 481.
14. Ibid., 628.
15. Brusilov, *Vospominaniia*, 15.
16. Ibid.
17. Semanov, *Brusilov*, 20.

18. The following comments are quoted in Rostunov, *Brusilov*, 19.
19. Ibid.
20. Ibid., 20.
21. Ibid.
22. Quoted in Ibid.
23. Semanov, *Brusilov*, 20.
24. Knox, *Russian Army*, 460.
25. A. Levitskii, "General Brusilov," *Voennaia by'*, No. 89 (January 1968), 34. On his graduation and attitude while in the Caucasus, see Brusilov, *Vospominaniia*, 16, 19.
26. "I read the military journals and a multitude of books by military specialists, Russian and foreign," he recalled; see Brusilov, *Vospominaniia*, 34.
27. Ibid., 16.
28. Ibid., 18.
29. The course of Brusilov's career can be followed most easily by referring to the chronology in Rostunov, *Brusilov*, 235–38.
30. Brusilov, *Vospominaniia*, 19.
31. Ibid., 18–22.
32. Ibid., 20–22.
33. Ibid., 25, 30.
34. Semanov, *Brusilov*, 43–44.
35. Brusilov, *Vospominaniia*, 26–27.
36. Ibid., 26.
37. Ibid., 61–62.
38. Ibid., 62.
39. Ibid., 28.
40. Suvorov's teachings are summed up in his famous *Nauka pobezhdat'*, of which there are numerous editions. Dragomirov's tactical precepts were enshrined in his influential *Uchebnik taktiki*, an early version of which appeared as early as 1867, and the last edition (as a tactics text) just after the Russo-Japanese War. This undoubtedly was one of the texts used by Brusilov during his military training with the Pages. On Makarov, his slogan, Dragomirov and Suvorov, see B. Ostrovskii, *Admiral Makarov, 1848–1904* (Leningrad, 1951), 185–86, 196–201; and Sergei Semanov, *Makarov* (Moscow, 1972), 154, 162–73.
41. Brusilov, *Vospominaniia*, 32.
42. Rostunov, *Brusilov*, 31.
43. Brusilov, *Vospominaniia*, 40. Solov'Eva apparently was the son of the famous historian, Sergei Solov'Eva.
44. Ibid., 33.
45. On Brusilov's later recognition of the value of aviation, and of the decreased role that cavalry would play in warfare, see Brusilov, *Vospominaniia*, 58–59; and Knox, *Russian Army*, 505–8. Typical of his views on the treatment of soldiers is the extract from his orders contained in an appendix to Brusilov, *Vospominaniia*, 247–51.

6

Hugh Trenchard:
Making the Unorthodox Orthodox

Scot Robertson

In branding an individual a heretic, one is generally casting aspersions on the person's character, beliefs, and values. Yet, in the vernacular of the military historian, the term "heretic" tends to be reserved for those who impose unorthodox views on a reluctant and conservative military to some positive end. Military heretics, therefore, are often held up as enigmatic and heroic figures. Russell Weigley has written: "In military history unlike most other branches of history, the hero in the fullest meaning of the word, the individual who by his own will and accomplishments alters the course of events, still strides across the record of the past."[1] Hugh Trenchard *may* have been such an individual. He still strides across the record of the Royal Air Force—the RAF—in particular, and of air power in general. Nevertheless, there remains scope for historians to examine the effects of his unorthodox—some would say—heretical views.

As the father of the Royal Air Force, Hugh Montague Trenchard had the rare opportunity to preside over the introduction of a new technology and the creation of a new and independent branch of the armed forces. Following the creation of the Royal Air Force, he was charged with the responsibility of honing the new technology into one of the principal weapons of war for the future. In short, Trenchard was granted the opportunity to make the first independent air service in his image. To his task, he brought unparalleled energy, sharp bureaucratic skills, vision, foresight, and a compelling personality. Such a unique combination of traits enabled Trenchard both to foster a group of air power disciples and, at the same time, overwhelm those opponents who stood in his path. It was through this combination of traits that Trenchard was able to ensure that his unorthodox ideas regarding this new form of warfare were at the center of the defense debate in the United Kingdom throughout the interwar period and, ultimately, beyond.

However, there was a negative side to Trenchard's efforts to build an air force capable of independent and, in the view of its proponents, decisive strategic air action. This is revealed in large part by the RAF's inability at the outset of World War II to carry out a strategic air offensive. Indeed, some have argued that the RAF was never able to carry out a strategic offensive at all. Still others argue that the operations of the Bomber Command in World War II were not unlike the trench stalemate of World War I, leading to the forlorn hope that just one more massed night-time raid would deliver the telling blow. This was similar to the situation that had confronted the High Command during the Great War.

In his highly readable account of Bomber Command's operations during World War II, Max Hastings described several of Bomber Command's first raids of the war.[2] On 4 September 1939, for instance, fourteen Wellingtons of Number 3 Group and fifteen Blenheims of Number 2 Group set out to attack German naval targets. Those attacks hardly marked an auspicious beginning for Bomber Command. The targets for the Wellingtons were the ships *Scharnhorst* and *Gneisenau* in the Elbe estuary. They failed to score a hit and lost two of their number. The Blenheims, whose target was the ship *Admiral Scheer* at Schillig Roads, pressed home their attack at low level. Although four hits were recorded, none of the bombs exploded. The cost was five aircraft. Thus, the scorecard was bleak. Twenty-nine aircraft set out. Of those, seven were shot down, or 24.1 percent. Such a casualty rate was very high. No military force can sustain 25 percent casualties and hope to maintain operations for long.

Be that as it may, Bomber Command persisted. On 12 December 1939, twelve more Wellingtons from Number 3 Group again took off to attack the Schillig Roads. That time the raid "ended in tragedy, with the loss of half the force."[3] Hastings said of those raids that they "were deliberately conceived as a means of testing Germany's defences and Bomber Command's tactics, rather than a serious assault on German sea power. There is no other way to explain the command's lack of concern about the failure of their aircraft to sink or damage a single enemy ship."[4] Despite the failures and the staggeringly high casualty rate, Bomber Command again threw itself into the breach on 18 December. On that occasion, twenty-four Wellingtons took off to attack enemy warships in and around the Schillig Roads and Wilhelmshaven. Twelve survived!

Those signal failures of the bomber forces of the RAF stand in stark contrast to the long-held expectations. From the last months of the Great War down to the outbreak of World War II, the notion of strategic bombing had held great prospect and at the same time cast a pall. On the one hand, the development of strategic bombing forces had apparently heralded a new era in which war would become a simpler task. Extensive land and naval forces were no longer considered necessary. Victory would go to the side that could master the skies and take the war to the very heart of the enemy nation. On the other hand, fear of a strategic bombing duel exercised a paralyzing restraint on British foreign policy.[5] That fear, furthermore, weighed heavily on the minds of British politicians and the public alike. Once it became evident that war loomed on the horizon, it was air war that terrified people most. Preparations would have to be made to both prosecute and endure a strategic bombing duel.

Those preparations were left to the Royal Air Force. It was the strategic bombing pundits of the RAF, after all, who had fostered the notion that Britain's fate in a future war would rest on the sturdy wings of the bomber. Even though Bomber Command eventually undertook a massive night-time area bombing campaign against Germany, the results of that campaign were neither decisive nor consistent with pre-war expectations. How was it that this transpired? There are no short, simple answers to this question. What emerges from an examination of the evolution of the idea of strategic bombing in the British context is a complex web of competing explanations. Yet when the many strands are unraveled, the pattern that remains is of disjunction between theory and doctrine. Our discussion in this chapter will concern the disproportionate effect of a military heretic whose unorthodox ideas and bureaucratic imperatives paid little attention to the drudgery of working out a doctrinal basis for making the idea a reality. What was once an unorthodox idea became, in itself, a form of orthodoxy.

Our focus on the doctrinal aspect of strategic bombing will look at the theory and development of an "idea" of war. This chapter is not a biographical study of Hugh Trenchard, nor is it an account of Royal Air Force operations. Rather, it is more of an attempt to consider how those responsible for the RAF as a collective body of "professionals"—the Air Staff—rationalized their experience and prepared their plans and doctrines for war. In essence, the core of this argument is that military heretics pushing unorthodox ideas have perhaps even greater responsibility to ensure that their views are well thought out before they, too, become accepted conventional orthodoxy.

Early strategic theorizing in the RAF drew heavily on the limited experience of "strategic" bombing in World War I. That experience profoundly influenced much of what followed in the two decades leading up to World War II. It must be noted, however, that many conclusions regarding the potential future use of air power were dubious at best, and dangerous at worst. Often they were derived from a cursory examination of the historical record. In that sense, then, the Clausewitzian dictum regarding the search for first principles through rigorous historical examination and critical analysis to determine cause and effect was flouted. While it is not necessary to delve deeply into the details of aerial operations during World War I, it is essential to review some of the important developments that emerged during that time as the air weapon began to make its presence felt.

At the outbreak of the Great War, expectations of what aircraft might contribute were modest. The general consensus was that aircraft could best serve as observation platforms, but beyond that, little was expected. With the emerging stalemate of trench warfare, the airplane began to show itself as a weapon of great potential. When it became obvious that aerial reconnaissance was invaluable for artillery spotting, and thus dangerous to troops on the ground, each side began to search for ways to drive off the enemy's observation aircraft. This was done first through groundfire and then by mounting machine guns on aircraft themselves. Hence the development of the pursuit role for aircraft.

The next development was to employ aircraft as ground support weapons. In this role aircraft either operated directly against troops or slightly to the rear, attacking supply dumps and communications facilities. It was a short step from this—what is now termed "close air support"—to taking up longer range operations, attacking targets far from the location of the fighting at the front. These operations, directed further to the rear, constituted the first attempts at "strategic" operations. Both Germany and Britain experimented with the "strategic" use of air power, but in strictly operational terms, neither achieved a great deal of success.[6]

This situation changed when Germany undertook raids on the United Kingdom, first with the Zeppelins and then with the Gothas. With this, Germany brought the war directly to London and the southeast. Up to then, the British public had not been directly threatened with physical harm by the war taking place across the Channel. In political terms, the German air raids against the British Isles produced a serious crisis of confidence that threatened to undermine the ability of Britain to carry on with the war effort. While the public was alarmed and outraged, the British government reacted with panic. The prevailing feeling in political circles was that if the German raids continued unabated, the British will to continue with the war would crumble. Hence, steps were taken to cope with the threat posed by German aerial raids.[7]

Again, it is unnecessary to tell this story in great detail. In the case of the Zeppelin raids, air defense measures had some limited success in dealing with the lumbering giants. Then, with the appearance of the fixed-wing Gotha bombers, the situation deteriorated. In particular, two raids on London stand out as important landmarks: the first on 13 June 1917, and the second on 7 July 1917. Both raids revealed the shortcomings of existing defensive measures. There was a shortage of fighters and anti-aircraft guns, and the organization of the warning system left much to be desired. As Webster and Frankland noted, "these raids and the subsequent . . . attacks of the autumn did much to determine the future of the British Air Service."[8] A political hue and cry resulted in which the air services were subjected to intense scrutiny and criticism. Air defense measures were branded as inefficient and ineffective, while the overall direction of the air war was questioned. It must be recalled that at this juncture the Cabinet and the High Command had engaged in a running battle with Sir Douglas Haig over the course of events on the Western Front. While politicians called for better defenses at home, Haig and his air advisor Major General Hugh Trenchard, the Commander-in-Chief of the Royal Flying Corps, resisted every request for the transfer of aircraft from the Western Front to the home front. Trenchard viewed defense as a misuse of aircraft, the only proper role being in the offensive. The compromise that was reached was the creation of the Royal Air Force.

Given that the RAF was created during wartime, partly as an expedient, its postwar direction or even its very existence was uncertain. It had to find a role for itself or perish. In doing so, however, the RAF created its own difficulties. It sacrificed the long-term objective of developing theory and doctrine to the short-term objective of developing alternative peacetime roles. I will illustrate how the search for a peacetime role resulted in ever-increasing claims for air power and at the same time detracted from the fundamental need to devise a doctrine for the employment of air power in war.

At the end of the war, the unbridled hostility of the two older Services and the equivocal attitude of the British government toward the continued independence of the RAF seemed certain to ensure that its existence as a separate service would be very short indeed. Despite this, Trenchard set out to protect the continued independence of the RAF. Perhaps recognizing that arguing for independence on the basis of the importance of strategic bombing was difficult, he cast about for alternatives. This search was colored by one major government policy designed to direct defense policy in the postwar period—the notorious and much vilified Ten Year Rule.[9] The Ten Year Rule stated: "It should be assumed for framing revised estimates, that the British Empire will not be engaged in any great war during the next ten years, and that no Expeditionary Force is required for this purpose."[10]

There can be no doubt that the object of the Ten Year Rule was financial. It came at a time of austerity, but also at a time when the responsibilities of the defense services had taken on even greater scope; the government had to find a formula to govern the financial call the defense services could make on the budget. In the political atmosphere of the time, one in which the prevailing sentiment was to get back to business as usual, it was politically dangerous to adopt a policy that would sanction "high" defense spending. It was against this backdrop that Trenchard set out to find new roles for the RAF, roles that would justify its continued existence.

Conscious of the need for financial restraint, Trenchard astutely shaped a policy that did not run foul of the limits imposed by the Ten Year Rule. In fact, Trenchard framed a policy that would yield the RAF new independent roles and save the government money. He outlined his views on the future of the RAF in an August 1919 memorandum: "Hostilities ceased before the evolution of the independent Air Force had reached a point which enabled sure deductions to be drawn as to the value of independent aerial operations. . . . but there can be no doubt that we must be prepared for long distance aerial operations against an enemy's main source of supply and Naval ports."[11] There is little in such a statement to which one can take exception. In fact, had Trenchard and the RAF adhered to its spirit perhaps they would not have lost sight of what should have been their central concern—the preparation of an efficient and effective air force capable of undertaking long-range aerial operations. Trenchard did pay lip service to this objective in a later memorandum, published as a Command Paper, in which he outlined the steps needed to create such a force. Research and development in navigation, wireless, photography, and engineering, along with the fostering of an "Air Force Spirit," were accorded special emphasis, as was the need for staff and training colleges.[12] In the financially strained circumstances of the time, however, Trenchard recognized that such projects were beyond the meager means of the first few peacetime budgets.

While the long-term objective was the creation of an air force capable of undertaking independent strategic operations, the immediate need was to blunt the attacks of the Army and Navy. "Air Control" or "Imperial

Policing" was the instrument Trenchard chose to employ. Malcolm Smith has attributed the inception of the scheme for "air control" to Winston Churchill, who gave backing to the idea at the Cairo Conference in March 1921, but the idea itself had been mooted much earlier in Trenchard's memorandum of 14 August 1919.[13] The memorandum stated that: "Since the Armistice . . . events in the near East and India have tended to show that against a semi-civilized enemy unprovided with aircraft, aerial operations alone may have such a deterrent effect as to be practically decisive."[14] Air control took on ever-increasing importance as it became apparent that Army and Navy attacks on the independence of the RAF would not diminish over time. In air control Trenchard saw the possibility of reducing the considerable cost of policing the Empire and the newly acquired Mandated Territories, thereby demonstrating to the government the value of the RAF.

It is important to understand the nature of air control operations, for it was in this sphere that virtually all the peacetime operational experience of the RAF was gained, and nearly all the later senior RAF officers served at one time or another in areas where they gained some experience with air control operations. While it would be foolish to attempt to deny the initial importance of air control operations, serving as they did to impress upon the government the importance of maintaining an independent air force, one might legitimately question the extent to which the operational experience gained in this role influenced later considerations of strategic theory and doctrine. It would seem that those in positions of responsibility within the RAF and the Air Ministry lost sight of the fact that air control operations were, in the first instance, an administrative tool in a bureaucratic battle. Had they not lost sight of this fact, the air control experiment would have remained just that—an experiment and an expedient. Instead, the experience gained in air control operations was to influence unduly the theory and doctrine of strategic bombing in the larger sense.

As mentioned, Trenchard first mooted the idea for air control operations in his memorandum of 14 August 1919. Shortly thereafter, the RAF undertook its first air control operation in Mesopotamia. Following the rebellion in Mesopotamia in 1920, the Air Officer Commanding, Middle East, Geoffrey Salmond, submitted a report on the possibilities of exercising air control in that region. In it, he envisaged considerable savings in terms of men, equipment, and infrastructure, and as such endeared the report to a cost-conscious government. Needless to say, the Army that had previously been responsible for exercising military control throughout the Empire was strongly opposed to the notion of air control. Despite this, Trenchard took Salmond's scheme to Churchill, who, as Colonial Secretary, gave it official sanction at the 1921 Cairo Conference. Thus, the RAF was given the task of exercising control in Mesopotamia. "The Mesopotamia experiment, which was immediately extended to Transjordan, proved to be a great success and, in due course, the Royal Air Force responsibility was increased yet again, to cover the Aden Protectorate, saving the British taxpayer some £35,000,000."[15]

Not content to rest on his laurels, and in the best tradition of bureaucratic empire-building, Trenchard sought to extend the air control experiment to the North-West Frontier of India. His success in attempting to exercise air control in India was not nearly so marked, as responsibility for security in India was vested in the India Office and the budget for the RAF in India came under the Army budget. Nevertheless, he managed to wrest part of the task of control for the RAF away from the Army.

Air control contributed markedly to the difficult and expensive task of policing the Empire.[16] Moreover, it did so at a reduced cost to the government, which in itself was important. Be that as it may, the operational experience gained in air control was never likely to provide much in the way of guidance to the larger and more central question of how to develop the aerial weapon for service against a first-class power in any future war. Air control was carried out in what can only be described as an artificial environment, one that would hardly exemplify the environment that would confront the RAF in operations against a major enemy. As Malcolm Smith has commented, "the success of Air Control lay in the fact that retaliation [against the British] was virtually impossible."[17]

This very fact should have limited the extent to which lessons were drawn regarding the efficacy of bombing. While it was one thing to bomb "recalcitrant tribesmen" who could mount no effective opposition, it should have been obvious that it would be a completely different thing to undertake bombing operations against an enemy capable of mounting some form of defense, either passive or active. Over time, this essential difference became blurred, first as the RAF began to rearm in the early 1930s and then in the later 1930s as it undertook the arduous task of preparing Bomber Command for its role as a strategic force. This should not be taken as a suggestion that air control operations were completely devoid of value to the RAF. Air control missions provided a valuable opportunity to acquire operational experience during peacetime. Furthermore, they allowed for experimentation with equipment and methods of bombing, despite the meager budget for research and development and the limited time available in an operational squadron.

It is important to understand the evolution of the Air Staff's theory given that belief in the offensive power of the bomber provided the rationale, at least in the collective mind of the Air Staff, for the independence of the RAF. This becomes all the more vital in light of the fundamental impact that notions of air power had on the overall approach to British security policy throughout the interwar period. Recent historical research has revealed the extent to which the bomber cast a long shadow over considerations of British security and foreign policy.[18] What remains to be considered is the extent to which this fear was self-generated. If it can be argued that the Air Staff contributed to the process whereby exaggerated fears of the bomber served to influence unduly British security policy throughout the interwar period, then the Air Staff must bear a considerable responsibility for the consequences of their actions.

Pursuing this line of inquiry is difficult for a number of reasons. In the first place, it is not possible to speak of a uniform theory of air power to which the Air Staff subscribed for most of the period in question. Rather, the theory of the strategic offensive in Britain evolved over time. The entire British approach was, to an extent, reflected in the thinking of Hugh Trenchard while he was Chief of the Air Staff from 1919 to 1929, and after his retirement when he continued to exert a powerful public and private influence. Trenchard's thinking evolved to such an extent that he soon became a Cassandra for the overwhelming power of the bomber. Unlike Douhet, however, Trenchard did not outline his theories of air power in a single volume; furthermore, he altered them substantially over time. His approach was one in which the claims made for the power of the bomber grew more and more extreme as he had to press constantly for the right of the RAF to exist in the face of Admiralty and War Office attacks on the air force's independence.

Another factor complicating any discussion of the Air Staff's theory of the strategic offensive is the extent to which unofficial ideas concerning aerial warfare began to compete with the "official" theory. In part, the rise of nonmilitary ideas stemmed from the fact that during the early years of the interwar period, the Air Staff was busily engaged in its internecine bureaucratic battles. Consequently, there was little time to devote to the task of developing a doctrine of strategic air power. Even so, non-Service commentators would undoubtedly have pressed their own views concerning the development of air power, for it had apparently altered the entire basis of British security policy. The notion that Britain was vulnerable—that it was no longer an island—had a profound impact on the British. Barry Powers wrote:

this cliche represented a generalised viewpoint; in this case that England's defensive security was lost with the development of the airplane and that England existed thereafter in grave jeopardy. This fundamental shift in England from confidence to insecurity about its defensive position was of major consequence during the interwar years.[19]

Such a viewpoint pervaded British society. Malcolm Smith has commented that "the idea of aerial bombardment was almost as haunting an aspect of contemporary culture as nuclear weaponry was to become later."[20]

A final factor to consider is that the development of theory of the strategic offensive coincided with the RAF's early successes in air control throughout the Empire. These operations were taken by the Air Staff as a vindication of their confidence in the overwhelming power of the bomber. When this was coupled with their interpretations and analysis of the contribution of air power during the Great War, the future, at least to the Air Staff, seemed clear. Air power, particularly strategic offensive air power, held the key. Defense against this new and potentially devastating weapon seemed impossible, and thus the only apparent recourse was to rely upon the counteroffensive potential of the bomber.

In retrospect, these analyses were flawed. They failed to take into account the totality of the brief experience of air power in the British context. Air power advocates chose to focus only on those aspects that sustained their views. The inability or unwillingness to subject their notions regarding air power to the kind of serious scrutiny suggested by Clausewitz was a major shortcoming that plagued the Air Staff's efforts. The role of strategic air power during the Great War was marginal, while air control operations, although providing a valuable opportunity to gain operational flying experience, resulted in a false understanding of what would be required to carry out a strategic offensive.

Despite these limiting factors, Trenchard and the Air Staff felt justified in developing a rudimentary theory of the strategic offensive. This theory turned on the potential of independent air operations directed against an enemy's morale and its economic resources. Its development was aided—even driven—by the desire to avoid the slaughter of trench warfare. Furthermore, the Air Staff emphasized that aerial operations would preclude the necessity for a "Continental" commitment. David MacIsaac wrote that the essence of the Air Staff's theory was that "air attacks aimed at the sources as opposed to the manifestations of an enemy's strength . . . would produce a much swifter and hence in the end more humane decision."[21]

Thus, the theory of the strategic offensive with its roots in the final years of the Great War flourished in the bureaucratic battles of the early

1920s. Although many things would change from the mid- to late 1920s until the outbreak of World War II, the essence of the theory was unchanged. What remains is to consider the means by which the Air Staff and the RAF sought to transform a theory of war into a doctrinal reality. At this point I put forward the argument that Trenchard's unorthodox ideas became, in and of themselves, orthodox. The theory of strategic air power evolved into a dogma of strategic air power.

Although it is clear how the Air Staff came to the "theory" of air power, it is equally necessary to understand how they set out to create a doctrine for its application. In modern warfare, theory without doctrine is a dangerous proposition. Without doctrine, the application of a particular theory relies on vague general principles, rather than on a previously worked-out method. As Clausewitz noted, the role of theory is not to prescribe but to act as a guide in the study of war. Theory is meant to yield the fundamental truths upon which doctrine can be based.

Given that the Air Staff placed the greatest emphasis on the offensive capabilities of strategic air power—that is, the employment of the bomber force against targets such as enemy industry and civilian morale—one would have expected them to devise and test the tactics necessary for such an offensive. But the consensus among historians is that tactics were by and large an underdeveloped facet of RAF policy during the interwar period. The Official Historians wrote:

Until two years before the war the operational and technical problems of the strategic offensive had been neglected, and even later no real attempt was made to solve them by more realistic operational exercises. . . . the result was that as late as 1939 the Air Staff had little realisation of the tactical problems raised by the strategic plans.[22]

It is true that only a major war could have provided the real test, not only of the tactics necessary for a strategic offensive but of the very theory as well. Deprived of a major war, deprived even of operations against an opposing air force, the Air Staff was left to develop tactics through exercises. Yet this was a curious aspect of the overall approach to air power adopted by the RAF. Considerable effort was expended in defining the theory, but almost no realistic effort was made at exploring the tactics necessary to translate the strategic hypothesis into sound doctrine.

Clearly, a revolutionary strategy such as the one expounded by Trenchard and his colleagues in the aftermath of World War I demanded a thorough consideration of the tactics required to put it into effect. If the net result of Trenchard's strategic thundering was that traditional British defense policy was no longer sufficient, and that British strategy would have to be remade to take into account the radical new threat from the air, then one would expect that the Air Staff's prescriptions for the future should have been based on more than mere hypothesis. Yet in sum, that was what emerged from the interwar period! The concept or hypothesis based on the experience of World War I was elevated to the level of dogma. Williamson Murray stated:

[T]he myopia of the Air Staff hindered the development of a broadly based conception of air power in Great Britain. . . . Moreover . . . the evidence of World War I did not provide clear, unambiguous evidence on the impact of air power. But when all is said and done, too many of those in higher positions in the Royal Air Staff [sic] between the wars allowed doctrine to become dogma and failed to examine the assumptions on which they based their air strategy in light of the current capability and the difficulties that emerged just in peacetime flying.[23]

Once strategy became overborne by dogma, tactics became dogmatic as well. The net effect was that the rudimentary tactics designed to effect the strategic offensive fell far short of what was required.

How did the Air Staff approach the development and testing of tactics? What were the parameters within which tactical development took place, and what were the results? During peacetime, one of the only available means to test a strategic theory is through exercises. An exercise can take a number of forms—the most commonly understood type is a full-scale operational exercise involving large formations engaging in a mock battle. Yet this is the rarest form of exercise due to the expense and the disruption caused to the regular training program. Furthermore, exercises of this type are more often designed to confirm rather than test theory.

Less ambitious exercises that have specific objectives, such as testing a particular tactic or the potential effect of a particular piece of equipment on existing doctrine, may have a greater influence on the development of tactics and doctrine. These forms of exercises and trials have, or should have, a more telling influence, and as such are of greater utility than their more glamorous counterpart, the mock battle. A note of caution about the role and value of exercises must be sounded. An exercise is fraught with many limitations, not least of which is its inescapably artificial nature. It cannot replicate wartime conditions, hence its value is limited by the degree of vision and foresight brought to the exercise by its planners. This being said, it would be well to consider the tests, trials, and exercises undertaken by the RAF.

Between 1927 and 1935, the RAF undertook a series of large-scale exercises, the very nature of which revealed the state of Air Staff thinking and also served to confirm their preconceptions. The stated objective of many of the exercises was to test the arrangements for the air defense of the United Kingdom.[24] One must, however, adopt a cautious attitude when considering the "defensive" nature of the exercises. In the strategic vernacular of the Air Staff, the term "defensive" had a complicated meaning. On one level, the object was to provide for the immediate defense of the country by engaging enemy attackers over Great Britain. This was not, however, viewed with favor, as the Air Staff believed it to be a misuse of air power. That they contemplated it at all was a response to public and governmental reaction to the prospect of a mutual bombing contest in which civilian morale was the ultimate objective of both sides. In effect, defense of this kind was to forestall the collapse of the public's will to continue a future war in the face of the anticipated casualties. The Air Staff accepted it as a political necessity, although not one that should swallow much of their scarce resources.

The other level on which the Air Staff considered the "defensive" capability of air power involved the notion of the "offensive-defensive," or the "counteroffensive," what Malcolm Smith has termed "the theory of strategic interception."[25] This form of defense relied upon the anticipated ability of the RAF to bring overwhelming pressure to bear upon the source of any enemy's offensive potential through aerial attack. The RAF would force the enemy from its own air attacks onto the defensive. This notion was at the core of the Air Staff's strategic thinking, and the object of most of the large-scale exercises was to test the RAF's capability to implement such an "offensive-defensive."

It should surprise no one that the results of the exercises were taken as evidence of the veracity of the Air Staff view, even though there were numerous shortcomings in exercise design, to say nothing of the interpretation of the results. Other doctrinal considerations also suffered from the tendency of theory to become dogma. Not least of these were the capabilities and tactics of bomber formations. To carry out a strategic offensive required the solution of a number of problems. Two stand out as fundamental to the "offensive." First, the question of how the bomber force would reach the general target area intact. Presuming that the Air Staff could work out a solution to the first question, the second question involved a consideration of how the attack itself would be delivered. For the Air Staff to give meaning to its theory, it had to come to grips with these issues. The means and extent to which they did so—or, more correctly, failed to do so—reveals just how far the Air Staff allowed theory to unduly influence doctrinal considerations.

It is possible to suggest a number of reasons why the RAF and the Air Staff failed to appreciate the difficulties and complexities of the doctrinal and planning processes. One explanation might be that the intellectual approach was fundamentally absent from the British experience. In fact, they lacked experience with the type of staff work that would have contributed to the development of an intellectually sound approach to air warfare. In the absence of this, the Air Staff were incapable of making the linkage between "strategy" and "operations." They persistently failed to understand the importance of defining precise targets, hence their predilection for abstractions such as "Germany" rather than a "real" target such as a factory or even a city. Had they been capable of progressing beyond this they might have been in a position to formulate plans that addressed the specific requirements of operations.

Another possibility is that the Air Staff were so enamored with the apparent simplicity of their theory of strategic air power that careful and detailed planning seemed unnecessary. A final possibility, one that may in fact be most instructive, is that very few of those on the Air Staff possessed any degree of experience with planning at the strategic level. For the most part, those who made up the Air Staff during the first few years of the RAF's independent life possessed only operational experience. In effect, the Air Staff drew primarily from a pool of operational flyers. During World War I, RFC, RNAS, and later RAF officers did not participate directly at the general staff level. Rather, they acted as air advisers to the general staff. As such, they did not benefit from the evolution of the general staff as a body.

This was further compounded by the means through which officers were prepared for Air Staff work. Attendance at the Staff College was determined by a qualifying exam in which candidates were required to consider the problems involved with large-scale air war. One recurring question concerned the "correct" policy or doctrine for the RAF. It is clear from the examiners' reports that they were seeking a particular answer, namely that the only appropriate use for air power was in the offensive against enemy morale. If admission to the Staff College depended on an unquestioning acceptance of established doctrine, then the Staff College merely turned out staff officers unprepared to critically examine the central tenets of their profession.[26] It can be said that this lack of experience of planning at the strategic and operational level contributed greatly to the deficiencies of the RAF in developing a realistic understanding of air power and consequently a doctrine for prosecuting air warfare.

At the outset of World War II, Bomber Command was forced to adopt a "gloves on" policy, as the government was unwilling to accept the risks contingent with a strategic offensive that might lead to a mutual bombing contest. As such, Bomber Command's earliest operations were of a severely restricted nature. This must have come as a grave disappointment to all those in the RAF who had long maintained that the advent of strategic air power had radically altered the nature of war. For the better part of two decades, air power advocates had worked to convince their masters that through strategic air power, Great Britain could avoid the prospect of a "Continental commitment." In many ways they were successful in their endeavor, but not, perhaps, in the way they had first imagined. One constant in defense circles throughout the entire interwar period had been the claims made by air power pundits, and those claims helped shape the overall approach to defense planning. Unfortunately, however, the net effect was that British air strategy was disjointed and crippled by the time the test of World War II was upon them.

Generally speaking, the literature dealing with the RAF has treated the interwar period rather casually, if at all. For the most part, the trend has been to discuss the emergence of the theory of strategic bombing during the Great War, and then leap over the next two decades to discuss the strategic bombing campaign of World War II. When historians have paused to consider the interwar years, they have done so through a peculiar set of lenses that focus almost entirely on the frustrations of limited finance, interservice bickering, the pressures to disarm, and general political malfeasance. Such emphasis is unfortunate and unwarranted, for it overlooks many of the important aspects of the development of the idea of strategic air power that are fundamental to an understanding of the shortcomings revealed during its first great test.

This chapter has suggested some of the underlying reasons for the RAF's flawed approach to strategic air power. The central conclusion is that the RAF as a collective body never fully appreciated that what emerged from the experiences of World War I was only a theory—a hypothesis that required considerable effort to transform it into a doctrine of strategic air power that could serve in operations. The belief that strategic air power would be "decisive" was elevated to an article of faith. One is forced to conclude, however, that the Air Staff had built their theory on the flimsiest of foundations. Had they followed through with some of the essential doctrinal development, they might have recognized this and Bomber Command might have been able to play a more direct role during World War II.

How, after twenty years of proselytizing, was the Air Staff only able to recommend "propaganda" raids and costly but ineffective raids on naval targets? Simply, the RAF's theory of the strategic offensive was not a theory in the Clausewitzian sense. Rather, it was merely a hypothesis. The Air Staff failed to appreciate the importance of applying critical analysis to the matter of air power and its place in the defense hierarchy. Instead, the air power advocates seized upon the experience with "strategic" bombing during World War I as a means of ensuring the survival of the air force as an independent service. This was not necessarily a negative factor, but in the absence of a thorough exploration of the record of air power during World War I it led to unwarranted conclusions. For instance, little attention was paid to the fact that British defenses had succeeded, ultimately, in coping with the German bombing offensive, albeit at a tremendous cost and effort. In the absence of such consideration, it was a fairly straightforward step to the conclusion that the "offensive" application of air power was the only possible course to take.

From such a dubious intellectual origin, the air power pundits used their "theory" of strategic air power for all manner of purposes. They used it as a tool in the fight against the Army and Navy, and developed the concept of air control to illustrate the power of aerial bombardment. Using crude calculations of the German offensive in World War I, the experience of air control, and the "Continental" air menace, the RAF ensured that it would survive. It is unfortunate that what first served as a tool in an administrative battle assumed the mantle of infallibility, when the suspect "theory" would ultimately have a profoundly unsettling effect on British politicians and the public alike. It was, however, a theory that lacked substance.

The effect of this lack of substance is most obvious in the area of doctrinal development. The Air Staff failed to comprehend the simple fact that "doctrine" does not flow automatically from theory. Yet, from the moment that Trenchard declared that the "moral" effect of aerial bombardment was vastly superior to the physical, and that the only proper use of air power was in the strategic offensive, the Air Staff assumed it possessed a "doctrine" to carry out its vision of air warfare. Upon reflection, however, those fiercely held convictions proved naive and unfounded. Again, the Air Staff lacked the intellectual rigor and insight to subject their hypothesis to test and experiment. Furthermore, they persistently failed to realize the deleterious effect their particular theory had on the development of the air force. The RAF was left with a hollow shell. Virtually every aspect of force development suffered. Doctrine in the true sense of the word was nonexistent. As a consequence, the more practical aspects of force development were not dealt with in a coherent and intelligent manner. Instead, when they were dealt with at all, they received the fleeting attention of an Air Staff not inclined to view the concept of strategic air power critically, nor prepared to come to grips with some of the more obvious shortcomings of their strategic thought.

The concrete manifestations of this uncritical approach revealed themselves in equipment policy, tactical development, and operational planning. In each case the dogmatic and doctrinaire attitude of the Air Staff to the larger idea of "air power" resulted in entire avenues of inquiry, research, and development being overlooked, closed off, or ignored. For instance, the prevailing belief that defense against the bomber was, if not impossible, then a misuse of air power, resulted in the design and production of bombing aircraft that were slow, lightly armored, and outgunned. Furthermore, a review of the operational exercises undertaken by the RAF throughout the interwar period reveals how faulty assumptions led to a simplistic notion of what was necessary to undertake a strategic offensive. This created a spillover effect that impacted negatively on doctrinal and tactical development. Not only did it suffer under the crushing burden of strategic orthodoxy, but the operational and other exercises that should have served as a test-bed for doctrine were used instead as a vehicle for the Air Staff to trumpet their own theory. Neither the Air Staff nor Bomber Command were fully aware of the requirements for a strategic offensive. When they did turn—belatedly—to consider the specific requirements, the magnitude of the task was too great. The failure throughout the 1920s and early 1930s to take up the larger questions of air power and examine them rigorously made itself felt during the period of rearmament and expansion, and well into World War II itself.

In drawing conclusions about the development of the theory and doctrine of strategic air power in the RAF during the interwar period, a number of points become obvious. First, the Air Staff's approach was one-dimensional. It focused only on theory to the detriment of the equally important question of doctrine. It was also one-dimensional in the overwhelming emphasis placed on the "offensive" aspect of air power. Thus, "defensive" potential and "tactical" air power took a back seat for the better part of two decades. A second point to consider is the disproportionate effect of the theory of offensive air power on overall government policy. The RAF stressed the power of the bomber to such an extent that in certain circles the idea of actually employing a bomber force became inconceivable. In effect, the RAF was viewed by some as a "deterrent" to war. Yet a deterrent requires credibility for it to deter, a fundamental truth seemingly overlooked by the Air Staff.

These two points serve to condemn the lack of intellectual rigor that the Air Staff brought to its task of developing the necessary supports for their theory of war. The neglect of the fundamentals identified by Clausewitz created an atmosphere in which the theory of strategic air power was rarely if ever subjected to serious and meaningful scrutiny. Instead of acting as a guide or framework for the study of the phenomenon of "air power," the Air Staff allowed its theory to become dogma. The consequences of this are all too apparent in the conduct of the strategic bombing campaign during World War II. While there is no doubt that the bombing campaign still poses many questions for historians, answers will always prove problematic and elusive. Be that as it may, there is enough evidence available to allow one to suggest that the strategic bombing campaign of World War II requires reevaluation. This chapter has demonstrated why Bomber Command was compelled to carry out its offensive in the fashion it did. The principal contention is that the failures during the 1920s and 1930s to develop a realistic conception of air power based on a firm foundation of theoretical and doctrinal inquiry are partly attributable to the influence of Hugh Trenchard's unorthodox ideas. More specifically, it was the manner in which ideas and theories were elevated to the level of strategic orthodoxy without the parallel development of a doctrine that stands out as perhaps the greatest shortcoming. The absence of doctrine made it difficult to develop and test the necessary hardware and weapons systems, and ultimately, operational plans. Thus, the RAF found itself caught in a vicious circle of ever-tighter confines, so much so that it was forced to go to war "on a wing and a prayer."

NOTES

1. Russell Weigley, *The Age of Battles: The Quest for Decisive Warfare from Breitenfeld to Waterloo* (Bloomington, IN, 1991), 77–78.
2. Max Hastings, *Bomber Command* (New York: 1979).
3. Ibid., 17.
4. Ibid.
5. Uri Bialer, *The Shadow of the Bomber: The Fear of Air Attack and British Politics 1932–1939* (London, 1980).
6. There are numerous accounts of the development of British air power during the Great War. See, for instance, Sir Walter Raleigh and H. A. Jones, *The War in the Air*, 6 vols. (Oxford, 1922–37); Neville Jones, *The Origins of Strategic Bombing: A Study of the Development of British Air Strategic Thought and Practice up to 1918* (London, 1973); and Sir Maurice Dean, *The Royal Air Force and Two World Wars* (London, 1979).
7. Those seeking greater detail on this should consult any of the following: Andrew Boyle, *Trenchard* (London, 1962); Raleigh and Jones, *War in the Air*; Sir Charles Webster and Noble Frankland, *Strategic Air Offensive against Germany*, Vol. I (London: 1961); Dean, *Royal Air Force*; Malcolm Cooper, *The Birth of Independent Air Power* (London, 1986); Malcolm Cooper, "Blueprint for Confusion: The Administrative Background to the Formation of the Royal Air Force 1912–1919," *Journal of Contemporary*

History, 22 (1987), 437–53; and John Sweetman, "The Smuts Report: Merely Political Window Dressing?" *Journal of Strategic Studies*, 4 (1981), 152–74.

8. Webster and Frankland, *Strategic Air Offensive*, 35.

9. Perhaps the best single account of the Ten Year Rule is provided by George Peden, *British Rearmament and the Treasury* (Edinburgh, 1979).

10. War Cabinet 'A' Minutes, 616A, CAB 23 (Cabinet Archives, Public Record Office, Kew).

11. Memorandum on the Status of the RAF by the CAS, 14 August 1919, AIR 8/2 (Air Staff Archives, Public Record Office, Kew).

12. Memorandum by the Chief of the Air Staff, 25 November, 1919, in Cmd. 467.

13. Malcolm Smith, *British Air Strategy between the Wars* (Oxford, 1984), 22–23.

14. Memorandum on the Status of the RAF by the Chief of the Air Staff, 14 August 1919, AIR 8/2.

15. Dudley Saward, *Bomber Harris: The Story of Marshal of the Royal Air Force, Sir Arthur Harris* (London, 1984), 29.

16. For details of some of the operations, see Saward, *Harris*; Air Marshal Sir Robert Saundby, *Air Bombardment: The Story of Its Development* (London, 1961); H. M. Hyde, *British Air Policy between the Wars* (London, 1976); and Jaffna L. Cox, "A Splendid Training Ground: The Importance to the Royal Air Force of Its Role in Iraq 1919–1932," *Journal of Commonwealth and Imperial History*, 13 (1985), 157–84.

17. Smith, *Air Strategy*, 29.

18. Uri Bialer, *Shadow of the Bomber*.

19. Barry Powers, *Strategy without Slide-Rule: British Air Strategy, 1914–1939* (London, 1976), 110.

20. Smith, *Air Strategy*, 1.

21. David MacIsaac, "Voices From the Central Blue. The Air Power Theorists," in Peter Paret, ed., *Makers of Modern Strategy from Machiavelli to the Nuclear Age* (Princeton, 1986), 633.

22. Webster and Frankland, *Strategic Air Offensive against Germany*, 107.

23. Williamson Murray, *Strategy for Defeat: the Luftwaffe, 1933–1945* (Maxwell, AL, 1983), 330.

24. See, for instance, the report on the 1927 exercise by Flt. Lt. W. T. S. Williams, "Air Exercises, 1927," *Royal United Services Institute Journal*, 72 (1927), 741.

25. See Smith, *Air Strategy*, 44–75.

26. For a full discussion of the recruitment of officers to the Staff College, see A. D. English, *The RAF Staff College and the Evolution of the RAF Strategic Bombing Policy, 1922–1929* (Master's thesis, Royal Military College of Canada, Kingston, Ont., 1987), particularly chapter 4.

7

Admiral Katō Kanji: Heretic, Hero, or the Unorthodox in Pursuit of an Orthodox Naval Policy

Ian Gow

Admiral Katō Kanji (1871–1939) remains one of the most controversial figures in interwar Japanese civil-military relations. The choice of this navy man for a case study of a military heretic is based on criticisms by contemporaries and by postwar academics of his role and actions in the evolution of the Japanese Naval General Staff within the interwar navy, and especially his role in opposing "inferior" ratios at the interwar naval arms limitation conferences. The position taken by Katō and others undoubtedly contributed to a major upheaval in Japanese interwar intranaval, intermilitary, and civil-military relations, as well as in other areas of Japan's domestic and foreign politics. In particular, his consistent and outspoken opposition to "imposed" and "inferior" naval ratios, and the application of his "realist" view of international relations in the context of so-called naval disarmament conferences, provides an ideal focal device for studying naval intervention in politics. It also permits the examination of the tendency of Western commentators and even Japanese contemporaries to label those holding opposing political views as narrow-minded, radical, and, indeed, heretical. Katō Kanji's opposition to policies pursued by the Japanese Cabinet, especially during the London Naval Conference of 1930, manifested itself as massive, overt political intervention in Japan's domestic and foreign policy. Even after his resignation as Chief of the Naval General Staff in 1930 over "infringement of the Supreme Command," the reverberations of his political maneuvering, and certain political machinations arguably wrongly ascribed to him, had an impact on Japanese civil-military relations throughout the dark valley (*kurai tanima*) of the 1930s. In the eyes of some, his actions provided the grounds for an increasingly violent intervention in the political process by young officers.

Admiral Katō Kanji was a figure of considerable controversy in the interwar period. He could, in terms of the conventional wisdom of the day, be perceived as heretical—by the Navy Ministry—for his views on the role of the Naval General Staff within Japan's maritime forces. He could be, and was perceived as, radical, narrow-minded, and even heretical in his views on arms control. In the eyes of key officers in the Navy Ministry in the 1920s, the protreaty camp within the Japanese elite, this was especially so. Their views were echoed by the American and British policymakers and conference delegates with whom he dealt. Subsequently, especially after 1945, foreign and Japanese commentators and academics who have been critical of his efforts have portrayed him in these dismissive terms. But before we examine the grounds for the evolution of this view and whether it is justified, it is useful to consider the changing approaches to the analysis of the Japanese military and its leaders.

These approaches were based initially on wartime propaganda and its residual memories and, later, on carefully selected documentation translated for the prosecution of the Imperial Military Tribunal of the Far East (IMTFE); they provided support for those interested in proving that pre-1941 Japan manifested a Schumpeterian primitive atavism. This meant that continuing feudal remnants of its samurai past dominated the thinking and the selection of Japan's military leadership and led inevitably to war with the modern and more rational West. The seminal *Taiheyō Sensō E No Michi* (The road to the Pacific War) and the first western monograph based on these sources, James Crowley's path-breaking study, *Japan's Quest for Autonomy*, were regarded by the traditional "praise and blame" school of Japanese militarism as heretical interpretations. Crowley's work provided considerable evidence to reinterpret Japanese military officers' behavior, particularly that of naval officers, as rational, modern, and leading to intervention in politics for a variety of acceptable reasons: for example, budgetary constraints, or in the case of arms control, the defense of their organization and strategic concepts. These actions had little to do with seagoing samurai rampaging across the domestic and international political arena in the 1930s. Crowley's study, intentionally or not, provided a much more sympathetic treatment of the problems and political realities confronting the Japanese officer corps, especially in the interwar years. It also provided more detail than ever before on key naval officers and their involvement in the interwar naval arms limitation debate.

However, in the 1970s, revisionist historians, or more accurately, neo-revisionist historians, purposely sidestepped the Crowley thesis. Central figures in this respect were Tsunoda Jun, a Japanese army historian; Stephen Pelz, an American diplomatic historian; and Sadao Asada, an American-trained Japanese diplomatic historian. They focused their efforts on the Japanese navy in politics and, since this is an area somewhat neglected in Western treatments of Japanese military affairs (there still exists no "academic" published study of a major naval figure), they provided new information that was a major contribution to military knowledge. Unfortunately, their work was marred by a rather one-sided and questionable reassessment of the historical materials. The crux of their argument holds that the Japanese navy was not the force for moderation accepted by scholars (heretical). Furthermore, it charges that a section of the navy, centered on the so-called Fleet faction (*Kantai-ha*) mainly based in the Naval General Staff, opposed naval arms limitation, took control of the navy, restarted the naval arms race, and bore considerable responsibility for drawing Japan into armed conflict with the West. It was a new twist on the old "praise and blame" approach—adeptly switching the emphasis away from condemning only the army for the Pacific War and, instead, apportioning some of the blame on naval extremists and hard liners. One might well question revisionist understanding of the political process involved in arms control limitation negotiations. Certainly they painted a very simplistic picture of the political schisms within the Japanese navy. On one side were the protreaty faction (*Jōyaku-ha*), supporting the government view of conceding on ratio issues to the Americans. These officers, mainly located in or supportive of the Navy Ministry, were almost always characterized as talented, balanced sophisticates, pro-Western and rational. In contrast, those opposed to major concessions, who argued against the naval treaty ratios, were and are invariably described as narrow-minded, traditionalist, and interventionist. The analysis seems to equate political intervention against the treaty as political interference in politics and, therefore, as wrong; at the same time, equally large-scale intervention by the protreaty naval camp was regarded as correct, devoid of political intervention, and perfectly legitimate. To this negative view of the antitreaty or fleet faction, they penned portraits of leading officers like Katō Kanji that were essentially character assassinations lacking objectivity and balance. However, these studies were followed by Roger Dingman's outstanding study of the naval arms race that culminated in the Washington Naval Conference of 1921 to 1922. In his monograph, Dingman returned to the path already pioneered by Crowley and the quasi-heretical view of Japanese military men as rational and modern rather than non-Western and feudal.

If we now focus more closely on Katō Kanji himself, Pelz's award-winning *Race to Pearl Harbor* shows clearly the problems inherent in the "neorevisionist" or "regressionist" approach influenced by Asada and Tsunoda. Pelz describes Katō Kanji: "Katō seems to have been a straightforward type of sailor. He had a traditional background: his father had commanded a squad of samurai spear bearers in the feudal domain of Fukui, and Katō received training in the traditional warrior virtues. Furthermore, he was influenced as a youth by a samurai teacher who had taken part in the Meiji restoration." Note the judicious use of emotive anachronism in terms such as "samurai" and "feudal," with the repetition of "traditional." In terms of historical fact, Fukui was hardly a feudal domain around the time of the birth of Katō Kanji in 1871. It was a highly progressive domain, having disbanded the spear-bearer squadrons long before Katō's father reached the age to join, let alone lead, a squadron. In fact, the quotation appears to have been taken in toto from one of Katō Kanji's biographies. The quote is accurate in terms of the textual translation. However, the subject of the chapter from which the quote is taken is Katō Kanji's father, not Katō Kanji himself! Not for the first time, in my opinion, have those seeking evidence for Katō as the seagoing samurai been too quick to (mis)interpret the evidence in their anxiety to prove a point. It was Katō Kanji's grandfather who led the spear squadron; thus, the whole characterization is highly misleading.

Common to this neorevisionist literature is the notion that Katō's countrymen held him to be a simple man. By this the Japanese were not commenting on his intelligence—as others have assumed—but upon his approach to issues. They did not mean that he was simple-minded but, rather, simple-hearted. He was highly emotional in certain issues; he was direct; he was usually unwilling to use the calculated indirectness so common to the Japanese bureaucratic type. With Katō Kanji, what you saw was what you got. He was far from being a simple sailor—in professional and technical terms, he was one of the outstanding officers of his generation. However, given his personality and his charismatic presence and direct style, in a society where his competitors for "flag rank" were often bureaucratic types, he was smooth and indirect. Katō was a straight-talking commander uninterested in the diplomatic niceties and intrigues of political maneuverings. Interestingly, one American attaché as early as 1921 stated that Katō Kanji was "one of the very best Japanese naval officers—a leader—but his enemies call him narrow-minded and a radical." Unfortunately for Katō, 1921 to 1935 were interwar years when the debate raged on naval arms limitation, and he had enemies in abundance among the protreaty camp in Japanese politics.

He has acquired severe critics among modern scholars who emphasize that his traditionalism and narrow-mindedness on the technical issues of arms control were negative qualities. Instead, his critics might consider that he was a curious blend of tradition and modernity, like many of his generation. Being stubborn on certain technical issues relating to naval arms control, he was not narrow-minded on the uses of new techniques or technology. He was narrow in his views on domestic politics but broad in his understanding of international relations, even though he subscribed to a view that might be classified as realist in a decade—the 1920s—when idealist views dominated. But he was an outstanding naval officer by any standards. He had been at the top of his class at Etajima, a key factor in promotion to Flag Rank in those days. He was closely associated with the major heroes of the Japanese navy, having been Chief Gunner on Admiral Togo's (to whom he was devoted) flagship, the *Mikasa*, in the Russo-Japanese war. He was decorated for his work in World War I by both the British and the Americans. And at one time or another, he occupied all the leading educational posts in the navy: commandant of the Gunnery School, president of the Naval Academy, and president of the Navy War College.

He was appointed chief technical adviser to the Japanese delegation at the Washington Conference, was Commander-in-Chief (C-in-C) of the Combined Fleet during the Geneva Conference of 1927, and Chief of the Naval General Staff and Supreme Military Councillor at the first London Naval Conference in 1930. He was, additionally, a Supreme Military Councillor at the abortive second London Naval Conference in 1934. In the 1930s he was considered for political posts, the governor-general of Formosa and even prime minister; but these were blocked by his political enemies, and it was political opposition by Admiral Prince Fushimi that prevented his promotion to Admiral of the Fleet. He was the Japanese navy's foremost Russian expert and a figure of immense popularity among young officers, greatly respected for his blend of traditionalism and technological leadership. Undoubtedly, however, his involvement in the naval arms limitation debate provided the negative image of Katō; hence, it is necessary to examine the evolution of Japan's perspective on naval arms control, especially after the Great War.

From 1871 to 1921, from the creation of an autonomous Japanese navy department to the opening of the Washington Conference, Japan's naval power grew at a remarkable rate. Its fleet, created after a ban of 200 years on ocean-going vessels, was transformed in those fifty years from a collection of hand-me-down ships into the principal naval force in the Pacific and the third-ranking navy in the world. Several factors contributed to the high standing and experienced Japanese navy of 1921: victories over China and Russia between 1895 and 1905; the Anglo-Japanese alliance of 1902 with its strong naval dimension; and considerable naval involvement in World War I in terms of ferrying Australian and New Zealand troops to Europe, supporting the British China squadron, protecting Allied vessels from German submarine threats, and chasing the German Fleet to the first battle of the Falklands. However, postwar plans in the navy department to create a fleet equal to those of Britain and the United States threatened to bankrupt Japan's economy. Civilian leaders and even some naval officers saw arms limitation as a possible way out of the naval arms race.

By 1919, it would have been reasonable to expect that the general revulsion against war, as well as the creation of the League of Nations, augured well for the world. However, despite the elimination of the German navy, the three major naval powers (the United States, Great Britain, and Japan) were locked in a naval arms race that appeared to have commenced during the war when they were allied powers. France and Italy were involved in a minor variation of this arms race, albeit on a reduced scale. But the race among the three major powers threatened to strain their economies, particularly that of Britain, which had been weakened by the war. It also contributed to a heightening of tension that seemed to endanger the foundations of the new world order that the Allies, and especially the Americans, were endeavoring to create. Thus, there was a push for a naval arms limitation agreement that received tangible form at the Washington conference of 1921 to 1922.

The Washington conference was really two conferences: one on naval limitation, and another on Pacific and Far Eastern questions, especially those relating to Pacific fortifications, China, and the Siberian intervention. The resulting naval treaty set out a capital ship and aircraft carrier building ratio of 5:5:3, respectively, for the United States, Britain, and Japan. This gave the Americans parity in these vessels with Britain while allocating Japan an inferior ratio and refusing them parity. This system, including agreements on Pacific fortifications and Chinese sovereignty, came to be known as the Washington system and lasted for just over a decade. For Pelz and Asada in particular, these conferences stopped the naval arms race. But they view this process through the tinted lens of the idealist and, indeed, appear to use the metaphors of arms control literature while subscribing to rather simplistic views about disarmament and dismissing realist views on international relations. It is certainly possible to view Washington as participating not in disarmament but in arms control. Therefore, Washington was a realist response to the naval question, with agreements on building levels and the like that arose in response to domestic budgetary problems faced by the three main competitors. This is in contradistinction to idealist views about a disarmed world. The conclusions of Pelz and those of like mind, who see Washington as halting the arms race, conveniently ignore the fact that it merely rechanneled the race into auxiliaries—vessels under 10,000 tons, such as cruisers. What is clear, however, is that the negotiations over these force levels split politicians and professionals in all three countries and produced a series of challenges to traditional orthodoxies.

The Japanese sent the navy minister, Admiral Katō Tomosaburō, as their chief plenipotentiary. He wore civilian clothing during the conference in response to the insistence of Charles Evans Hughes, the American Secretary of State, that civilians be sent as chief plenipotentiaries. The prime minister, Hara Kei, a civilian, was appointed navy minister pro tem—a heresy for which he was assassinated later (infringing on the Supreme Command). As their Chief Naval Aide, or chief technical delegate, the president of the Naval War College was selected. This was Admiral Katō Kanji. When one looks for reasons for his appointment, at a time when he was most certainly *not* a controversial figure, one sees immediately the problems of accurately and objectively assessing him. His appointment puzzled certain scholars of the Washington conference, causing one to write: "Katō was associated with a Captain Suetsugu, as an advocate of the big fleet and an opponent of naval limitation." He therefore concluded that: "Katō's inclusion is therefore something of a mystery and can only be explained on the hypothesis that the Japanese in their desire for consensus wished to include discordant elements within the navy."

Since Japanese scholarship frequently indicates that Katō was a member of the Hard-line faction (*Kyooko-ha*) or Fleet faction (*Kantai-ha*), the hypothesis does have a certain plausibility. It seems, however, that Ian Nish and others are drawn to this solution because of Katō's later behavior in the naval limitation debate. In other words, the grounds for his appointment were determined before the Washington conference. In addition there were actually two Fleet factions: one prior to the Washington conference comprised of advocates of the big fleet in a ratio of 8:8:8, and one afterwards that opposed the Washington agreements. To label the first group "anti-arms limitation" is questionable since it would have supported arms limitation provided it was advantageous or, at the very least, not disadvantageous to Japan.

There were many positive reasons for selecting Katō Kanji as the chief technical delegate. His technical expertise was second to none, and he had recently led a major technology mission to Europe and the United States. He had an international reputation as a gunnery expert, and as his period as naval attaché in England showed clearly, he was an authority on naval construction and had an excellent command of English. Katō had also been a member of the tri-ministerial conference on naval limitation convened by the Japanese Foreign Ministry three days after Tokyo received the official invitation to the Washington conference. Just as crucial, Katō had had experience in negotiating military-related diplomatic issues. He had been a member of the Anglo-Japanese team that drafted the military agreements in the second Anglo-Japanese alliance, something that helped him during complex negotiations with the British during World War I, especially concerning the China Squadron. He had later been at the center of three-way discussions with the Americans and British when he served as C-in-C of the naval squadron dispatched to Vladivostock in 1918. Siberia was on the Washington conference agenda, and Katō was the Japanese navy's foremost Russian expert and a fluent Russian speaker. Helping him was the fact that he was on excellent terms with many leading British officers and, through Admiral Archibald Lucius Douglas, founding father of Japanese naval education (portrayed as a typical English officer but in fact one of those excellent hybrids—a Canadian Scot), had made friends with many officers at the Navy Club. Katō held the British KCMG (Knight Commander of the Order of St. Michael and St. George) for service in World War I, as well as the American DSO (Distinguished Service Order). In addition to his linguistic skills and these other impressive qualifications, which included an excellent knowledge of the literature on arms limitation and disarmament, he may have been selected because of his ability to argue forcefully, directly, and effectively with foreign officers, an unusual trait for a Japanese delegate in an era when they were inexperienced in international negotiations.

Katō was not opposed to naval limitation at this time. He was opposed to disarmament. He did, however, regard naval arms races as a symptom rather than a cause of the problem. He also was skeptical about the reasons for the Americans calling a conference—namely, that they could no longer afford to build or plan because of economic constraints and congressional opposition—not on any quest for world peace disarmament. Hughes launched his naval limitation proposals on an almost totally surprised audience. He had not even carried out discussions with his own navy's General Board. He stated loftily that all competition in naval armaments must cease immediately, that a naval holiday be instituted in ship replacement, and that any agreed ratio for capital ships and aircraft carriers be extended to auxiliaries.

The complexities of naval arms limitation need not detain us here; suffice it to say that the Japanese, like the Americans, believed in the orthodoxy of parity in principle and, unlike the Americans, that naval power should be based on national need. Not surprisingly, the American delegation proposed and began to limit the debate to ratios based on "existing strength" rather than national need. This resulted in Japan having to agree to a ratio that was, according to American statistics, 10:10:6 in capital ships. Katō, involved in complex and often heated arguments and discussions throughout the conference, did not at any time push his own personal opinions on "national need" and parity in principle. He did, however, continually challenge the figures on which the ratios were based and especially the American definition of "existing strength."

One reporter, totally bemused by the statistical arguments, proposed the following formula for naval arms limitations:

Divide the number of American submarines, by the number of Japanese cruisers. To this result add the cube root of the sum of the coastlines of America, Japan and Great Britain. Multiply by the maximum distance between the rate of exchange between pounds and dollars: divide by the sum of the national wealth of Japan, Great Britain and the United States and place the decimal point four figures from the right!

In the Committee of Technical Experts, Katō was confronted by a chairman, the American Secretary of the Navy, Colonel Roosevelt, who brought to bear a considerable expertise garnered during his career in the army against Mexico. The Japanese were therefore negotiating with a civilian-led U.S. delegation, an army man chairing the technical subcommittee on naval armaments, a definition of "existing strength" based conveniently on figures and definitions most advantageous to the Americans, no consensus among the American team alone on their own figures, and no consensus on anyone else's figures or even an agreed definition of "existing strength." Just for good measure, the Americans were operating with intelligence gained from breaking the Japanese diplomatic traffic between Tokyo and Washington.

The Japanese team, which had prepared thoroughly on naval limitation issues, had predicted the U.S. position relatively well; but they were disappointed, if not surprised, by the definition of "existing strength" put forward by Hughes and his advisers: ships built and building. The Japanese were well aware of a statement in 1916 by the American secretary of the navy, Josephus Daniels, who "categorically insisted that the

United States would fare better in arms control talks if it had a large naval building programme." Katō Kanji continually questioned any definition that included ships being constructed and argued that naval strength meant ships on the water. Katō was prepared to argue that ship building might be called "potential strength" but not "existing strength." It is of course clear that regardless of how well Katō and others argued in technical subcommittees on technical issues, the real decisions would be made elsewhere—and on political, not technical, grounds. It was Hughes, the lawyer and politician, who was utilizing political criteria to achieve ratios. To adduce failure to Katō's intransigence in the subcommittees is deliberately to misread the documentation—or not read it at all and rely on journalistic, impressionistic data. Here Katō was orthodox and not heretical, whereas the Americans were unorthodox, especially through the *faits accomplis* of American civilians such as Hughes leading the conference and nonnaval men such as Roosevelt in the Technical Committee.

Katō, it has been argued, fought with his chief plenipotentiary and publicly with an Imperial prince in the delegation, and was often (mis)quoted in the press. He was even rumored to have committed suicide. He did at times argue strongly with his navy minister. There were numerous reports of differences within the mission, but the public falling out with Prince Tokugawa, who was regarded by all as incompetent, is best seen in the light of the fact that Katō was immediately invited to dinner by him on his return to Tokyo. Katō has been castigated for returning home early because of his great dislike of the results of the conference. He was, as many other naval professionals were, very frustrated by the negotiations and probably by their results as well. However, he did not say anything controversial on his return. He left only prior to the ceremonies, and he was in fact ill and entered a hospital immediately on his return. If the navy minister was so angry with him at the conference for pushing his own ideas, it seems surprising that the minister immediately appointed him to the key position of vice-chief of the Naval General Staff after the conference. Katō Kanji's appointment as a senior delegate at Washington, and the way he behaved in the technical committees, are possibly exactly what Katō Tomosaburō, the chief plenipotentiary, navy minister, and politician, wanted.

Called to extend the Washington treaty capital ship ratio to lesser craft, the Geneva Naval Conference of 1927 significantly failed to halt the construction race in auxiliary vessels. The immediate cause of the failure was the inability of the United States to obtain concessions on cruisers issued from Great Britain. Negotiations at Geneva showed that a simple extension of the Washington agreement was out of the question and that extending existing ratios to all other warships created a great number of strategic-technical problems that were virtually insoluble. It has been stated that Geneva failed because weak politicians were dominated by the naval specialists within the delegations. This may have been true of the Americans but not so for the British and the Japanese. Katō Kanji was C-in-C of the Combined Fleet in 1927, and his role was peripheral. No diary for the period exists, and records of the C-in-C Combined Fleet were destroyed at the end of World War II. Traditionally, the C-in-C Combined Fleet position was a professional, military one, and Katō therefore could not speak out on Geneva. Adolph Clemensen has stated that Katō Kanji headed the Naval Committee in Tokyo that produced the Japanese plan for the Geneva Conference. There is no extant evidence for this, and Clemensen provides no source—Katō did, however, influence the 1923 National Defense Plan, which laid down plans for the post-Washington building program. Katō was actually vice-chief of the Naval General Staff when the 1927 committee was formed, but he was not active in its deliberations. He did write a most interesting letter to Admiral Saitō Makoto, governor-general of Korea and the plenipotentiary-designate for Geneva, attempting to dissuade him from going to Geneva.

Asada has stated, on the basis of this letter: "The move to appoint Saitō as Chief Plenipotentiary caused Katō Kanji deep concern. . . . in an exceedingly audacious manner he requested Saitō decline the offer." According to Asada, Katō Kanji's reasons were twofold: first, the chief American civilian delegate, Hugh Gibson, was young, lacking political weight, and could not be compared in any way with Saitō; second, Katō made reference to the most powerful lessons of the Washington conference that, from the position of the navy, suggested that sending a leading figure as chief delegate was disadvantageous. Asada believes that Katō thought that Saitō, like Katō Tomosaburō at Washington, would place political considerations above narrow strategic military needs. Asada also states that Katō believed Saitō to be lacking in both experience and ability, and that Katō's offer of an additional delegate—a confidant to assist Saitō —turned out to be a hard-liner who would in effect be a watchdog. Asada concludes that Katō placed very little value on Saitō's diplomatic ability and that Katō implied that Saitō lacked the requisite qualities for the job.

There is no substantiation of any of this in the letter. There is no evidence of arrogance, no intemperate tone. Rather, it is best seen as a well-balanced, thoughtful, perceptive communication that actually turns out to be accurate in some of its predictions. Moreover, it was written to a senior colleague he had known well for almost two decades. He was undoubtedly trying to persuade Saitō not to accept the appointment. He pointed out that Gibson was inexperienced and of low caliber, that one of the British co-leaders, Viscount Cecil of Chelwood, was an idealist, and that the conference would fail. Katō believed that the United States was not serious about arms limitation because it had sent a low-ranking representative. Katō therefore recommended, in the light of these observations, that Saitō had more important things to do in Korea "on which the fate of the Empire depended." Katō also pointed out that as had happened at Washington, the appointment of a leading naval figure such as Saitō would be disadvantageous. Katō did concede, however, that by appointing someone of Saitō's stature, Tokyo would express Japan's wishes for peace and this would benefit the Empire. Still, the conference might well fail, and then it could be said that Japan had ruptured the conference by sending a naval figure. Katō urged Saitō to consider the complexities involved in negotiations, saying that he might benefit from a confidant, which Katō recommended. Katō finished by saying that if Saitō went to the conference and it brought no results, it would damage Saitō's career.

Katō's prediction about the conference's failure proved true. His assessment of Gibson was shrewd and correct, since the absence of a heavyweight on the American delegation like Hughes weakened the American bargaining position. This being the case, Saitō was wasting his time and tarnishing his reputation. Katō was, of course, aware that Saitō might have to agree to a deal that would be unpalatable to naval authorities in Tokyo—Saitō had long since retired from the navy. From a narrow professional perspective Katō, in charge of the Combined Fleet and trying to remedy inferior capital ship ratios with auxiliary build-ups, would have feared this; but his preconference letter indicates his great respect for Saitō—not the reverse. The offer of a specialist adviser was born out of Katō's own experience. At Washington, he knew better than anyone else how important good and timely technical advice was—even if ignored eventually—and the adviser recommended by Katō, Admiral Kobayashi Seizō of the Navy Ministry, was hardly a hard-liner.

Katō did make some bland, public statements to the press, but they give no insight into his own real position. However, talk of another naval conference as the decade ended saw Katō pitched into a major battle and an ensuing domestic political crisis. This conference was to extend the life of the Washington treaty; extend the capital ship-building ratio to auxiliaries, especially cruisers; and, perhaps, reduce battleship displacement and gun calibers. The constitutional and political crisis that resulted from the negotiations at London in 1930 cannot be fully addressed in this chapter. However, the point to consider is that Katō Kanji was not a member of the Japanese delegation. He was by this time chief of the Naval General

Staff and remained in Tokyo, with then–prime minister Hamaguchi Osachi, again acting as navy minister pro tem. This was a heresy in the eyes of the ultra-nationalists that, as at Washington, resulted in yet another assassination of a premier. Still, Katō argued the orthodox naval position, based on three principles that had been accepted by the government as Japan's minimum prior to the conference. These were: a ratio in heavy cruisers of 70 percent vis-à-vis the United States; an overall ratio of 70 percent in auxiliaries; and autonomy in submarines.

The Americans once more redefined the criteria for negotiation, namely "existing strength" to ships built, building, and authorized. Rear-Admiral H. E. Yarnell, an American technical expert, had stated categorically that it was ships built and building that counted at an arms conference. Despite this, it seemed as if the United States wanted to "waive the rules." On Japanese definitions of ships built, Japan had eight heavy cruisers—10,000 tons with eight-inch guns—and the United States just one; on the American definition of existing strength, based on the Washington formula of ships built and building, Japan still had a superior ratio against the United States of 12:10. It was only on the criteria of a paper-building program that the Americans were able to get a superior ratio for existing strength. It is argued that the three principles only emerged after Katō Kanji became chief of the Naval General Staff. This is based on comments made by his predecessor, Admiral Suzuki Kantarō, who became Grand Chamberlain at the Imperial Palace: "When I retired from CNGS [Chief of Naval General Staff] last year [1929] such things did not exist." He went on to indicate that it was a matter for the government to decide. This is surprising since Suzuki, chief of the Naval General Staff at the time of the 1927 Geneva Conference, had then stated on public record "the size of armament is a matter to be decided by the Chief of the Naval General Staff."

But the instructions for the delegation to Geneva in 1927 had stated that Japan could accept only a cruiser standard not lower than 70 percent of that allowed either the United States or Britain, and retention of Japan's strength in submarines—70,000 tons. By 1930 a consensus between the civilian and military decision makers had emerged over the three principles prior to the London conference; moreover, it had been publicly stated beforehand. However, the instructions were altered after negotiations began in London without Katō's approval. When he challenged the revised instructions by appealing directly to the throne, he was blocked until after the instructions had gone by none other than his predecessor and now Grand Chamberlain, Suzuki, who conveniently found the Emperor's diary full. Suzuki had no authority to block Katō, since the appropriate military official with direct access to the Emperor was the Chief Military Aide-de-Camp. It was Suzuki's heretical interference with Katō's appeal that was to trigger massive right-wing protests and, eventually, contribute to radical right-wing violence in Japan. Katō was outmaneuvered at every turn by a prime minister who, as acting navy minister, was determined to secure a treaty at all costs to improve his nation's economy; thus, Katō was left with no alternative but to resign. He became a Supreme Military Councillor and became heavily involved in fighting for a post-London treaty budget for the navy, but he gradually found himself marginalized and isolated. His name was constantly associated with and often utilized by others to justify certain developments within the navy relating to the reform of the Naval General Staff, the purge of naval officers in the mid-1930s, and the violent actions of radical younger officers who opposed civilian control of government. He cannot be directly linked to the politics of violence, although young officers and ultra-nationalists frequently cited his mistreatment by the authorities. This had added piquancy when his nomination as Admiral of the Fleet was blocked, and when his chances to hold political office—as the premier, the navy minister, and the governor-general of Formosa—were ruined by his enemies. Certainly he was given important naval duties from time to time, both real and ceremonial, but this never included the kind of recognition his supporters believed he deserved. He was also widely considered for reappointment as chief of the Naval General Staff if war broke out; but he died in 1939, having completed his account of the 1930 London Treaty crisis the night before.

Katō probably would not have been a good choice for political posts. While he was well versed in foreign policy, he often showed naiveté in domestic politics. He might have been manipulated by others relatively easily—but, to be fair, he never really had the experience or the opportunity to gain experience in the art of political compromise in terms of major political appointments as opposed to major naval, especially "command," appointments. As a principled man, he probably would have disliked being a politician. Nonetheless, he does not appear to have been a heretic but, rather, a good example of a realist in international relations when idealists (and realists disguised as idealists) held sway. He was as much a victim of the unorthodoxies and heresies of arms control strategists, especially American ones, and of heretical acts by protreaty (*Jōyakuha*) forces within the Japanese navy and within the government. He was orthodox in military terms, and one could make a strong case for him being orthodox and conventional in naval limitation terms.

However, there is perhaps one area where he did challenge naval orthodoxy: the relationship between the Naval General Staff and the Navy

Ministry over peacetime powers, and the relative positions of these two bodies in internal naval politics. This development was a direct result of the efforts of civilian politicians to control the military in Japan and from military efforts to expand their influence in the domestic and foreign policy arena—a trend accelerated by developments from the Washington conference onward, but evident even before 1914. His advocacy of a stronger Naval General Staff, though unorthodox, was a defense mechanism to combat a more threatening challenge to the orthodoxy, especially prominent in the army, of political insulation from direct political intervention. Focusing on which power had the right to decide the size of the fleet, arms limitation was at the heart of the controversy. However, if we focus on organizational politics within the navy and on civil-military relations, arms limitation emerges as a symptom rather than a cause of overt political intervention in politics by the navy, especially in 1930.

It might be useful here to summarize the development of Japan's military autonomy. In the initial period after the creation of the modern state, which was complete by 1878, civilian control, modeled on the French system, was in effect. The top military officers were required to go through the premier (*Dajo Daijin*)—almost always, but not exclusively, a civilian—to the Emperor. In 1878, with the creation of the Army General Staff, its chief was permitted direct access to the Emperor in both peacetime and in war. The practice of only appointing serving officers as service ministers also appeared at this time; therefore, especially after the cabinet system was developed, the military authorities could prevent cabinets being formed or could bring them down. In addition, new military command (*gunrei*) regulations that permitted internal changes in matters like service organization without cabinet approval were introduced prior to the Russo-Japanese war.

By these developments the military were effectively insulated from political control and could bypass the cabinet. By refining national security to include foreign policy, and even by defining domestic political developments in an era of total war as matters of national security, they were able to intervene in politics. The military role in policy making expanded dramatically. In terms of Katō and the navy, it was the *gunrei* regulations that enabled power to be transferred, without cabinet approval, between the general staffs and their ministries, which is the most germane. Major efforts to control the military by the political elite began in earnest in the years immediately preceding World War I. The then–prime minister, Admiral Yamamoto, in order to halt the fall of cabinets over budgetary battles revolving around navy and army rivalry (the so-called Taisho political crisis), managed to change the service minister qualification to allow the appointment of reserve officers. This triggered plans to strengthen the General Staff system, especially in the navy.

In the Japanese navy, the General Staff had been created later than its army counterpart and was, therefore, a younger organization. Moreover, the Japanese naval organization was closer to the British than the German model; the Naval General Staff was subordinate to the Navy Ministry in peacetime and only gained some autonomy, although it was technically subordinate to the Chief of the General Staff in wartime under Imperial Headquarters (*Dai Honei*). The Naval General Staff had actually been embarrassed at the beginning of World War I: when hostilities broke out but the *Dai Honei* was not set up, it could not exercise the command function over the disposition of fleets and had to go through the Navy Ministry. Together with the threat of reserve officers occupying the Navy Ministry portfolio—a civilianizing measure, one could argue—this caused General Staff planners to consider strengthening the organization. No major changes ensued, but at the time of the Washington conference, another flurry of activity occurred around plans to strengthen the General Staff vis-à-vis the Navy Ministry. When the invitation to the conference was issued, there were discussions regarding the civilianization of the Navy Ministry portfolio; these efforts received the support of Navy Minister Admiral Katō Tomosaburō. At Washington, all the other leading figures were civilians, which increased the pressure for a non-uniformed man as service minister. During the conference, the prime minister, Hara, as acting navy minister had taken the civilianization of the post further forward. By 1923, the vice-chief of the General Staff, Katō Kanji—assisted by a Captain Katō (no relation)—began proposing the transfer of powers from the Navy Ministry to the Naval General Staff to preserve the right of command (*gunrei*) in the hands of the uniformed officer corps. These efforts ceased after the death of Katō Tomosaburō, who had become prime minister following his tenure as naval minister and chief plenipotentiary at Washington.

The London treaty crisis of 1930 brought the weakness of the Naval General Staff to the fore again; it was consulted on naval strength issues but its agreement was not required. Hamaguchi outmaneuvered the naval staff; in this, he was aided by two former naval staff chiefs: Suzuki and Admiral Okada Keisuke. The former, as previously noted, had been a strong advocate of the autonomy of the chief of the Naval General Staff on naval strength issues when he was the incumbent but changed his position dramatically after his postretirement political appointment to the Palace. In discussions with the navy minister, Admiral Takarabe Takeshi, on his return from London, Katō insisted that a letter be written by Takarabe agreeing to jurisdictional parity in terms of determining the size of the fleet in peacetime. Previously the Navy Ministry had agreed that the Naval General Staff should be consulted in such matters but did not require the latter to agree.

The developments after 1930, which led to a purge of the naval officer corps—"the Osumi Purge"—were not, as is often supposed, the work of Katō Kanji. Rather, they came from Admiral Prince Fushimi, then-chief of the Naval General Staff. The appointment of Imperial princes as chiefs of both general staffs after 1930 can be seen as a clear effort to use the Imperial family to strengthen the command organizations against the service ministers. Fushimi had at times been close to Katō, but their relationship, which dated back to academic days when Katō was his official companion, deteriorated during the treaty crisis. Fushimi had as his vice-chief the other Captain Katō. This Katō, together with Fushimi, was determined to purge officers who had, by their opposition to the London treaty ratios, undermined the position of the Naval General Staff. The Naval General Staff was revamped, achieving parity not only with the Navy Ministry but also with the Army General Staff in wartime at Imperial Headquarters. Since there was no effective coordinating body above them other than the Imperial Institution (which was not permitted to be involved in "political" matters), this meant that inter- and intramilitary rivalry was unresolvable.

This state of affairs had dramatic consequences for the Imperial forces in wartime. Katō had not been active in Fushimi's appointment; and although he was concerned over the position of the Naval General Staff, he had not been directly involved in its changed position or the purge of protreaty officers within the navy. Nonetheless, these changes did mean that any future agreements on naval limitation would require the consent of the Naval General Staff. Katō Kanji was symbolically important, but he was not an active instigator as some portrayed him. Still, the "germanification" of the Naval General Staff system was the result of all these debates and crises and, over a decade, can be directly linked to Katō. For a naval officer corps trained under the British-unified naval structure, with the commanders subordinated organizationally to the administration, Katō and others of like mind would seem heretical in their views. The developments that ensued were a challenge to naval organizational orthodoxy, as well as to the orthodoxy of overall command and supremacy of the Army General Staff in wartime. However, it was fueled by another challenge to Japanese orthodoxy, namely those who wished to see greater civilian control over the military. In the end they failed to achieve such control and actually increased the political insulation of the military from civilian political elite control. This course of events arguably increased military intervention in the political process.

In conclusion, Katō Kanji was undoubtedly a controversial figure. Over naval limitation in particular, he took the initiative to guide the development of policy. Given the political dynamic, he was also a symbol and a pawn in other people's strategies. However, in naval and technical terms he was orthodox; his views were representative of many of his officer colleagues, especially those of the "command" type rather than the political types, who tended to gravitate to the Navy Ministry. His views on foreign policy were orthodox in terms of the realist camp on international relations. It is simplistic, if not misleading, to conclude that Katō and others like him, who were skeptical about arms control measures dictated by the Americans, were either explicitly or implicitly supporters of war because they opposed arms limitation. It is even more reprehensible to characterize, by overt stereotyping, highly intelligent officers like Katō as irrational and simple, while characterizing those who supported inferior ratios as rational, Western, and highly intelligent. Katō seems in many respects to have been caught in the midst of a major series of political debates, especially those engendered at London in 1930, where it has been permissible to interpret his actions as opposing the American position (from an American perspective) and being over-reliant on the idealist, protreaty camp and newspaper versions of events. Such a flawed approach has given Katō Kanji a stereotyped negative image that owes more to wartime propaganda than the political realities of peacetime civil-military relations in prewar Japan.

Katō was one of the outstanding officers of his generation and, indeed, of the prewar Japanese navy. He was technically superb. Blending tradition and modernity, as did many other Japanese leaders of the prewar period, he enabled the Japanese navy and the Japanese state to develop at a remarkable pace and in a unique way. It is true that he involved himself in politics to defend the navy; and there have been accusations that he acted improperly at times, made a number of mistakes, and was occasionally manipulated. Although he was somewhat naive in domestic politics, he was not so in foreign policy. His role, and indeed the role of all those who opposed arms limitation on the terms being offered at Washington and London, must be distinguished from the extremist, ultra-right in Japanese politics that is often associated with these political events. A new look at the opponents of interwar naval arms control, armed with the tools of arms control and arms race literature rather than mere metaphors, will produce a more objective view of both sides. There were changes in view during the 1920s and 1930s on disarmament, on arms control, on the role of cruisers, on aircraft carriers, and more. Whether one side or the other is open to the charge of heresy is, at the very least, questionable.

APPENDIX

The literature on the interwar naval limitation conferences and especially the London Naval Conference of 1930 abounds with references to two opposed groupings: the *Kantai-ha* (Fleet faction) and the *Jōyaku-ha* (Treaty faction). Other terms often used interchangeably with the above are *Kyooko-ha* (Hard-line faction) or *Gunrei-ha* (Command faction) versus *Onken-ha* (Moderate faction) or *Gunsei-ha* (Administrative faction). In general, these labels are attached to the two sides that emerged from splits in the Imperial navy during or after the Washington conference. The former grouping (Fleet faction/Command faction/Hard-line faction) usually refers to those officers who opposed naval limitation and especially the ratios agreed on at Washington and, particularly, London. They are usually assumed to be located within the Naval General Staff or supportive of the rights of that organization above the Navy Ministry or civilian bodies like the cabinet. The latter group, usually located in or supportive of the Navy Ministry, endorsed the government's decisions to accept the treaty restrictions agreed on at Washington and London. The Fleet faction and its variants are generally regarded as being guided by narrow, professional, and technical/strategic imperatives; the Treaty faction and its equivalents are regarded as more internationalist, cosmopolitan, and biased toward political imperatives.

These distinctions are at best inappropriate and at worst positively misleading. First, the opposing forces in the naval limitation debate were not limited to naval officers, active or reserved, or other military personnel. Second, the Fleet faction/Treaty faction dichotomy was not used or recognized by naval officers of the time, although there was also a well-defined Fleet faction that was acknowledged by naval officers and had existed since the Meiji period (1868–1912). Third, these distinctions do not take account of changes over time experienced by both individuals or organizations. The distinctions may have limited utility at the macrolevel, but, as with many such devices, they prove less useful at the microlevel, even impairing an understanding of or oversimplifying exceedingly complex matters and perspectives.

There can be little doubt that there was in the 1920s, or even before, a growing schism within the navy along organizational lines as the younger and essentially junior Naval General Staff officers began to challenge the historical domination of the Navy Ministry in command-related (*gunrei*) matters. This split is often labeled "Command faction versus Administrative faction." Although not totally limited to naval officers, until the naval arms limitation conferences, this competition and schism constituted essentially an internal naval matter. Viewed from this perspective, it is linked with the naval limitation debate but is so pervasive that, especially concerning the London Treaty of 1930, the political crisis over the treaty issue may be seen as a symptom of organizational rivalry rather than a cause, as Pelz, Asada, and others have thought. Awareness of the Command versus Administrative factions, loosely clustered around the Naval General Staff and the Navy Ministry supporters, should be kept in mind when discussing the naval treaty political maneuverings. This is a more rewarding distinction for naval limitation politics within Japan based on the protreaty and antitreaty factions.

Protreaty factions denote those people important to the decision process, whether civilian or military, who ultimately believed that a treaty must be concluded for Japan's domestic or international well-being and security. This group can include those who approved or disapproved of the lower cruiser ratio Japan obtained at London in 1930 since their principal aim was a successful treaty. Using this approach, it is easier to differentiate between "hard liners and soft liners" even within the protreaty faction. The former group may include those who did not wish to accept the treaty based on the "American proposals," believed the compromise made in 1930 was not the final offer, and held that standing up to the Americans would result in further concessions. They wished to push harder and probably went into the negotiations believing the "three principles" represented something very close to what they would ultimately receive—that it was the maximum they would agree to in the negotiations. Soft liners, on the other hand, thought almost entirely in terms of a successful treaty, accepted the 1930 ratio as a final offer, and feared (especially after Geneva in 1927) calling the American bluff and placing the responsibility for lack of success firmly on the shoulders of the Japanese delegation. This would be detrimental to Japan's image and might have perilous domestic implications. This group regarded the three principles as the ceiling, the best they could possibly achieve in any negotiation—an ideal—therefore, they expected to make considerable concessions. Prime Minister Hamaguchi and other politicians like the foreign minister, Shidehara Kijurō, clearly were soft liners. On the other hand, Okada is normally grouped with these men but initially seems to have been a hard liner who continually advocated that the Japanese negotiators "push again." An even bigger shift took place concerning Prince Fushimi. He certainly moved from the antitreaty to protreaty faction in late March–early April 1930 before returning to the antitreaty grouping.

Ranged against these men (and often their organizations such as the Court and the Navy Ministry) were the antitreaty forces. Here again, it is useful to distinguish between hard liners and soft liners intrafactionally. Many hard liners took the extreme stand that there should be no treaty at all limiting either capital ships or auxiliaries, and they even advocated scrapping the existing Washington ratios. They certainly held that the "three principles" were the absolute minimum, the floor, in terms of negotiations. Nevertheless, the documentation shows that even this group, including Katō Kanji and the General Staff, was willing to concede on the "three principles," just *not* on all three. Compromises, they held, were possible on overall ratios in light cruisers and destroyers. Concessions were even possible on submarines, but emphatically not on heavy cruisers. They believed strongly that Japan must push again after the 1930 compromise, which was another American variant plan and not a compromise. They felt that the Americans were bluffing and believed that the United States would be prevented from making good its threats to massively expand its navy by the strictures of both international opinion and domestic opposition to increased expenditure.

These distinctions, which allow for intrafaction and interfaction shifts over time, may prove more useful than the existing distinctions. Past analyses of cleavages in the navy, arising out of the London naval treaty crisis in particular, have tended to assume a static permanency unwarranted by the available documentation. It is suggested here that it would be possible (indeed, not difficult) to identify officers in the Naval General Staff who felt that naval limitation would be beneficial to Japan and could even be beneficial to the navy. They might have believed it was beneficial prior to Washington, still felt so after Washington, but did not like the actual treaty arrangements and decisions—the inferior ratio or limitation to capital ships—so gradually shifted to the antitreaty camp. Organizational transfers of personnel between the Naval General Staff and the Navy Ministry might radically alter a personal perspective (*honne*) or, more important, an official position (*tatemae*). Such things as awareness of the impact of the Washington agreements, or the nature of emerging U.S. foreign policy perspectives and their impact on Japan in the 1920s, may have caused shifts in individual and institutional positions as well.

Moreover, one can discern shifts between factions and within factions in 1930 after the "revised instructions were sent," after the treaty was signed, and after the treaty was ratified. Hence, Katō Kanji's actions, whether heretical or not, offer insight into the evolution of Japanese naval policy in the interwar period, a period when the domestic and international implications of that policy affected Japan's position as one of the three great naval powers in the world.

8

Moshe Dayan: Above the Rules

Michael I. Handel

> Or again one may appeal to genius, which is above all rules, which amounts to admitting that rules are not only made for idiots, but are idiotic in themselves.
> Clausewitz, *On War*[1]

Moshe Dayan was born on 4 November 1915 and died on 16 October 1981 at the age of sixty-six.[2] He led an adventurous and varied life as a soldier, politician (he was, in turn, Minister of Agriculture, Minister of Defense, and Foreign Minister of Israel), an author and journalist,[3] an amateur archeologist and notorious robber of ancient graves, and was known as a womanizer on a scale approaching, though never quite reaching, the level of Mussolini or John F. Kennedy.[4] Although it is possible to learn much about the feelings and thoughts of Dayan—who has been the subject of a number of detailed biographies,[5] an autobiography (which added nothing to what was already known about him), and other books by relatives and mistresses[6]—he will forever remain an enigma. He probably never fully understood himself, nor was he ever understood by others. Throughout his life, he was not one to evoke a measured response in others, who either admired him as a legend, sometimes to the point of adulation, or hated him and made him the focus of endless controversy and jealousy. The love-hate relationship between the Israeli public or media and Dayan became even more acrimonious after his death. Symbolically, and in more than one way, he left nothing to his children although he was very wealthy. In like manner, he bequeathed no political or ideological legacy or vision to Israel. Yet, without exception, his admirers and detractors agree that for better *and* worse, his character and style made a lasting imprint on the Israeli identity and modus operandi, particularly with regard to the Israeli Defense Forces (the IDF). In fact, the IDF cannot be understood properly without reference to Dayan's influence.

The growing intensity of the public debate in Israel concerning his personality and influence on the course of Israeli history became more evident than ever on the tenth anniversary of his death. In October 1991, numerous essays and special supplements on Dayan appeared in all Israeli newspapers and magazines: many were vitriolic, often petty, attacks by jealous enemies who still felt the need to settle accounts with him. It is significant, however, that those who worked closely with him (particularly during the years that he was Chief of Staff and Minister of Defense) had more positive memories of Dayan (for instance, General Gazit, General Tal, Colonel Bar On, as well as his children—as did, by the way, Arab acquaintances and statesmen).[7]

The ferocity of the debate undoubtedly indicates that consciously and subconsciously Dayan had become a symbol of Israel, both in life and in death. The debate, therefore, is as much about the hopes, dreams, failures, and disappointments of modern Israel as it is about Dayan himself. Approaching its fiftieth year, Israel is no longer a nation of pioneers and idealists but a nation in search of an identity. The transition from youth to maturity and old age is not easy for an individual or a state. Dayan, who in his youth was a vigorous man of action, who appeared invincible, died as a frail, bitter man. He is now equally remembered as the hero of the Sinai Campaign and the Six-Day War as well as the man "responsible" for the initial costly setback of the Yom Kippur War. Surely, in a period of uncertainty about the future, many Israelis must ask themselves if Dayan's life and death were a metaphor for their own fate, or whether the state can be rejuvenated through a change in direction.

In his later years, Dayan became increasingly convinced that Israel must make a renewed effort to establish a lasting peace with its neighbors. As he put it, a nation cannot live "by the sword alone."[8] But Dayan's striving for peace was tempered by his search for security. While peace required the return of territories occupied during the Six-Day War (notably, the return of the Sinai to Egypt in 1978), it also meant that Israel may have weakened its security. For both ideological and security reasons, Dayan was not ready to return the West Bank to Jordan and the Golan Heights to Syria—nor was he prepared to agree to the establishment of a Palestinian state. He died as he lived—in the process of changing his mind, in transition from one position to another. Many believed that had he lived longer, he would have eventually recognized the need to accept greater risks for peace. Despite all of the criticism heaped upon Dayan, Israel has yet to produce another leader of his caliber—with his pragmatism, wisdom, openness, knowledge of the Arabs, and prestige.

Most of this chapter will examine Dayan as a military leader, beginning with a few observations on his character and temperament. This is followed by a brief survey of his ideas on military affairs and his contribution to the evaluation of the Israeli military doctrine and Israeli security in general. This chapter will end by asking a few more general questions about the temperament of unconventional/eccentric military leaders in military organizations, exploring the conditions under which they can operate and the attitudes of military organizations toward such leaders.

Before a discussion of Dayan's military career is possible, a few words on his character and personality are in place. Since there is no need to repeat the well-known story of his life even in an outline, I will select a number of key facts and traits that throw light on his military (and political) careers.

Moshe Dayan was the first baby born in Kibbutz Deganya, an idealistic commune, where he lived until the age of five, at which time his parents left to help found Moshav Nahalal—a cooperative settlement. The distinction between a kibbutz and a moshav is important in the context of Dayan's life, for in a kibbutz the individual must submit his private interests and ambitions to those of the group and can own no private property, whereas in a moshav the individual farmer can possess his own property, accumulate wealth, and serve the community on a voluntary basis. The moshav was built by those who did not wish to subordinate their interests or lives entirely to those of the community. Typical of this more individualistic type of personality, Dayan was always described as a loner. He was an individualist who needed to contribute to the community of his own free will—not become part of a larger group. This may have been encouraged by his parents, who built him a small hut where he could sit and read—a luxury not available to any of his friends. Many of his childhood friends and later colleagues considered him to be antisocial, although he was respected, but not loved, for his courage, intelligence, even sense of humor. He was never "one of the gang" or "a team player." Naturally, these characteristics did not endear him to his peer group, and he could not be described as a particularly well-adjusted member of his community. His extreme individualism explains in part his pragmatism bordering on opportunism (in the positive sense), his nondogmatic character, his flexibility, and his capacity for change.

His individualism and difficulty in adjusting to the society and group to which he belonged were recognized by all. Thus, when he and his first wife applied for membership in a new kibbutz, his wife Hanita was accepted immediately but he was put on probation. Dayan was so insulted that he withdrew his application. While in a British jail as a member of the Hagana (from October 1939 to February 1941), Dayan was selected as the representative—but not the leader—of his group (the so-called '43) to the authorities. This was done in recognition of his intelligence and leadership qualities, not his popularity. He never tried to lead by consensus or by being nice to all. As he once put it, "I believe in decisions, not in consensus. . . . a decision always involved danger."[9] "Groupthink" was a disease to which he was immune.[10] Under all circumstances, he never compromised in the pursuit of his own idea of truth or his own interests. (Even as a politician later on, particularly in the 1970s, when his views were not always accepted, he never compromised; he simply dropped his ideas or policies and did not fight for them.) In this sense (much like Woodrow Wilson),[11] it was always all or nothing for him. (In fact, he never quarreled with people, he simply cut off all contact with them.)[12]

This was demonstrated by the fact that he always refused to accept a position as second-in-command—the position of a deputy. When Ben Gurion considered appointing him to be deputy chief of staff in 1952 in preparation for his appointment to be chief of staff, he refused and said that he would only agree to be chief of operations. He told Prime Minister Ben Gurion that as a deputy he would have to support his chief and therefore could not be true to his own ideas. Dayan nevertheless agreed that as chief of operations he would stand in for General Makleff, the chief of staff, in his absence. He thus had his cake and ate it too.[13] Similarly, on the eve of the Six-Day War, when Prime Minister Levi Eshkol offered Dayan the position of deputy prime minister (as a result of public pressure), Dayan immediately refused. He said that unless he could be directly responsible for national security affairs as either prime minister or minister of defense, he would rather join the army and accept any independent command position the chief of staff would assign him. He was ready to accept orders but always in an *independent command position*, which involved at least some freedom to make his own decisions.[14] He once said, "My self has significance only as long as I remain myself."[15]

Part of Dayan's charisma resulted from his habit of expressing his opinions as *honestly* and simply as possible whether his audience liked it or not. In this he could go to extremes, and honesty could quickly become tactlessness or outright rudeness. In his youth, he had a cruel streak to the extent that he did not tolerate fools lightly and at times mocked those who were weak or inferior. Later in life, particularly during his years in the foreign ministry, he was known to be increasingly rude and insulting to his subordinates and others around him.[16] His insistence on speaking the truth may have had something to do with his attitude toward his father, Shmuel Dayan, who could best be described as a small-time political operator. Shmuel always tried to appoint himself to political positions of power in his community, whether it was Kibbutz Deganya or Moshav Nahalal. This occurred at a time when working the land was considered the most important, "virtuous" occupation, while political duties were supposed to be an unpleasant and unpopular chore. Even if one enjoyed political pursuits, he had to pretend that he felt obliged or forced to do it as part of his duty to the community. Despite all his attempts to *pretend* that he wanted only to till the land and had been forced to become a politician, everyone knew that Shmuel Dayan wanted to be a politician. An opinionated man, he incessantly preached to others about what to do while consistently failing to live up to his own advice. In short, he was perceived by those in his community and also undoubtedly by his son as a hypocrite. (For example, when Kibbutz Deganya was founded, Shmuel Dayan demanded that all the members delay having children for at least five years to allow the kibbutz time to become more prosperous. A few months later his wife became pregnant with Moshe, who was the first baby born in Deganya.)[17]

A perception of his father as a hypocrite may have pushed Moshe to the opposite extreme. As a father, Shmuel did not provide Moshe with a positive role model. He was away from home during most of Moshe's youth, often leaving the family for long trips abroad. His mother, who was chronically ill, had to carry the burden of taking care of the farm and raising the children. This clearly generated repressed resentment in Moshe and in his mother toward the father. Moshe, in turn, proved to be a poor father. On the positive side, Dayan was creative, imaginative, and had some talent for poetry and drawing. He was known for his dry sense of humor, which served him in good stead in later years. Like many intelligent men, he was willing to work and spend time on subjects that were close to his heart. He had little patience for details, wasting as little time as possible on things that did not interest him. Thus, while he could deal well with the broad picture, he lacked the discipline and patience necessary to develop knowledge in greater depth in many areas. This becomes evident from his written work, which has good style, is never boring, reflects a good *intuitive* understanding of problems but lacks thoroughness and depth (for example, see his *Vietnam Diary* and *Living with the Bible*). These traits in particular were simultaneously his major strengths and weaknesses, for they were clearly more suitable for action than for reflection, short-run thinking rather than long-run planning, and operational command more than staff work.

In his youth, Dayan was often in the fields around his settlement and loved to spend as much time as possible outdoors. He felt happy and comfortable being surrounded by nature. He loved traveling alone or with a few friends to remote areas that were dangerous and inhospitable. He was very familiar with the topography and geography of northern Palestine—and indeed got his first job as a guide for the British Army in that area. This love for nature and the outdoors at least partially explains his passion later in life for archeology and his impatience with staff work, as well as his Rommel-style desire to be out in the field with the troops. In contrast to his father and many of his own generation who feared and despised the Arabs, Dayan came to respect and appreciate the Arabs and their culture. He never hated Arabs; he even tried to learn from them as he found their life simpler and more in harmony with their environment. Paradoxically, it was this familiarity with the Arab culture and mentality that made him such a formidable Arab enemy. He knew their weaknesses, fears, and vulnerabilities more than most. As we shall see, throughout his military career it allowed him to prepare more daring and realistic plans for war—and as a diplomat allowed him to understand and communicate with Arab leaders. Not surprisingly, he was also respected by the Arabs more than any other Israeli leader.

Both Clausewitz and Jomini agree that the most important and necessary condition for the military genius, that is, the outstanding military commander, is *courage*. After stating that "courage is the soldier's first requirement," Clausewitz goes on to explain that there are two types of courage: "courage in the face of personal danger, and courage to accept responsibility either before the tribunal of some outside power or before the court of one's conscience." Courage in the face of personal danger is in turn divided into two types. The first was an indifference to personal danger that stemmed from within the individual himself and could be considered a permanent condition. However, the second type of courage came, according to Clausewitz, from ambition, patriotism, or an enthusiasm of any kind. Each of these two types had different characteristics; the highest kind of courage was a compound of both.[18]

As for *personal courage,* it can be said that Dayan was an exceptionally courageous soldier—as his friends and foes alike would agree. As a boy, a sergeant, chief of staff, or even minister of defense, he was always at the front of the front line. He led a commando unit into battle during the War of Independence, during which he showed great daring and a willingness to exceed his instructions and take very high risks.[19] Even as chief of staff he was often found at the front leading the troops on the battlefield, not at General Headquarters where he was supposed to be.[20]

During the most intensive period of reprisal raids (1953–1956), he always waited on the battlefield to interrogate the troops returning from action. While in Vietnam as a reporter for the *Washington Post*, he insisted on accompanying patrols into the jungle and observing combat at close quarters, thus causing his hosts a great deal of concern for his wellbeing. As minister of defense, he always went down to the field, to the fortifications of the Bar Lev line; during the Yom Kippur War, he was the only minister to appear on the battlefield and talk to the troops, which, as General Sharon commented, did much to boost the morale and confidence of those around him.[21]

Dayan's courage was no less evident at the lower levels, whether as a guide for an Australian commando unit in a raid in Lebanon where he lost one eye in action, or when he entered Baghdad alone on a dangerous mission to deliver weapons to the local Haganah organization and smuggled two illegal immigrants back to Palestine under the noses of the British, or his clandestine missions to King Abdallah of Jordan. As all his biographies indicate, his life abounded with episodes of fearless action under fire and highly dangerous circumstances. Some believe that his fearlessness sprang from a subconscious death wish, or because, after he had lost one eye, he wished to prove that he was still as fit for military service as in the past.[22] Regardless of the reason, Dayan's bravery under fire put him on an equal footing with military leaders such as Nelson or Rommel. Although he was rarely afraid (he could take catnaps on the ground while the battle was raging around him), Dayan remarked that he was not a fatalist, thus suggesting that he did not believe in some superior forces that would protect him, that he was "lucky" or immortal. He also implied that he knew when to avoid unreasonable risks.[23] This last statement appears to be reliable and therefore refutes the speculations about his supposed death wish.

As a general, Dayan insisted that his subordinates exhibit similar levels of courage through leadership by example: to this end, as chief of staff, he introduced reforms in IDF doctrine stipulating that no mission should be aborted unless at least 50 percent casualties had been sustained. This did not mean that he did not do his utmost to reduce casualties by careful planning, deception, and so on. Dayan had little patience with officers who were not brave or who lacked the motivation to fight.[24] On the other hand, Dayan was much more forgiving and tolerant of mistakes committed by those whom he considered to be courageous, who showed initiative, or who failed while disobeying orders attacking or setting more difficult or ambitious objectives than had originally been planned. He thought that courage and bravery under fire should always be encouraged even if they involved high costs or failure. Two famous examples of this attitude are reported in his Sinai *Diary*. The first occurred during the opening phase of the Sinai Campaign when the commander of an entire task force decided to defy orders instructing him not to begin his attack until forty-eight hours *after* the beginning of the campaign. The officer, Colonel Asaf Simchoni, decided not to stay on the sidelines and launched his attack in the opening hours of the campaign. His decision made Dayan furious since the intervention as originally planned was politically motivated, allowing the campaign to be presented as a reprisal raid and a withdrawal in case the British and French decided not to become involved in the war—or if the operations did not go as well as planned. Colonel Simchoni's purely military/operational decision (and a major act of insubordination) was taken on the basis of his belief that any delay could prove too costly later on. Unaware of the underlying political considerations, he not only recklessly endangered the entire political preparations for the campaign but also made it necessary for the IDF to improvise extensively in all its operational plans. Despite Simchoni's irresponsible behavior, Dayan finally agreed to go along with his fait accompli (Dayan concealed the entire episode from Prime Minister Ben Gurion during the war). He later explained that it is "better to be engaged in restraining the noble stallion than prodding the reluctant mule."[25]

Similarly, when Colonel Arik Sharon, the commander of the paratroop regiment that was dropped near the Mitla Pass in the Sinai, entered the pass in disobedience to his orders (which again for political as well as operational reasons forbade him to advance into the Mitla) and suffered the heaviest and most unnecessary casualties of that war (39 paratroopers were killed—while 171 Israelis were killed in the entire war).[26] Upon publication of Dayan's memoirs, the families of the soldiers who had fallen in that battle were enraged by his assertion that this particular battle was not only contrary to orders given but also fulfilled no useful military purpose. In the Sinai *Diary*, Dayan asserted that what was most disturbing for him about the capture of the Heitan defile at Mitla was not that the paratroop command had disobeyed his orders with such bloody consequences (for Dayan himself had found it necessary in the past to disobey orders in order to achieve a tactical position). What Dayan found particularly galling was the attempt by the paratroop commander to cover up his actions and to report these actions in such a way as to satisfy the General Staff. Further, Dayan was even more angry because the paratroop unit had failed to fulfill its battle task, which he felt was equally as grave as disobeying orders.[27]

MOSHE DAYAN

Dayan's reaction showed him at his best as a soldier and military leader. He was brutally honest, true to himself, recognized himself in a similar situation, and encouraged and rewarded bravery. His reaction to the breach of orders was certainly not typical. The acceptance of such an act of insubordination is rather unusual and could set a dangerous precedent. Yet the morale and élan of the troops was first and foremost on Dayan's mind. This type of behavior was subsequently repeated many times by Israeli officers in action. Dayan wanted to encourage initiative, dedication, and motivation for taking action—the success of building a first-rate combat-oriented army may have occurred at the expense of civilian control, obeying orders, and so on.

Perhaps unfortunately for the Israel's later history, Colonel (later General) Sharon was not court-martialed; instead, he was, on Dayan's initiative, summoned to a discussion with Prime Minister Ben Gurion, at which he told Ben Gurion that this was the nature of warfare. He stated that mistakes were inevitable and that had he known then what he knew later, he would not have acted as he did. These sagacious words on the nature of war, however, only served to conceal a brazen lie.

Insofar as Clausewitz's second type of courage is concerned (the courage to accept responsibility), Dayan's record is mixed. Here we must clearly distinguish between his role as soldier and that of politician. As a military commander and chief of staff, he had a good record. He did not hesitate to make forceful recommendations and try to convince his superiors to accept them. On the whole, when he or his subordinates made a mistake, he did not hesitate to accept responsibility. In fact, part of his charisma was based on his ability to disarm his opponents and appeal to his supporters by admitting his mistakes. This honesty allowed him to learn from his mistakes, change his mind, and improve. Two examples will help to clarify this point.

Israel was, and still is, divided into three military regions, each with its own organization, command, and force structure. Soon after Dayan became the IDF's chief of staff, he decided that in order to conserve resources and improve the tooth-to-tail ratio (that is, combat troops to support troops ratio), he would eliminate the Southern Command, organizationally speaking. But eliminating such a large organization could not be carried out as simply as he had first thought, like some exercise on paper. His order was carried out, but it created immense chaos and confusion and completely failed to achieve the desired results. True to his character, Dayan admitted his mistake one year later and rescinded the order.[28] As chief of staff, he did not hesitate to admit the failure of certain policies or of inadequate achievements in military operations, as one can see clearly in his Sinai *Diary*. After two or three years of intensified Israeli reprisal raids, primarily against Jordan and Egypt, it became clear that they had failed to achieve their desired ends of deterring acts of Arab aggression against Israel,[29] and that the cost in casualties had become intolerably high. Although Dayan was one of those who had initiated the entire policy and led to its escalation, he now (September/October 1956) admitted its failure. He felt that there was a general agreement that the then-current system needed to be changed. The practice of Israeli forces launching an attack on Egyptian or Jordanian military installations in reprisal for every murder committed by the fedayun in Israel had lost its element of surprise. Now the Egyptian or Jordanian forces stood ready for any Israeli attack. Dayan asked the question " 'what now ?' I expressed the view that we cannot continue in this state of no-peace and no-war."[30] Dayan had learned a lesson he ought to have known before—that there is nothing more dangerous and self-defeating in military action and planning than establishing a repetitive, predictable pattern of action.

In a critical analysis of one of the most crucial battles of the Sinai Campaign for the positions of Um Katef and Um Shihan, Dayan blamed the Southern Command, the GHQ, but most of all himself as chief of staff, for failing to launch a combined and coordinated attack with all forces available. Failure was not the fault of the combat units that had been sent forward against the objectives in dribs and drabs.[31] Dayan's willingness to accept responsibility as a military commander stands in contrast to his reluctance to do so as a political leader. Early in his political career, as the minister of agriculture, for example, he rather peremptorily decided to change all the tomatoes grown in Israel to a new variety called "Moneymaker," which he thought would be more suitable for export. The decision proved to be a mistake and caused many complaints. Dayan, in this instance, refused to accept the responsibility and blamed his staff at the Ministry of Agriculture.[32]

The most famous example of Dayan's refusal to accept responsibility for his actions as a politician occurred after the Arab surprise attack in the opening phase of the Yom Kippur War, for which Israel paid very dearly and which caused a serious setback for the Israelis. Public opinion and many of the leaders of the IDF claimed that Dayan was responsible for the failure to put the army on alert and mobilize for war. The public demanded his resignation. Dayan stubbornly claimed that he was not responsible and that he would not resign. In my opinion, based on many years of studying the problem of strategic surprise, Dayan was right.[33] Those who wanted his resignation were looking for a scapegoat. No strategic surprise at the opening of a war has ever been avoided. The failure to anticipate an attack is the result of numerous complex factors, all of which were present before the Yom Kippur War—a confusing plethora of signals and noise, wishful thinking and a variety of preexisting concepts that distort intelligence, misperceptions, overconfidence in the potential of the intelligence community to provide an unambiguous warning, political considerations making mobilization very difficult, and underestimation of the consequences of strategic surprise. Clearly, no individual—but only an entire community—can be blamed under such circumstances.[34] (In fact, Dayan had ordered a partial mobilization and alert in the Golan Heights when provided with reliable information.) Indeed, the Agranat Commission did not find him *directly* to blame but only *indirectly* responsible by virtue of his position as minister of defense.[35] Perhaps his responsibility as an elected official in a democracy should have convinced him to resign on general political and moral grounds. Dayan is still viewed by many as refusing to accept the responsibility for the disastrous early phases of the Yom Kippur War. For those familiar with the problem, however, his position in this case was not unreasonable.

As a politician, though, Dayan did not stand as firmly behind his opinions as he did when he was chief of staff. He was known, even when he thought he was right, to bow prematurely to the views of the prime minister and Cabinet, and he was not as ready to fight for his opinions. This at least on one occasion may have led to the Yom Kippur War. In 1972, Dayan, after much reflection, proposed to Golda Meir a plan for unilateral withdrawal in the Sinai away from the Suez Canal. His old archenemy, Minister of Education Yigal Allon (who was jealous of Dayan's success throughout his career) leaked the entire plan to the press and torpedoed it.[36] Golda Meir had earlier rejected the plan out of hand, but Dayan chose not to fight although the implementation of his plan may have delayed or prevented the Yom Kippur War.

How can the difference in his behavior as a soldier and as a politician be explained? Perhaps by the different nature of the worlds of military affairs and politics. In the military, a position is held for a specific period of time (the chief of staff in Israel is normally appointed for a period of three years) and is hierarchical (with the commander-in-chief being the ultimate decision maker). In the Hobbesian world of politics, no position is permanent or certain, and survival calls for constant bargaining, negotiations, and compromise with other politicians and public opinion. It is a world where decisions are reached by consensus, not by edict. As a loner in the political world without any substantial party or organizational support who relied instead on his popularity and personal relationship with the prime minister, Dayan was in no position to enforce or even fight for his views. On another level, it is possible that his age and, later on, ill health may have also reduced his readiness and eagerness to fight for his opinions.

Dayan was living proof that a formal military education is not a prerequisite for military success. Hence the insistence of Clausewitz, Jomini, or Napoleon that military genius is an innate quality that can perhaps be sharpened by education but does not depend on it. It can even be suggested that a standardized military education designed to develop a solid, average staff or combat officer might actually have a regressive effect on the talent of a military genius whose superior performance is based on intuition—that is, on ad hoc improvisation and on breaking the rules of war at the right moment. As in every other profession, *greatness depends on a readiness to deviate from the norm*, on creative change and attempting to solve old problems by finding new solutions, and on being willing to risk rejection and failure. Most high schools, colleges, universities, military schools, or war colleges are designed to deal with the average student—not to encourage genius or deviations from the norm. Yet genius and unique talent can only operate outside the normal framework. In this sense, genius and creativity may often be considered a threat to most organizations.

Dayan certainly was not the product of a West Point or Sandhurst. He was, so to speak, an autodidact whose military knowledge sprang from hands-on experience and intuition rather than a theoretical knowledge of military affairs. At the Haganah he did attend a number of lower-level squad and platoon commanders courses (1937). He also attended a course for sergeants run by the British army in Sarafand (1937)[37] and after the War of Independence, a course for higher-level regimental commanders in Israel (January–February 1952) and later in England.[38] In all these courses (including a course for higher-level officers that he initiated, developed, and participated in as chief of staff) he never accepted the "academic" solution; instead, he always tried to develop an original approach and loved to argue against the conventional wisdom of the instructors.

Most of his understanding of military affairs, which was superior *on all levels* from tactics and operations to the highest strategic political levels, was based on his experience in the field and his intuitive understanding of military affairs. Two military experts in particular influenced Dayan, perhaps setting some sort of a role model for him.[39] The first, known only in Israel, was Yitzhak Sadeh, an unconventional, individualistic military instructor. Sadeh was responsible for the education of many young soldiers who subsequently became leaders of the Haganah Palmach (an elite commando unit of the Haganah) and who later served as senior officers in the IDF. Sadeh stressed the need for an active defense, even the offensive, which was uncommon at the time (the mid-1930s), and was interested in developing a highly mobile defensive force. Dayan was impressed by him and appreciated his originality, directness, and above all his demand for daring action—sometimes bordering on the irresponsible.[40]

The second man to influence Dayan in that period was Captain Orde Wingate, one of the most eccentric and controversial British officers of World War II.[41] Dayan served on Wingate's so-called Palestine Special Night Squads (S.N.S.), which emphasized daring long-range night operations, maintaining the offensive, initiative, and carrying the war to the bases and villages of Arab terrorists and guerrillas. From his first meeting, Dayan was greatly impressed by Wingate, whose personal appearance, bearing, and eccentric idiosyncrasies appealed to him. Dayan saw that Wingate was driven by an iron will and capable of enduring great hardship in order to achieve a given military end. Dayan was even attracted to Wingate because of the latter's unshakable belief in the Bible, which he would read before going into battle. Dayan wrote about Wingate that "judged by ordinary standards, he would not be regarded as normal. But his own standards were far from ordinary. He was a military genius and a wonderful man."[42]

It is difficult to ascertain the degree to which Dayan was influenced by Wingate's example. It is clear, however, that much of what Dayan said about Wingate could also have been said about himself—Dayan would have been pleased to have been described in that manner. Wingate's dislike of ceremonies, parades, and formalities in general, as well as his idiosyncrasies, may have led Dayan to understand that a military organization could be more than just spit and polish. From Wingate, Dayan learned to lead with an aggressive spirit and offensive-minded planning. Above all, he learned that others, as well as himself, should be measured by their actions, not words.

Finally, yet another "school" has been mentioned in Dayan's career: the "Abraham J. Baum School." Dayan first met Abe Baum in a hotel bar in New York City in July 1948 on his return from escorting the coffin of Colonel Micky Maraus to West Point to be buried. Baum was a manufacturer of ladies' garments in New York who had, during World War II, served as a captain with the U.S. 4th Armored Division under (then) Colonel Creighton Abrams. Baum was known as a brave soldier who had had extensive combat experience; and before Dayan returned to the war raging in Israel, Baum briefed him about his own wartime experiences. Although not exactly a J. F. C. Fuller or a Liddell Hart, Baum gave Dayan a "lecture" in which he summarized his principles of war and armored warfare in particular. Dayan reported these principles to be as follows:

1. If there is an opportunity—exploit it.
2. Use a much larger force to attack an objective that you believe would fall even at the hands of a smaller force (that is, maximum concentration of force at the decisive point). At every turn, try to create the impression that your force is much bigger than it actually is.
3. For a breakthrough, use narrowly organized formations—preferably in a single column.
4. Use firepower primarily for its psychological effect rather than to inflict casualties. A frightened enemy is second only to a dead enemy.
5. With a smaller, inferior force you must be constantly on the move. As soon as you stop moving, you forfeit your advantage as an armored force.
6. Forget about reserve forces. Deploy your forces in such a way as to give the enemy the impression that you have even more troops.
7. Introduce infantry to occupy ground.
8. Keep your armor for a counterattack.

Learning can take place in the most unexpected settings—Dayan liked what he heard and never forgot this advice. Later on, Dayan very successfully implemented his own version of Baum's doctrine in a "deep" penetration raid as the commander of a number of jeeps, some half-track vehicles, and one captured armored vehicle (Regiment 89). In this raid and with a very small force, he exceeded his orders and occupied the Arab cities of Lod and Ramallah (July 1948).[43] Baum inspired Dayan to develop his own blitzkrieg type of war. By taking great risks and succeeding, Dayan established his reputation as a daring commander. He used similar methods and techniques on a much larger scale in the Sinai Campaign.

As we have seen, Dayan's understanding of military affairs was based on his intuition and experience, not on formal education or the study of theory. (In this sense, he was very much a self-made military man—more so, for example, than Napoleon or Rommel, who were also men of action who based much of their military leadership on daring action and intuition. But at one stage in their careers, they at least had the benefit of a formal military education.) As a military leader and chief of staff, Dayan was, on the whole, open-minded, flexible, and ready to learn and change his mind if the evidence so indicated. His lack of formal military education, like that of most of the Israeli senior military officers of his time, was a weakness; but at the same time it gave him one great advantage. A lack of familiarity with the military history, experience, and theories of war as well as with the military doctrines of other nations forced him (and the Israeli military in general) to develop their own original military doctrine and planning—rather than mechanically imitating foreign military organizations. While learning by trial and error was costly and prolonged, it allowed the Israelis to develop innovative ideas about waging war. Instead of the wholesale adoption of the British, American, or Russian doctrines as the Arabs had done—doctrines of little relevance to conditions in the Middle East—the Israelis devised an original doctrine suited to their own temperament and tailored specifically to fight their Arab opponents.

Early in his career, Dayan evinced an appreciation for intelligence and deception. In planning for war, he was able to put his lifelong interest in Arab culture and his Arab neighbors to good use. In the Sinai *Diary*, for example, he makes it clear that the Sinai Campaign was premised on the taking of very high risks because of his specific estimates of the weaknesses and qualities of the Egyptian armed forces. He insisted that fighting the Egyptian army was not comparable to fighting the German Wehrmacht. Dayan saw the task of the Israeli forces as bringing about the collapse of the enemy forces and gaining control of the Sinai Peninsula as quickly as possible. He felt that the Israeli units had to stick to their "maintenance of aim" and continue to advance until their objective was gained. In order to do that, they had to be self-contained and carry all their supplies with them. The Israeli advance was possible, even though Egyptian forces would be bypassed, because Dayan believed that the Egyptian army would not behave as European armies would in similar circumstances.[44] He saw that the Egyptians were "schematic in their operations" and that it took them time before any decision involving changes in dispositions could be reached. This played into the Israelis' hands because they were used to acting with greater flexibility and less military routine. While Egyptian command headquarters were often in the rear, far from the front lines, Israeli commanders were forward with their troops. Thus, the Israelis could issue orders to exploit the situation after the initial breakthrough of the Egyptian front. Dayan believed that the campaign could be run in such a way that the enemy would have no time to reorganize after their front was assaulted and would be given no pause in the fighting to allow them to regroup. Dayan noted that when he said "the objective is the Sinai Peninsula and the enemy is the Egyptian Army. It also suits the character of our Army and of our officers."[45]

It would be easy to imagine Rommel issuing similar orders at different phases to the Afrika Korps fighting the British. Perhaps one of the principal factors in the making of unconventional soldiers is their tendency to see opportunities where others see only obstacles—to avoid thinking in terms of the worst-case analysis, and, as Sun Tzu puts it, to "know the enemy and know yourself; in a hundred battles you will never be in peril."[46] In contrast to Dayan's ability to "know the enemy," the British and French overestimated the Egyptian forces during the Sinai Campaign, when they launched a 72-hour bombardment of Egyptian targets as though they were facing the Nazis in Normandy. In so doing, they wasted considerable time and were forced to quit operations before they could achieve their objectives. To some extent, overestimation of the enemy also occurred in the Gulf War, when U.S. preparations and plans were conducted as though the enemy were the Wehrmacht or the Russian army. This overestimation was at least understandable in light of American sensitivities after the Vietnam War (and other factors).[47]

Undoubtedly, none of Dayan's predecessors as chief of staff would have been ready to accept such risks. Most conventional soldiers would have opted for a more conservative, traditional plan. One point that needs to be emphasized is that Dayan, in planning for the Sinai Campaign (unlike the British and French), was extremely conscious of the *time factor* and did his utmost to accelerate the pace of the campaign. This later became a key element of the Israeli military doctrine.[48] (There were two main reasons for his stress on *time* and *speed*: first, there was the fear that the United States and the Soviet Union or the United Nations would intervene politically before the operations could be brought to an end and all objectives achieved; second, as mentioned in the preceding quotation, speed, rapid and deep penetration, and being constantly on the move would throw the slower Egyptian army off balance.)

Dayan also saw deception as critical for the achievement of strategic and operational surprise, which he considered an ideal way to facilitate a quicker and more decisive victory at a lower cost. He did everything he could to use deception to achieve surprise in the Sinai Campaign. Strenuous efforts were invested in creating the impression that Israel was planning an operation on its eastern border against Jordan and Iraq: the mobilization of reserve troops was delayed until the last possible moment; the mobilized troops were told that operations were being planned against Jordan; and troops in the Negev, for example, that were designated for operations in the Sinai were concentrated on the Jordanian, not the Egyptian, border. The deception succeeded so well that some sections of Israeli intelligence not in the know started to believe that an attack against Jordan was going to take place. And two messages that President Eisenhower sent to Prime Minister Ben Gurion urging him to avoid war indicated that he was afraid of an attack against Jordan.[49]

Another aspect of the deception plan was to slow or delay the Egyptian reaction by presenting the whole operation not as a war but as a large-scale reprisal raid. This was Dayan's own brilliant solution to a complicated situation. Despite the coordination of the war with the British and French governments (at the Sèvres Conference), the Israelis were not convinced that the British and French would, in the end, join the operation. It was therefore important not only to slow down the Egyptian response by creating a deliberately ambiguous situation but also to allow Israel (if necessary and if things went wrong and Israel found itself alone) to withdraw and to pretend that only a raid of limited scale had taken place. (This is why the 7th Brigade, as discussed earlier, was ordered *not* to attack until forty-eight hours after the beginning of the attack at the Mitla Pass.) For this reason, the entire Sinai Operation was planned by Dayan and his staff to begin at the end, that is, with a parachute jump deep in the Sinai and not with a direct frontal attack across the border. Dayan personally wrote the carefully and ambiguously worded radio bulletin announcing the beginning of the war:

The Army spokesman announces that Israel Defense Forces entered and engaged fedayun units in Ras en-Nakeb and Kuntilla, and seized positions west of the Nakhl cross-roads in the vicinity of the Suez Canal. This action follows the Egyptian military assaults on Israel transport on land and sea designed to cause destruction and the denial of peaceful life to Israel's citizens.[50]

Such an announcement was certainly not meant to be construed as a declaration of war. (A similarly ambiguous announcement was initiated by Dayan at the opening of the Six-Day War.) In assessing the deception plan before the outbreak of the war, Dayan hoped that the Egyptians would interpret the paratroop drop at Mitla as merely a raid. He did not believe the Egyptians would think that the Sinai could possibly be conquered without first attempting to secure control of the two northern axes, those of El Arish and Bir Galgafa. Moreover, he felt that even as late as the second day when the Israeli mobile brigade would capture Thamad and Nakahl, points of defense on the Mitla axis, the Egyptian High Command would still think that this was done in order to reinforce the paratroops cut off at Mitla and that the Israeli intention remained to withdraw and return to Israel.[51]

This sophisticated deception (1) enabled the Israelis to present the attack as a raid and not as the outbreak of war, thus giving Israel more political and strategic flexibility, and (2) allowed the planners to gain more time by confusing the Egyptian High Command. There was, however, one more reason for the deception plan. When Dayan met with Guy

Mollet and Selwyn Lloyd in Sèvres, the British foreign secretary refused to coordinate any military operations with Israel. This created a serious problem, and Ben Gurion, who was suspicious of British intentions, was ready to leave the conference and return home. Characteristically, Dayan found a creative solution acceptable to all participants, which made the British and French participation in the operation much easier: he suggested that by dropping paratroopers at the Mitla Pass, Israel would pose a threat to the safety of the Suez Canal, which would give the British and French a pretext to issue "both" sides an ultimatum to withdraw ten miles from the Suez Canal. This indeed was the plan as later implemented.

As a result of this deception plan, Israel achieved complete surprise, gained needed time, and brought the campaign to a quick and decisive conclusion. Dayan was certainly most unusual in his enthusiasm for deception, for most conventional military leaders show little interest in this type of approach.[52] Dayan demonstrated his flair for deception at one more critical juncture, on the eve of the Six-Day War. Following a prolonged crisis and three weeks of troop concentration by both Egypt and Israel, Dayan was invited to join Levi Eshkol's Cabinet as minister of defense. His presence immediately raised the level of confidence in the new national emergency government and boosted the morale of the IDF. It was correctly suggested that with or without Dayan, the war would have been won. Yet Dayan made a significant contribution. After three weeks of crisis, the problem was that if Israel did not go to war on its own initiative, its entire deterrence posture, which had been built up since the Sinai Campaign, would collapse; the crisis would remain unresolved; and not having a war would clearly be a victory for the Arabs. Furthermore, the danger of an Arab surprise attack was increasing daily. Dayan thought that Israel must go to war and, this time, *destroy* (not just dislocate) the Egyptian army in the Sinai. But how could Israel achieve surprise when all sides had been fully mobilized for some time? Dayan was convinced that strategic surprise was absolutely essential for an Israeli victory. This was so important because Israeli strength was very limited, and Dayan believed that the first strike would determine who would have the greater casualties and that the power ratios of Egyptian and Israeli forces could be quickly changed. For Dayan, to attack first was to initiate and to conduct the war according to Israeli direction. If Egypt was allowed to open fire first, then Israel would be at a grave disadvantage for it would have to fight the war on Egyptian terms. In order for Israeli forces to win, it was necessary for them to achieve surprise with the first strike.[53]

It is interesting to note that this time Dayan had a higher estimate of the Egyptian army and was aware of the greater danger posed to Israel. He also recognized the importance of achieving surprise as a force multiplier—and not allowing the Arabs to benefit from attacking first (which is what he "allowed" to happen in 1973). Once again, he emphasized the question of time. By achieving surprise, maintaining the initiative, and being continuously on the move, Israel might be able to accomplish its objectives before the United Nations or Great Powers interfered. Above all, he understood that this war could only be fought in terms of all or nothing, and on a large scale. At this point, he made a decisive contribution to the achievement of surprise through the use of deception. On 1 June 1967, Dayan met with a journalist, the grandson of Winston Churchill, who at the end of their interview asked whether war was going to break out in a day or two or if he should forget about waiting in Israel for a war and return to London. Dayan told him that it was now both too late and too early to open fire, and that Israel must continue to try to solve the crisis by diplomatic means.[54] Two days later, he repeated the same message to local and foreign correspondents. The *Jerusalem Post* reported the next day: "Defence Minister Dayan . . . said that it was too late for a spontaneous military reaction to Egypt's blockade of the Tiran Straits—and still too early to draw any conclusions about the possible outcome of diplomatic action. 'The government—before I became a member of it—embarked on diplomacy; we must give it a chance,' Dayan declared."[55]

By this time, everyone was convinced that Israel had missed the boat. Consequently, this ruse (in combination with a number of other deceptive measures to lend it an air of authenticity) enabled Israel to achieve surprise.[56]

Many senior Israeli military experts consider Dayan to be the most successful chief of staff (1954–1959) the IDF ever had.[57] For better or worse, he left a lasting imprint on the IDF, to which he made his most important contribution, recognized by all commentators without exception. When he took over command of the IDF in 1954, it was demoralized and its standard of combat operations was poor. He set a personal example and worked tirelessly to imbue the IDF with a fighting spirit and improve the performance of combat operations. By establishing a number of elite units to set high standards for the rest of the armed forces, Dayan started a tradition that is still very much alive in the IDF today. In the long run, however, Dayan's emphasis on battlefield performance may have led to the relative neglect of supporting and logistical units. On a personal level, he was never interested in the details of staff work and other "routine" matters. He was always concerned with the broader picture and let others deal with the finer points. The advantage of such an attitude is that it focuses the leader's energy on key tasks, preventing him from becoming mired down in secondary or tertiary issues. Like Rommel or Wingate, he spent as much time as possible with the troops in the field—and as little as possible in his office. In wartime, he was continuously at the front—following or leading the troops right into the thick of battle. Dayan admitted that there were times when his desire to be with the forward units instead of staying with the GHQ command post did cause difficulties for his staff officers and upset the ordered organization of staff work.[58] This was certainly the case during the Sinai Campaign when he joined the units attacking Rafah and stayed with them until El Arish was captured. Dayan, however, was unable to change his ways. He liked being up with the troops.[59]

Indeed, Dayan's Rommel-like hyperactivity sometimes caused him to arrive at the front ahead of his own troops, endangering himself unnecessarily. While he raced along with the troops, his absence was acutely felt at GHQ when decisions needed to be made on sensitive higher-level issues.[60] His presence on the battlefield inspired the troops, and on occasion (as in the battle of Rafah) allowed them to radically change plans and improvise; at the same time, his presence, as he admits, may have put the local commander in an awkward position.

Dayan was adamant in his belief that a commander must be on the battlefield to view the situation for himself—to stand on the hill Napoleon-style—in order to get an immediate impression of all developments and make faster real-time decisions. The question of whether a commander should lead from the front or rear has no perfect solution: each approach has its advantages and disadvantages. If a great leader takes command from the front lines he can enjoy resounding tactical and even operational successes, but there is a price to pay; namely, he is not always available to make urgent, higher-level decisions. The question as to what is the most rational and effective style of command depends on the particular circumstances as well as on the temperament and qualifications of the military leader. Clearly, Dayan's temperament made his presence on the battlefield inevitable.

Dayan's frequent presence on the battlefield also made it necessary for him to be able to trust his subordinates and delegate authority. This he did extremely well. Once he had delegated authority, which he did on most issues, he gave his subordinates a free hand. Similarly, once he had assigned an objective to a unit, he refrained from interfering directly in the commander's decisions. Such commanders were therefore able to improvise as long as they were determined to achieve their assigned objectives. Dayan thus believed in developing the initiative of lower ranking commanders within a general framework: this is what the Germans refer to as *Operieren*.

A military environment that values and encourages initiative in the lower ranks must also have a greater tolerance for mistakes—as long as the proper lessons are learned. Such conditions will result in the design of a flexible, decentralized military doctrine that encourages offensive planning and initiative, allows the taking of greater risks, quickly adapts to changing circumstances on the battlefield, and exploits success to the fullest extent possible. Thus, the very unpredictability of those who implement this type of doctrine confounds the enemy. This was the legacy that Dayan left to the IDF. However, these qualities, as positive as they are, do have their drawbacks. Ad hoc improvisation can be very effective in a dynamic, mobile, and offensive war, but it is less suitable for a defensive war. Excessive reliance on the belief that "every plan is a basis for a change" can result in inadequate preparations, confusion, poor coordination, and difficulties in command and control—all problems that to a greater or lesser extent afflict the IDF even today.

One shortcoming frequently identified with military geniuses who perform superbly on the tactical and operational levels is that they almost automatically turn to military means to solve problems on all levels. For example, the careers of Napoleon and Rommel reveal their weaker understanding of strategy; that is, they won most of the battles but lost the war. The same cannot be said of Dayan, whose "military genius" was equally astute on the tactical, operational, and strategic levels throughout his career. His critical comments on U.S. battlefield tactics and strategy in Vietnam are extremely perceptive, and seem even more impressive when one remembers that he did not have the benefit of hindsight. And as evidenced by his contribution to the planning of the Sinai Campaign and the Six-Day War, his grasp of the political considerations that determined military strategy was outstanding, as was his talent for strategic and operational planning. In the Sinai Campaign, his entire plan was brilliantly and creatively designed to fit the unique political circumstances at hand. Moreover, his recognition of the time factor in military operations and consequent emphasis on the importance of speed was based on an almost uncanny understanding of political constraints imposed on every Israeli military planner. Although his later career as a foreign minister need not concern us here, it is worthwhile to note that Dayan's creativity and imagination did not fail him in the diplomatic arena either.

Although Dayan encouraged initiative and daring—and tolerated even outright disobedience for the "right" reasons—he strictly adhered to the instructions and guidelines of the political authorities in his own career. Under his command, the IDF was at all times a loyal and effective instrument at the disposal of the Israeli government. Some have accused him of fascist tendencies, but they were likely to have confused fascism with charisma and individualism. But Dayan's intuitive understanding of the political dimensions and the constraints imposed by political factors on the formation of strategy were not always shared by later Israeli military leaders, who tended to see military operational action as a panacea—the solution to all problems. Many had absorbed the lessons pertaining to success in military operations but failed to weigh, or even comprehend, higher-level political-strategic considerations in war. An excellent example of this narrow military vision is Arik Sharon, whose war in Lebanon would never have been acceptable to Dayan.

Another example of the effect of Dayan's military legacy on his own policies is instructive. Before the beginning of the Six-Day War, Dayan warned all commanders who were likely to spearhead the advance toward the Suez Canal that they should stop well before reaching the Canal. His reasons were political. Remembering the Sinai Campaign and the sensitivity of the Great Powers regarding any threat to free passage through the Suez Canal, Dayan wanted to avoid undue political pressure on Israel. Another reason was that he wanted to avoid direct contact with the Egyptian armed forces; he believed that if his plan were followed, Egyptians would not see any need to cross the Suez, but that if they did so, their military positions, upon crossing, would be too weak to be defended successfully. Furthermore, he thought (and this may have been wisdom after the fact) that a large Israeli military presence on the banks of the Suez Canal would be psychologically unacceptable to the Egyptians and goad them on to full-scale war. (Dayan was especially concerned about Soviet intervention, and for this reason he was also very reluctant to launch a major attack on the Golan Heights or, later, to come within artillery range of Damascus.) Nevertheless, the Israeli commanders—the "noble stallions" who had been weaned on Dayan's own tradition of aggressive combat—conveniently forgot his orders in the heat of battle and advanced all the way to the eastern bank of the Suez Canal. Blinded by purely operational considerations and therefore without regard for the political consequences of their *fait accompli,* these commanders viewed the Suez as no more than the best antitank defensive ditch available. Once the war had ended, Dayan was unable to convince the government and the IDF to withdraw somewhat from the bank of the Canal. During the War of Attrition and later in the outbreak of the Yom Kippur War, Israel was to pay a heavy price for this mistake.

Dayan's legacy as chief of staff and as a military leader in general was mixed: he inspired the development of a highly motivated army but at the same time neglected the humdrum details of proper staff work and routine procedure. The IDF therefore excelled at maintaining combat initiative and developing imaginative offensive operations, while its record on combined arms cooperation and the development of mobile artillery and other support units was much weaker. Further, the fighting spirit that flourished under his tutelage sometimes tended to the extreme and became difficult to control. To some extent, he also created an army with a strong anti-intellectual bent. Yet Dayan's enthusiasm for offensive operations was tempered by his political wisdom. The same cannot be said of many other Israelis, who, under the heady influence of operational successes, seemed oblivious to political, diplomatic, and other nonmilitary types of action. This was the Pandora's box that Dayan's success inadvertently opened. This may be why many Israeli intellectuals are now so critical of Dayan's record, although the fault is more that of human nature, for which there is sometimes no greater failure than success.

Was Dayan a heretic or an eccentric? These terms have been defined in Webster's *Third New International Dictionary*: *eccentric*: A person that deviates from conventional or accepted conduct, especially in odd or whimsical ways; a person or thing that varies from some established type, pattern, or rule in any way. *heretic*: One that dissents from an accepted belief or doctrine of any kind: INNOVATOR, NONCONFORMIST.

Adjectives such as "average," "typical," or "conformist" could never be applied to any aspect of Moshe Dayan's military career and personal life. He was a lone wolf by choice and willingly paid a price for this aloofness in his social life, in general, as well as in his political life. His eye patch established a physical barrier—perhaps imparting an aura of mystery or glamor to his persona (although he tried at least three times in his life—unsuccessfully—to be fit with a glass eye). He was intolerant of foolishness and unusually direct, often to the point of being blunt and tactless. Still, he could not be accused of the type of odd behavior exhibited, for example, by Wingate (for instance, sitting naked in a kibbutz kitchen while munching raw onions).

Dayan also liked to think of himself as direct and honest, but his behavior was rife with contradictions and tensions. Apparently immune to the normal compunctions of conscience, Dayan had numerous affairs while married (which he made no effort to conceal) and did not hesitate to break the law when it came to the appropriation of irreplaceable antiquities. Tensions that arose as a result of this behavior must have been alleviated to some extent by his strong defense mechanisms. He was far more willing to accept responsibility as a military leader than as a politician, for in the latter occupation his behavior seemed to become less principled and more compromising. Being an independent, individualistic man, Dayan naturally liked to operate as free from authority as possible. He went to extraordinary lengths not to accept positions as second in command that would force him to compromise his beliefs or the truth as he saw it. He had his own inner light and felt no need to follow others or seek consensus. Dayan's nonconformism, direct style, mannerisms, and insistence on being himself for most of his life may also explain his charisma.

As a soldier, Dayan can best be described as unconventional—but not eccentric in the sense of being odd. First and foremost, he was fearless. Of course, this quality is a sine qua non for any great military leader, but in Dayan it was developed to an unusual degree. His courage in the thick of battle and his insistence on being at the front (which may have been indicative of a subconscious death wish) impressed all who observed or heard of it. Second, Dayan never insisted on unusual deference to his rank and showed no interest in organizational or routine matters. In this sense, he was definitely not typical of the average modern officer serving in a large military organization. Surely, he would have been a failure at the Pentagon, Whitehall, or even in the Israeli army of today. A David or a Gideon (to whom he would probably have liked to compare himself) can flourish only within a small and relatively young military organization lacking in tradition. He was, therefore, both the product and representative of a young Israeli army as yet undominated by modern military technology and bureaucratization.

Dayan's readiness to accept high risk in planning military operations was also atypical; indeed, most military commanders would think in terms of the worst-case analysis and try to reduce risks accordingly. But Dayan's intuitive grasp of military affairs, his exceptional *coup d'oeil*, meant that his readiness to accept risks was simply the mark of a great commander. Dayan's intelligence, temperament, impatience for routine work, and courage inevitably made him an ideal soldier, a superior leader of men in battle who was unconventional but not eccentric militarily.

Large, modern military organizations are based on routine bureaucratic procedures, well-established career patterns, hierarchy and obedience, and a solid and stable performance of duties—not on individual brilliance. Survival in such a setting demands the sacrifice of one's ego, concealment of likes and dislikes, the cooperation of a "team player." It is therefore no surprise that most military organizations strongly discourage deviations from the behavioral norm. This is self-defeating in many ways, since only those who dare to think creatively can break out of the predictable routine that is so devastating in war. An important methodological question that has no simple answer is, then: What is the relationship between the environment or so-called *strategic culture* on the one hand,

and the military heretic on the other? Which is more important and under what circumstances? How does it encourage, limit, or define the role of the unconventional soldier?

In a military organization with a long, venerable tradition and highly developed military doctrine, the influence of the unconventional soldier would inevitably be restricted to the periphery, to specialized matters far removed from the centers of decision making. On the other hand, his influence would be much greater as a commander within a young military organization or new service branch whose roles and doctrines have still not been firmly established. In a military where no orthodoxy (a tradition or inflexible doctrine of operations) exists, there are no heretics—only more creative and daring soldiers. Dayan was fortunate enough to begin his military career at a time in Israeli history when he could take part in building its tradition or strategic culture. Therefore, the impact of his unconventional outlook was much greater than it would have been in older, more established military organizations. On balance, Dayan's influence was for the better: he created a tradition that stressed openness and flexibility; the readiness to accept very high risks on the operational level but less so on the strategic; trust in intelligence work; the indispensability of deception and surprise; a decentralized command that granted more initiative to local officers; and, finally, the clear subordination of the military to the political authorities. As mentioned earlier, though, these achievements were not without cost. At times, improvisation was carried to an extreme, leading to the neglect of detailed planning and staff work; whereas the promotion of a high-risk, offensive strategy inevitably led to poor defensive thinking and some "trigger-happy" attitudes. For this reason, a flexible, "open-ended" doctrine that is ideal for a small military force is often ill-suited to a larger one. As the IDF grew and moved from wars dominated by platoon-sized formations (1948) to regiments and battalions (1956), divisions (1967), and even larger formations (1973), Dayan's legacy has become less relevant. Yet like the German military, the IDF has managed to preserve an unusual degree of openness and flexibility on the operational level despite its much larger size. This is what has made it such a formidable force.

Finally, could a military heretic such as Dayan have the same impact on the IDF today? Here the answer has to be "no"; there is little place for a Nelson, Patton, Rommel, or Dayan in large, bureaucratic military organizations that value micromanagement, consensus, and stability more than anything else. Under what circumstances, then, are military organizations prepared to accept innovative, unconventional individuals who do not fit the mold? Toward answering these questions, a few hypotheses can be suggested:

1. The smaller the military organization, the more tolerance there is for heretics or eccentrics.
2. The newer a military organization, the less influenced it is by tradition. The resulting flexibility makes an unconventional or innovative approach more acceptable.
3. The threshold of tolerance for eccentric or unconventional behavior rises the farther one is from the administrative centers of command (such behavior is tolerated in the colonies or on a remote front but not in GHQ or the Pentagon).
4. In crisis situations, when more accepted methods of waging war have failed, openness to unusual ideas or solutions will increase in direct proportion to the level of desperation.
5. The degree to which national or cultural influence affect individualism and creativity varies. For example, the British accept eccentric behavior to a greater extent than the Americans or Germans.
6. Finally, to survive within a military organization, the military innovator or unconventional soldier needs the protection of a sympathetic benefactor or mentor. (Wingate had Churchill's support; Dayan, that of Ben Gurion. Without Ben Gurion's backing, Dayan would not have been able to survive or flourish as he did in the IDF.)

APPENDIX

Dayan's Contribution to Israeli Military Style	Consequences
As chief of staff, focused on combat and operations. Concentrated on the "big picture"; neglected details and smaller issues.	Strong morale and offensive spirit. Weak staff work; neglect of noncombat and support mission. "Strong teeth, weaker tail."
Creative, high-risk, offensive, operational planning. A non-dogmatic, flexible military doctrine. A knack for improvisation.	Good offensive planning; weaker on the defensive. Too much left to improvisation, too little to careful planning.

Personal presence on the battlefield. Leading from the front.	Very good for morale and for success on the battlefield, but led to neglect of staff work, overall control, and direction.
Delegation of authority. Decentralized command.	Good for initiative and the exploitation of opportunities but difficult for centralized command and control.
Intelligence, deception, and surprise.	Very positive record. Set an excellent example. Are still considered essential for all strategic and operational planning. Heavy emphasis on knowing the enemy.
Political control.	Set an excellent example. Government and politicians always in control; no interference in political affairs. Only problem—difficulty in controlling local initiative.
Special doctrinal issues. Time factor.	Paid careful attention to the role of time and speed in the conduct of war.

NOTES

1. Carl von Clausewitz, *On War*, Book 3, eds. and trans. Michael Howard and Peter Paret (Princeton, NJ, 1984), 184.
2. Although Dayan was born on 4 November 1915, in later years he inexplicably gave his date of birth as 20 May 1915. See Avner Falk, *Moshe Dayan: Ha'Ish Ve Ha'Agada* (Jerusalem, 1985). This book is an excellent example of how not to write a psychoanalytical biography. The author's methodology is crude and simplistic: he chooses only the facts that support his preconceived "theoretical framework" and even then often bends the facts to support his arguments. The book has not, however, been translated into English, although the reader can get a clear idea of Falk's belabored theories in: Avner Falk, "Moshe Dayan: Narcissism in Politics," *Jerusalem Quarterly*, (Winter 1984), 113–24; and Avner Falk, "Moshe Dayan: The Infantile Roots of Political Action," *Journal of Psychohistory*, 11 (1983), 271–88.

For more balanced, less speculative biographies in this growing field of research, see Alexander L. George and Juliette L. George, *Woodrow Wilson and Colonel House: A Personality Study* (New York, 1964); Anthony Storr, *Churchill's Black Dog* (London, 1989); and Erik H. Erikson, *Young Man Luther: A Study in Psychoanalysis and History* (New York, 1962).

Most noteworthy in the context of this book are biographies of unconventional soldiers such as John E. Mack, *A Prince of Our Disorder: The Life of T. E. Lawrence* (Boston, 1976); John Willett, *Popski: A Life of Lt. Col. Vladimir Peniakoff* (London, 1954); or Christopher Sykes, *Orde Wingate* (London, 1959). Wingate, the very eccentric and unconventional officer under whom Dayan had his early military instruction in the field, is still a highly controversial figure like Dayan himself. See Peter Mead, "Orde Wingate and the Official Historians," *Journal of Contemporary History*, 14 (1979), 55–82; Shelford Bidwell, "Wingate and the Official Historians: An Alternative View," *Journal of Contemporary History*, 15 (1980), 245–56; Peter Mead and Shelford Bidwell, "Orde Wingate: Two Views," *Journal of Contemporary History*, 15 (1980), 401–4; and Sir Robert Thompson and Peter Mead, "Wingate—The Pursuit of Truth," *Army Quarterly and Defense Journal*, 108 (1981), 335–40.

3. Among his books are: Moshe Dayan, *Diary of the Sinai Campaign* (New York, 1967), which is still an excellent account of the Sinai Campaign, its planning, and some of the major battles; Moshe Dayan, *Moshe Dayan: Story of My Life* (New York, 1976) is a good read but adds little that is new and, probably, is more interesting for what is omitted; Moshe Dayan, *Breakthrough: A Personal Account of the Egypt-Israel Peace Negotiation* (New York, 1981); and Moshe Dayan, *Living with the Bible* (Jerusalem, 1978). In Hebrew, he also published a perceptive analysis of the war in Vietnam as a result of a trip there from July–September 1966; see Moshe Dayan, *Yoman Vietnam* (Tel Aviv, 1977). See also Moshe Dayan, "Israel's Borders and Security Problems," *Foreign Affairs*, 33 (1955).

4. A detailed "monograph" on Dayan's sex life in the context of the Israeli society of the 1950s has yet to be published. Dayan's most recent biographer, Robert Slater, claimed in an interview that in his *Warrior Statesman: The Life of Moshe Dayan* (New York, 1991), he discussed only Dayan's three or four most important love affairs, since including all of Dayan's affairs could fill ten volumes. (See in particular pp. 319–25.)

Dayan was married to his first wife, Ruth (Schwartz) Dayan, for thirty-six years (married in 1934; divorced in 1971). For eighteen of those years, he also had an ongoing affair (which he did not conceal from his wife) with Rachel Rabinovich Korem, who later became his second wife. While his affair with Rachel continued off and on, he had another affair with a much younger woman in her early twenties, who was encouraged by her mother to initiate the relationship with Dayan (1968–1970). He also had a stormy affair with the wife of one of his senior officers who was also a boyhood acquaintance. This David and Bath Sheba affair was faithfully recorded by the woman, Mrs. Hadassa More, in a book entitled *Derakhim Lohatot* (Tel Aviv, 1963), which was published and widely read in Israel after Dayan ended the affair. Unfortunately, the bizarre psychoanalytical biography by Avner Falk has almost nothing interesting to offer on this problem. See also Sharit Rom, "The Organ of the State," *Hadashot*, Special Yom Kippur Supplement (17 September 1991), 16–18; and Dvora Shapiro, "Rachel, Hadassa, Elisheva," *Ma'ariv*, Special Supplement (22 September 1991), 15.

5. The best biography by far is still Shabtai Teveth, *Moshe Dayan: The Soldier, The Man, The Legend* (Boston, 1973). This is, however, an abbreviated and inferior version

of the Israeli edition, which is much more detailed (over 600 pages in Hebrew while the English translation is only 350 pages long). This book also lacks objectivity and only takes the reader up to the late 1960s; nevertheless, it is very readable and contains an excellent account of Dayan's life until the time of the Six-Day War. While not hagiography, it is very partial to Dayan's point of view and is "too clean" and uncritical. (For example, none of Dayan's well-known sexual escapades are mentioned.)

6. Among those that should be consulted are: Ruth Dayan and Helga Dudman, . . . *Or Did I Dream and Dream* (Jerusalem, 1973); and Yael Dayan, *My Father, His Daughter* (New York, 1985). Also worth consulting are More, *Derakhim Lohatot*; and Yael Dayan, *The New Face in the Mirror* (London, 1959).

7. See Meir Pail, "The Most Successful Chief of Staff until Today," *Ma'ariv*, Special Supplement (22 September 1991), 25; Shlomo Gazit, "He Made No Excuses," Ibid.; and a more critical assessment in Shlomo Gazit, *Yediot Achronot*, Special Supplement (September 1991), 6–7; Ariel Sharon, "This Myth Should Not Be Destroyed," *Yediot Achronot* (3 October 1991); Alex Schifman, "Missing the Commander," *Hadashot*, Special Yom Kippur Supplement (September 1991), 22–24; and Major-General Ehud Barak, "In the Field He Was at Home," *Yediot Achronot*, Special Supplement (22 September 1991), 5.

On Dayan's attitude toward the Arabs, see Hayim Hamegbi, "Our Brother Moussa," *Hadashot* (17 September 1991), 25–27.

8. This is the title of Dayan's last book. It is taken from Samuel II, Chapter 2:26: "Then Abner called to Joab, and said: 'Shall the sword devour forever? Knowest thou not that it will be bitterness in the latter end?' "

9. Quoted in Falk, *Moshe Dayan*, 228.

10. On "groupthink," see Irving L. Janis, *Victims of Groupthink* (Boston, 1972).

11. See George and George, *Wilson and House*. Cf. Sigmund Freud and William C. Bullitt, *Thomas Woodrow Wilson: A Psychoanalytical Biography* (Boston, 1967); and Edwin A. Weinstein, *Wilson: A Medical and Psychological Biography* (Princeton, 1981).

12. Shabtai Teveth, *Moshe Dayan* (Tel Aviv, 1971), 371. This is the Hebrew edition, and all subsequent references are to this volume.

13. Ibid., 370–71.

14. Ibid., 504. See also Dayan, *My Life*, 46; and Falk, *Dayan*, 250–51.

15. Teveth, *Dayan*, the epigram to both the Hebrew and English editions.

16. Michael Karpin, "Longing for Moshe Dayan," *Davar Ha'Shavua* (7 September 1991), 4.

17. Teveth, *Dayan*, 10–40.

18. Clausewitz, *On War*, Book I, especially Chapter Three, "On Military Genius."

19. Teveth, *Dayan*, 247–99; and Dayan, *My Life*, 57–75.

20. See Dayan, *Diary of the Sinai Campaign*.

21. Sharon, "This Myth."

22. I could not find any interesting analysis of or study on the possible impact of the loss of an eye on personality, but of anecdotal interest is T. C. Barras, "Vice-Admiral Lord Nelson's Lost Eye," *Transactions of the Ophthalmological Societies of the United Kingdom*, 105 (1986), 351–55.

23. Falk, *Dayan*, 350.

24. For example, see Dayan, *Diary of the Sinai Campaign*, 126–27.

25. Ibid., 96.

26. See Ibid., 102–3.

27. Ibid., 101–103.
28. Teveth, *Dayan*, 411–12.
29. On this, see Jonathon Shimshoni, *Israel and Conventional Deterrence: Border Warfare From 1953 to 1970* (Ithaca, 1988).
30. Dayan, *Diary of the Sinai Campaign*, 56–57.
31. Ibid., 124.
32. Falk, *Dayan*, 232.
33. Michael I. Handel, *Perception, Deception and Surprise: The Case of the Yom Kippur War* (Jerusalem, 1976); and Michael I. Handel, *War, Strategy, and Intelligence* (London, 1988), 229–81.
34. Handel, *War, Strategy, and Intelligence*, Chapter 5.
35. This was the conclusion of the Agranat Commission that was formed to investigate the reasons for Israel's surprise in the opening phases of the Yom Kippur War.
36. Yigal Allon and Dayan had been competing with one another since 1937, and particularly after the 1967 Six-Day War, much energy (perhaps more on the part of Allon) was spent on weaving political intrigues against each other. See "A Duel as a Zero-Sum Game," *Davar* (3 October 1991), 9; and Amnon Denker, "Life Under the Shadow," *Hadashot* (17 September 1991), 13. The latter is revealing on the intrigues of Allon in which he undermined a plan Dayan proposed in 1970 for the separation of the Egyptian and Israeli forces in the Sinai; if implemented as proposed, this plan may have ultimately prevented the 1973 war.
37. This is how Dayan described his experience in the British course for non-commissioned officers: "Even though I did not like the tough parades, drill exercises and polishing shoes, I found it interesting.... I did understand [nevertheless] that from an imperial point of view, the British knew what they were doing. There was something in this bullshit." See Dayan, *My Life*, 37.
38. On the time he spent in England, see Teveth, *Dayan*, 146–49; and, later, at the Senior Officers School in 1952, see Falk, *Dayan*, 192–95; and Dayan, *My Life*, 105–7.
39. Dayan, *My Life*, 37–39.
40. Ibid., 37.
41. Ibid., 37–39.
42. Ibid., 45–47; and Teveth, *Dayan*, 170.
43. Teveth, *Dayan*, 285–94.
44. Dayan, *Diary of the Sinai Campaign*, 39.
45. Ibid., 35.
46. Sun Tzu, *The Art of War* (New York, 1963), 84.
47. See Michael I. Handel, *Masters of War: Sun Tzu, Clausewitz and Jomini* (London, 1992), Chapter 1.
48. See Michael I. Handel, *Israel's Political-Military Doctrine* (Cambridge, MA, 1973).
49. See Dayan, *Diary of the Sinai Campaign*, 32–38.
50. Ibid., 73.
51. Ibid., 62.
52. See Michael I. Handel, ed., *Strategic and Operational Deception in the Second World War* (London, 1987), 1–92.
53. Dayan, *My Life*, 427–29.
54. Ibid., 425.
55. *Jerusalem Post*, 2 June 1967.

56. See Michael I. Handel, "Crisis and Surprise in Three Arab-Israeli Wars," in *Strategic Military Surprise: Incentives and Opportunities*, eds. Klaus Knorr and Patrick Morgan (New Brunswick, NJ, 1983), 111–47; and Barton Whaley, *Strategem: Deception and Surprise in War* (Cambridge, MA, 1969), A572–A604.
57. Pail, "Successful Chief of Staff," 25.
58. Dayan, *Diary of the Sinai Campaign*, 121–22.
59. Ibid., 142–43, 149.
60. Ibid., 121–22.

9

Afterword:
The Mark of the Heretic

John A. English

> Heresy is the lifeblood of religions.
> It is faith that begets heretics.
> There are no heretics in a dead religion.
>   André Suarès

There is something about a soldier who marches to a different drummer. Indeed, such an overt act of choice (the original meaning of heresy) can evoke the admiration of others: first, because it takes a certain amount of courage to do so within the regimented fellowship of an army; second, because the force behind the soldier's tread may spring from the musings of an active and intelligent mind in full pursuit of professional knowledge. In short, the true military heretic is likely to be a dedicated and creative thinker as well as a person of principle. While prepared to stand firm against the pressures of the mainstream, even to the detriment of career advancement, he is also likely to be a mover and shaker, his own music-maker.[1] Of course, one can hardly expect an armed force filled with heretics to be a disciplined and effective fighting organization. Given the requirement for teamwork and common approaches in military operations, there is much to be said for Benjamin Disraeli's admonition, "Damn your principles! Stick to your party."[2] The soldier who is constantly out of step can be a menace. On the drill square he can spoil a good parade and cause tears to well in the eyes of the most hard-bitten regimental sergeant-major; on far more important planes, especially those involving doctrine and the cooperation of arms, he may even bring disaster on his fellows in the field.

The nature of military heresy, like war itself, constitutes something of an antinomy. The heretical beliefs and ideas of yesteryear can become the doctrine of tomorrow, though the degree to which they are later considered heretical may be directly proportional to the time taken for them to win universal acceptance. In other words, heresies adopted relatively quickly are likely to be remembered as but conventional orthodoxies or, in extreme cases, dogma. Such general observations should not, however, obscure the importance of the individual military heretic who, like the religious martyr, usually deserves some credit for sowing the seeds of a new school of thought or faith. Yet, while yesterday's heretic is often hailed as today's saint, establishing the criteria by which to determine who is or is not a military heretic remains a daunting task.[3] Inevitably, subjective judgments have to be rendered. Not the least is that it is the pen rather than the sword that distinguishes the military heretic, who is most apt to be a scribbler bent on contesting doctrine and the accepted written word. Common sense suggests placing inspired commanders such as Horatio Nelson, Erwin Rommel, Bernard Montgomery, and George Patton in the league of practitioners rather than heretics. Except for the likes of Heinz Guderian and T. E. Lawrence,[4] and possibly Charles de Gaulle, Orde Wingate, and Evans Carlson,[5] it is a rare bird who is also a practitioner and a heretic. The individuals discussed in this afterword have been selected because of the depth of their military thought, the challenges they posed to contemporary services doctrine, and the career wounds they suffered in consequence.

One can hardly begin to discuss military heretics without first recognizing that doctrine long ago supplanted drill as the chief means of coordinating the field deployments and associated activities of modern armies. As Napoleon discovered in Russia, there were definite limits to the size of an army, however well drilled or disciplined, that could be controlled by one person. Military genius alone was no longer sufficient to shore up generalship. The solution, first instituted by the Prussians to compensate for lack of military competence in royalist appointees, was to provide field commanders with general staff advisers capable of offering expert counsel and overseeing the detailed execution of orders. The function of the general staff, declared its Hanoverian creator, Gerhard von Scharnhorst, was to provide the energy that set the motor of the army in motion. In solving the increasingly complex problems of modern armies related to people, things, and fighting, the staff also acted as a lubricant to the chain of command. An equally significant advantage conferred by this collectivity was that it enabled armies to study these and other aspects of war in peacetime and devise a "doctrine for war fighting" that would otherwise take too long to fashion in the event.[6]

The Prussian-German General Staff, which comprised both "Great" (War Ministry, *Grosser Generalstab*) and "troop" (*Truppengeneralstab*) elements, was both corporate and decentralized. Its *Kriegsakademie* dispensed a collective practical expertise, based on continuous critical analysis, to ensure that individual officers would be similarly capable of responding independently and sensibly to the often unexpected challenges of the battlefield, making the best use of resources available. Higher commanders were thus able to allow subordinates greater initiative and freedom of action in the execution of operations. Helmuth von Moltke issued only the most essential orders, which as a rule included everything that a subordinate commander could not do himself, but nothing else. Such decentralization reduced the bureaucratic friction inherent in hierarchy and encouraged innovation at lower levels, which permitted the army at large to adapt more quickly to changing circumstances. Uniformity of doctrine pertaining to the employment of all arms of the service increased command efficiency and made possible massive field army deployments. Loosely defined as the fundamental principles by which the various parts of military forces are guided in the attainment of objectives, doctrine also came to mean in practical terms that corpus of knowledge officially sanctioned to be taught.[7]

Though the German General Staff served as the model for all others, it differed in several important respects from its imitators. Under the first "great Chief of [the General] Staff," General August Count Neidhardt von Gneisenau, Prussian General Staff officers acting as chiefs of staff at corps level and above gained the institutionalized right to participate in the operational decision-making process. As "commander's advisers" or *Fuehrergehilfe*, they could communicate directly with the Chief of the General Staff on all matters related to their functional areas. The advent of the telegraph strengthened this link, which eventually enabled central headquarters to monitor operational and strategic deployments day by day, and, if necessary, even hour by hour. *Fuehrergehilfe* thus not only advised their respective commanders until such time as decisions were taken but assumed joint accountability for those decisions. Up to 1938 it was an unwritten rule that corps chiefs of staff were permitted to enter their opinions in war diaries when they disagreed with the responsible commander's decision. In fact, the Great War witnessed the development of the "Chief System" in which highly competent first general staff officers actually commanded the armies of nobles and princes.[8]

The unique responsibility of the Prussian-German General Staff officer in tendering advice and assuming accountability for its relevance with respect to decisions taken distinguish him from his counterparts in other armies. Unlike normal subordinates who often tended to give as little offense as possible in their advice to superiors, the chief of staff or first general staff officer was duty bound by Prussian tradition to press his candid and unsolicited advice upon his commander and urge him to make a rational, dispassionate decision based on the facts as presented. The latter, in turn, was obligated by established convention to listen to this advice prior to taking that decision, which the general staff officer then adopted as his own. This system, which to the uninitiated appeared to countenance insubordination, had the wider effect of elevating intelligence and expertise over rank, and it was not uncommon for junior general staff members to give orders to higher-ranking officers and have them obeyed. In September 1914, for example, Lieutenant-Colonel Richard Hentsch after personal deliberation ordered the commanders of the First and Second German Armies, against the wishes of the former, to break off action and withdraw during the First Battle of the Marne.[9]

For obvious reasons, tampering with military doctrine was not a thing to be taken lightly in any army. At the same time, technological advances in weaponry and modes of transportation demanded that doctrine reflect the realities of change. The Germans especially seem to have regarded operational doctrine not as dogma but as a dynamic process that represented a means to an end rather than an end in itself. Nowhere was this more clearly illustrated than during the Great War when the German army after the Somme battles radically revamped both its defensive and offensive tactical doctrine. Significantly, most of the progressive changes introduced (which included "elastic defense-in-depth" and storm-trooper offensive tactics incorporating new weapons like flamethrowers and trench mortars) directly reflected the deliberations of a small group of general staff officers, at least one of them a captain whose ultimate influence belied his modest rank.[10] As might be expected, the process of doctrinal and structural change sparked a heated tactical controversy, one actually fueled by General Erich Ludendorff; it ended, remarkably, with senior officers being converted by the arguments of their juniors. This triumph of expertise over rank was largely due to the pragmatic German staff approach that not only solicited ideas from the field but validated them through realistic training for their practicality in situationally specific situations. Doctrine that could not be applied was considered useless.[11]

The French and British armies by comparison proved less adept in adapting their tactics to the conditions of the Great War. To some extent this reflected the fact that neither really possessed a viable doctrine in 1914. The *offensive à outrance* adopted by the French as a means of countering German material and numerical superiority, although based on certain verified observations related to the superb 75-mm artillery piece, was less a military doctrine than an extreme form of chauvinism. Seeking to imbue French conscripts with the offensive spirit of the nation-in-arms through sociopolitical indoctrination used up valuable training time, with the result that their field performance suffered. German emphasis on the offensive, also sociologically rooted, at least related to the doctrine of flank attack and envelopment (albeit disastrously when it translated into the *ideé fixe* of the Schlieffen Plan at the strategic level). During the Great War, the French did nonetheless attempt to introduce combat innovations, although all too often bright ideas percolating from the front simply got lost in the bureaucracy of a hierarchical chain of command. In consequence, tactical change in the French army tended to reflect the exclusive imprint and extremes of single dominant commanders, such as Ferdinand Foch, Henri Pétain, and most disastrously, Robert Nivelle, who deluded himself into thinking before the debacle of his 1917 offensive that he alone possessed a formula for success.[12]

Unfortunately for the British, experience in smaller colonial conflicts had not provided their volunteer army with the requisite doctrinal foundation for the conduct of "great" war. Although widespread reforms had been carefully introduced after the painful experience of the South African War, the British army tended to deprecate doctrine on the grounds that it encouraged stereotypical methods and stifled initiative and flexibility. Common sense seemed preferable to doctrine, which continued to be regarded as something foreign—not entirely without justification, as many British pamphlet writers habitually plagiarized entire tracts from German manuals without fully comprehending their implications. The doctrinal shortcomings of the British army became more apparent after the deployment of its legendary "contemptible little army" in 1914. Without the conscript school infrastructure of the German or French armies, it now faced the task of training mass armies raised after the outbreak of war. While dogged in the defense, it proved less adept in the more difficult tactics of the attack. The art of coordinating different arms and orchestrating the fire of disparate weapons had not been studied in any depth, and everything consequently had to be learned in the less than desirable circumstances of never-ending battle.[13]

Although fresh thinking was badly needed in both the French and British armies, their senior staff structures do not appear to have been capable of accommodating constructive criticism. New ideas were not always welcome at higher levels. The corporate and collective approach that characterized German army doctrinal endeavors does not seem to have been widely emulated, though this is not to suggest that Allied soldiers did not succeed in innovating at lower levels. Official changes merely evolved in more amateur fashion. The British army, perhaps even more than the French, continued to underscore hierarchy and subordination at the expense of function and expertise. Commanders, regardless of competence, retained an authoritarian preeminence over both subordinates and immediate staff officers. As the latter could rarely speak with the frankness of the German general staff officer, their advice was not as readily forthcoming. Changes deemed worthy of mention had furthermore to be suggested discreetly, without provoking personal confrontation, in order to increase their chances of being approved. Though the British general staff was not entirely dysfunctional or without influence, its primary focus was reactive and executory rather than proactive and advisory.[14]

Instituted in the aftermath of the South African War, the British general staff did not for various reasons constitute a distinct and separate caste like its German counterpart. Nor was it "unified" like either the German or French model in which staff branches reported to one chief of the general staff for direction. In contrast, the British general staff was but the senior of three autonomous staff branches roughly corresponding to operations (*General,* or "G"), personnel (*Adjutant-General,* or "A"), and materiel (*Quartermaster-General,* or "Q"). The head of the British general staff, from 1909 the Chief of the Imperial General Staff (CIGS), was only one of four military members on the Army Council. This body, chaired by the Secretary of State for War, included the Adjutant-General, Quartermaster-General, Master-General of Ordnance (MGO), and two civilian members. Though as *primus inter pares* the CIGS assumed responsibility for all military staff coordination, he was in reality neither "general" nor "imperial," for he headed little more than an operational staff. Indeed, the absence of the collective predilection that so characterized the German general staff can readily be detected in the remark of one CIGS, who in 1926 answered his own rhetorical question, "Who is the General Staff?" with an authoritarian, "I am the General Staff."[15]

Paradoxically, the foregoing quotations first issued from the pen of a British regular officer who must surely rank as the quintessential military heretic against whom all others can be fairly measured. Indeed, it is difficult to think of a more striking example of a military heretic than J. F. C. Fuller. While his frankness alone might have marked him as being of the German general staff, his professional outspokenness from a British army career perspective led ultimately to the stake. Having once stated "that he was already a heretic by the age of five," he stood out throughout his army service as a totally unconventional soldier who likened himself to a "military Luther." In 1897 he railed against the "canting hypocrites" of Sandhurst with its "Crimean" and "cricket-complex" atmosphere.[16] The tedious "flunkeydom" of regimental service in Ireland left him similarly underwhelmed for the "intellectual standardization" and sheer amateurism it fostered. Reflecting on the initial defeats suffered by British forces in the South African War, he wrote: "Slap dash and bang may be all very well sometimes but that it constitutes war is absolutely ridiculous." He further charged that there was but "one officer out of a dozen" whose military education extended beyond knowing the names of their commanding generals.[17]

By 1907, having served in India as well as in Ireland and South Africa, Fuller began to write prolifically on professional matters. An idealistic autodidact, he strongly believed that war was a serious subject that required rational analysis and detailed study. He doubtless approved of and envied the systematic research and thorough preparation conducted by the German general staff. As might be expected in the essentially anti-intellectual atmosphere of the British army of the time, this got him into trouble at staff college during 1913. His paper on "The Tactics of Penetration: A Counterblast to German Numerical Superiority," which proposed a practical alternative to the accepted doctrine of envelopment on the heretical grounds that artillery had become the superior arm, was not well received (though it was subsequently published in the *Journal of the Royal United Service Institution*, or *JRUSI*, of November 1914). When called before the Commandant to explain himself, Fuller was told to "study the *Field Service Regulations* more closely, that envelopment and not penetration would dominate in the next war and that infantry not artillery would be the main arm."[18]

The dogmatic pronouncements of his superiors failed to move Fuller, who had in fact studied *Field Service Regulations* in great depth. Having previously noted that these referred to the "principles of war" in the earlier established sense of myriad fundamentals, he took it upon himself to elaborate six basic ones—objective, mass, offensive, surprise, security, and movement—which he used in another staff college essay. But because these principles, defined by Fuller as "generalizations of observed facts," were not specifically enumerated in *Field Service Regulations*, he was informed by his instructors that they were incorrect and that his ideas were dangerously unsound. Upon inquiring what the correct principles were, he was curtly told that it was not the business of a student to amend regulations. No doubt Fuller was an infuriatingly opinionated and irritating student, but within a decade the codification of principles in the modern sense of a short definitive list as he conceived them found expression within *Field Service Regulations*. In time, notwithstanding his later reservations about their slavish use, they became firmly rooted in the military doctrine of the British and American armies.[19]

Fortunately for Fuller, his staff college tour was cut short by the Great War; during the conflict he earned an international reputation as a military thinker of note. It is probably fair to say that his was the main intellectual driving force behind the development of the tactics and organization of the Tank Corps in France from 1917 to 1918. As principal general staff officer of the Tank Corps, he was clearly the mastermind behind the innovative tank attack at Cambrai in November 1917. He was also instrumental in planning the tank support for the smaller yet more technically advanced Battle of Hamel on 4 July 1918. Fuller's most outstanding achievement, however, was drafting his visionary "Plan 1919"; its most remarkable feature was that it called for a weapon, the Medium D tank, that did not yet exist. Conceptually, it amounted to a brilliant attempt to shape the future by forcing improvements on existing technology so that it fitted the needs of the plan, rather than vice versa. The plan was even more revolutionary for having as its objective the strategic paralysis of the enemy.[20] Through a surprise and sustained deep penetration by some 5,000 tanks supported by artillery, motorized infantry, and air, "Plan 1919" aimed to capture, destroy, or paralyze enemy headquarters and communication centers, thereby psychologically destroying the German will to resist and ending the war in one masterstroke. It possessed all, and more, of the theoretical underpinnings of blitzkrieg.

Between the wars Fuller continued to write in his spare time with increasingly controversial impact as he sought the reform of the entire defense machine. He published scathing attacks on the conduct of the Great War and virtually singlehandedly forced the British military establishment to consider the place of the tank in battle. In a futuristic article anonymously submitted to the *JRUSI*, he argued that mobility based upon machine fighting power counted for more than sheer numbers of men. Recognizing that the tank could be made gas-proof, he advocated the creation of a new model mechanized army in which airplanes would cooperate with armor as the main striking force, and all supply vehicles would be motorized. This army, in turn, was to be backed by an efficient national mobilization of manpower, industry, and associated economic resources. Fuller additionally called for a single Ministry of Defense and a "thinking" general staff headed by one chief rather than an Army Council. He further suggested that as educated men were easier to train, the army should become a "People's University." Although Fuller won the Royal United Services Institution 1919 Gold Medal for his essay, such talk proved too much for many readers who considered it "military Bolshevism." When the article was eventually published in the *JRUSI* under Fuller's name, it created a minor furor that caused Fuller's concerned superior, Major-General A. L. Lynden-Bell, to demand of him, "Boney! Boney! What *have* you done?"[21]

From the mid-1920s onward, while he was a staff college instructor, Fuller came to be publicly identified as a military radical, the heresiarch of the "tank school" and archenemy of the cavalry establishment and military conservatism. Yet, while he exerted influence far beyond what his rank belied, Fuller lacked (and later alienated) the patronage that would have enabled his school to effect reform. When he applied for War Office approval to publish a distillation of his staff college lectures in a book entitled *The Foundations of the Science of War*, the then-CIGS, Lord Cavan, refused him permission. In an interview subsequently requested by Fuller, Cavan explained that he considered it harmful for officers to publish books on military subjects, because they might call into question the validity of military manuals. "I cannot enforce this as regards the Army generally," he informed Fuller, "but as regards General Staff officers I intend to do so, and whilst you are at the Staff College I cannot give you permission to bring this book out."[22]

In 1926 Fuller assumed the position of Military Assistant to the CIGS, newly appointed General Sir George Milne. That such a relatively low posting caught the attention of the *Sunday Express*, which observed that he was "probably by far the cleverest man in the Army," attested to the strength of Fuller's reputation. Unfortunately, Fuller's last chance to reform the army from within foundered on his inability to retain Milne's confidence—undoubtedly shaken in the controversies aroused by Fuller's dazzling, irreverent, and revolutionary writings, which shocked the establishment to its core. Nonetheless, in December 1926 Milne selected Fuller, judged to possess the requisite "touch of . . . divine fire," to command the Experimental Mechanized Force then being formed. When Fuller discovered that he was not to take over a dedicated organization, but rather a garrison and ordinary infantry brigade within a division from which an ad hoc experimental force would be raised, he began to doubt the seriousness of the initiative. Fearing that routine duties and administrative concerns related to such triple-hatting would detract from experimentation, Fuller resigned on principle, which indirectly resulted in a higher priority being assigned to the Experimental Force.[23]

Though Fuller later withdrew his resignation, largely in response to friendly pressure to remain in for the good of the army (which he was also assured would be modernized), the knives were already out for him. The publication of his controversial *Foundations of the Science of War* in 1926 also drew fire that damaged his career prospects. Indeed, from this point until his retirement in 1933 he was relegated to the military outer darkness. That he advanced in rank from colonel to major-general during this period only camouflaged this reality. Within the British army, Fuller the field officer wielded more influence than Fuller the general. As a Rhine Army brigade commander in 1930, he complained of the peacetime routine that made "command in this country . . . the nearest approach to zero that any scientist has ever got down to."[24] The next year he refused an offer of an Indian district command, which he regarded with some justification as the ultimate insult:

As presumably most of my duties will be connected with communal riots and boycott disturbances, and as I have no confidence in the Government of India, which, in my opinion, through weakness and lack of insight are largely responsible for the present turmoil, I do not consider that I am a suitable officer to serve in that country. Further, from a purely military point of view, I consider such an appointment a pure waste of time.[25]

In declining a posting on political grounds, Fuller committed his final career sin.

Between 1931 and 1933 Fuller lived on half-pay and royalties from numerous published articles and books, among them *Lectures on FSR II* and *Lectures on FSR III*, which represented his apogee as a military theorist. After General Sir Archibald Montgomery-Massingberd took over as CIGS in early 1933, Fuller received notice that he would be retired that December. Montgomery-Massingberd openly detested Fuller and refused to read his books for fear they would make him angry. On learning that Fuller's *Grant and Lee* had been included on the reading list for officer promotion examinations that year, he altered their scope so that the book did not apply. Like many of his ilk, Montgomery-Massingberd genuinely feared the pernicious influence of Fuller's heretical writings on the minds of younger officers. Ironically, Fuller's cutting yet stimulating *Generalship: Its Diseases and Their Cure* appeared the same year. Others, especially foreigners, better appreciated the hard thinking behind Fuller's works. A Russian edition of *On Future Warfare* reputedly sold over 100,000 copies. It is equally clear that many German soldiers—including Heinz Guderian, who corresponded with and actually met Fuller in 1939—were familiar with the latter's writings. Fuller additionally influenced Charles de Gaulle, Bernard Montgomery, and George Patton, who considered Fuller one of his favorite authors.[26]

According to his biographer, Fuller "was, on balance, too clever, too rigid, too intellectually arrogant and self-reliant to be highly successful in a military career—at least in peacetime."[27] At the same time, General Sir Edmund Ironside, who admitted Fuller could be difficult to handle, described him as "straight and fearless and ingenious."[28] Unlike many of his career-minded contemporaries, Fuller remained a professional soldier in the truest sense of the word. Like the Germans, he prized expertise and function over position. His subject field, the study of war, mattered more to him than army social life and careerist advancement in rank. Ever contemptuous of "spittle-licking," he refused to prostitute himself for the sake of success. Sadly, his idealistic compulsion to tell the truth as he saw it aroused resentment and cast him in the light of a disloyal troublemaker. Yet Fuller's loyalty was to the army as a profession and not, as others evinced, to the army as a bureaucratic institution. The frustrated reformer thus turned rebel, intentionally resorting to exaggeration to argue his case and learning to refute by ridicule as much as by reason.[29] His sardonic wit and acid pen (which are exemplified by the inscription "Asses prefer refuse to gold" on the title page of his *Memoirs*, a saying that is attributed to Heraclitus, the "Dark Philosopher" who had contempt for mankind and held that the tension of opposites contributed to the unity of the one) guaranteed the eternal animosity of Fuller's detractors.

Still, Fuller was in many respects decades ahead of his time; and had British soldiers and governments followed his advice in the 1930s they would have been better prepared for World War II. Much of what he sought to achieve has long been accepted. A tireless advocate of mechanization, he was unquestionably the most original thinker who tackled this subject. One of the few significant figures in the history of the British army in modern times, Fuller, the professional soldier who was also a scholar, ranks among the greatest of the world's military theorists.[30] Although he may actually have failed as a military reformer in his day, his stimulating writings retain a continuing relevance and may still be read with great profit. In contrast, Montgomery-Massingberd's far grander career success, now hardly remembered for its relative insignificance, proved ephemeral. Fortunately for purposes of this chapter, Fuller's dedicated service, unequaled professional knowledge, noncareerist sense of vocation, selfless challenge to received doctrinal wisdom, and final bureaucratic martyrdom provide five characteristics by which to measure the military heretic.

The name most often associated with Fuller has been that of the renowned military theorist and journalist, Basil Liddell Hart, whose initial development as a defense critic owed much to the former. In terms of spreading influence, Liddell Hart was generally more successful than Fuller because he was less abrasive and intolerant of others. As he was not in the service for the greater part of his working life, however, it is questionable whether he merits being called a military heretic. Though equally imbued as Fuller with a sense of mission, Liddell Hart could write about military affairs relatively free from fear of career reprisal. His severe criticism of the British high command nonetheless partly reflected a traumatic personal experience in the Great War. A subaltern in the King's Own Yorkshire Light Infantry during the first day of the 1916 Somme offensive, he had witnessed firsthand the destruction of his regiment. He was the only officer in two battalions to survive unscathed. Later wounded and eventually invalided out of the British army, he spent the rest of his life pondering the twin questions of why such slaughter occurred and how it could be avoided in the future. Until his retirement in 1924, he directly influenced army doctrine through his work on official training manuals. Thereafter, as military correspondent with the *Daily Telegraph* from 1925, he regularly commented on army maneuvers and War Office affairs. From 1935 to 1939 he served as defense correspondent with the *Times*, reaching the peak of his direct influence as an unofficial, but principal, adviser to Leslie Hore-Belisha, the Secretary of State for War.[31]

With Fuller and other progressive officers, who often used him as a mouthpiece, Liddell Hart zealously fostered the mechanization and reform of the British army. There is no doubt that he exercised considerable influence among British junior officers, many of whom became his disciples. His writings, like those of Fuller, also reached readerships beyond Britain. Guderian, the German officer most responsible for the creation of the panzer arm, certainly read his works on infantry and the future structure of field armies. Many senior British army officers, on the other hand, greatly resented the influence of the former infantry captain who as *éminence grise* behind Hore-Belisha assumed a greater role than the CIGS and General Staff in molding army doctrine, organization, and senior appointments between 1937 and 1938. Liddell Hart's strategy of the indirect approach, most specifically detailed in *The British Way in Warfare* (1932), proved particularly attractive to politicians anxious to avoid another continental bloodbath. His advocacy of a return to Britain's traditional "blue water" strategy based on naval blockade, and his earlier flirtations with strategic bombing, likewise appealed to sailors and airmen. The overpowering strength of the surface defense, Liddell Hart argued, meant that Britain would be better off committing an RAF fighter contingent rather than an army to shore up continental allies. If absolutely required, however, a small professional mechanized force would be sufficient to tip the scales of any land war in their favor. Although official British policy roughly reflected such thinking until the spring of 1939, when it was rejected, this "doctrine of limited liability" and its defensive overtones proved Liddell Hart's undoing as a military adviser. He was now cast aside, his concepts discredited. Fortunately for his reputation, the war validated many of his ideas concerning the employment of infantry and armor, and in time that helped to restore his status as a notable military sage.[32]

Within contemporary naval circles, the mantle of heretic fell most fittingly on the shoulders of Admiral Sir Herbert Richmond, whose stormy career approximated Fuller's. A professional officer who was also a prolific writer, Richmond "became the fountainhead of British naval thought in the twentieth century."[33] His first book established his reputation as a serious scholar and won him the 1926 Royal United Services Institution Chesney Gold Medal, a distinction previously accorded only one other naval officer, an American, Captain Alfred Thayer Mahan. Although the clear-thinking but abrasively outspoken Richmond reached higher rank than Fuller, he was similarly forced into premature retirement. Like Fuller, he was unable to subdue his critical faculties and refrain from offering unsolicited advice, a tendency that within a more anti-intellectual service than the army inevitably marked him as an unpractical theorizer and troublemaker. Richmond's overbearing intolerance, uncompromising personality, and intellectual arrogance further estranged him from peers and superiors, who came to regard him as an unsettling gadfly not to be trusted.[34]

Richmond's leadership of an "intellectual revolution" within the Royal Navy started in 1912 with the foundation of the Naval Society and publication of the *Naval Review*. From that point on, he and his disciples, the "Young Turks" of the Grand Fleet, worked to bring about major changes within the navy. Despite having been a former captain of the revolutionary battleship and technological marvel, HMS *Dreadnought*, Richmond persistently challenged materialist influence in the shaping of naval policy. The highly technical reforms of Admiral Sir John Fisher had left Britannia well armed, but no one knew for certain whether she could wield her trident wisely. In Richmond's view, educational mismanagement lay at the root of naval ills; the brain of Fisher's great technical creature had failed to grow with its body. For lack of a properly trained war planning staff, Richmond maintained, the Royal Navy during the Great War not only failed to exploit its considerable and costly resources but actively courted disaster. To his credit, he was instrumental in effecting the 1918 reorganization of the naval staff, which saw incumbents selected on ability rather than social qualification. The principles that he enunciated in this process also formed the basis of all subsequent staff structures, including those used in World War II.[35]

Once described by General Sir William Robertson, CIGS, as "the first naval officer who seems to have a General Staff mind,"[36] Richmond constantly sought to promote constructive debate on naval affairs and inculcate among service officers the habit of reasoning things out from first principles. After the war, Richmond criticized what he perceived to be the blind faith of his superiors in the future of big battleships. This reflected his earlier opposition to the 1917 "Sea-Heresy" school of thought, which held that preoccupation with the protection of Britain's sea lines of communications distracted naval minds from the principal object of naval strategy; namely, the destruction of the enemy fleet. Prior to the 1921 Washington Naval Conference on arms limitations, Richmond questioned the wisdom of continuing building programs that took insufficient account of either the implications of submarines and aircraft or the economic realities upon which Britain's maritime ascendancy rested. He disputed the tendency to define maritime security mainly in terms of fixing relative battleship strengths and setting upper tonnage limits of 35,000. In 1929, Richmond mounted a concerted attack on the big ship advocates. Convinced of the soundness of his ideas, he publicly denounced the doctrine of material parity and called for more rational arms reduction approaches, based on qualitative measurements and smaller ship sizes, to meet the naval security requirements of individual nations. For what amounted to a personal act of conscience in opposing the battleship orthodoxy of the Admiralty, Richmond paid the career price.[37]

Richmond the ambitious reformer and service heretic was the intellectual heir of the gifted naval historian, Sir Julian Corbett, whose well-researched writings made him Britain's greatest maritime strategist. From his historical studies, Corbett concluded that the importance of maritime power lay in its capacity to influence military operations. The fleet and army of a maritime state constituted one weapon. Wherever the sea represented a substantial factor in war, maritime strategy dictated naval strategy, which in turn determined the movements of the fleet, in relation to the action of land forces. Thus, in Corbett's view, there was more to naval strategy and warfare than big fleets seeking big, decisive battles with other fleets. Although he believed that the *supreme* function of a fleet was to win battles at sea, he considered it strategically cramping to assume it to be the *sole* function of a fleet. Foreseeing that an unwilling enemy might choose not to do battle, as occurred after Jutland, he subtly argued that the first preoccupation of the fleet would almost always be to bring about such engagements by interference with the enemy's military and diplomatic arrangements. In the Great War, unfortunately, the Royal Navy's fixation with the concept of large-scale fleet action in the North Sea hampered naval planning for the Dardanelles expedition, invited the British naval defeat off Coronel, obscured the question of commerce protection, and prevented the early adoption of more effective methods for dealing with the submarine menace.[38]

The foregoing shortcomings all resulted, indirectly, from an obsession with materiel and the service view that big ships meant big fights. As Corbett pointed out, however, the inherent flexibility and mobility of naval forces meant that they could be assigned multiple tasks, including luring enemy ships onto them, while still retaining their ability to concentrate in time for major fleet actions that were means and not ends in themselves. Both Corbett and Richmond were at one with the doyen of naval writers, Mahan, that the true purpose of sea power was to control and regulate the movement of ships at sea. They differed with him over his command of the sea concept by which he envisioned maritime commerce being controlled. To Mahan, world power was based on oceanic power, and the paramount objective of naval action was (1) the destruction of the enemy fleet, and (2) the establishment of command of the sea. The principal means by which this was to be accomplished was the fire of armored capital ships concentrated in a great battle fleet that was never to be divided. Unlike Corbett, the thalassic Mahan treated naval strategy almost as a thing apart, an autonomous instrument of policy operating independently of land forces. He disregarded amphibious operations and discounted the value of the *guerre de course*. In contrast, Corbett saw the sea as being in a perpetual state of dispute, the focus of naval strategy that included diplomatic, financial, commercial, and military dimensions.[39]

During the reincarnation of the 1917 Sea Heresy debates in the Jutland controversy of the 1920s, the "Victory" school apportioned blame for the indecisiveness of that battle to Corbett's prewar teachings at the Naval War College. Corbett was publicly accused of preaching heresy, of suggesting that victory could be attained without hard offensive fighting. By 1923 he was dead, partly from being hounded over his interpretations in writing the official naval history of the war. Regrettably, the theories of neither Corbett nor Richmond received the professional and public attention showered upon Mahan. When the latter's *Influence of Sea Power upon History* appeared in 1890, it received instant acclaim in Great

Britain. Ironically, it also furnished the final blow that extinguished an existing heresy, that of the *jeune école*. This innovative doctrine, advocated by French Admiral Théophile Aube during the 1880s, contended that technological advances in mines and torpedoes had rendered battleships obsolete and command of the sea meaningless. Since navies had little affected the outcomes of the short wars of the late nineteenth century, the *jeune école* additionally assumed that the time factor would preclude amphibious operations and limit the effectiveness of commercial blockade. Against a Britain highly dependent upon overseas trade, however, it proposed waging a vicious *guerre de course*. The alarmed British responded in 1889 by initiating a massive ship-building program aimed at producing a balanced fleet of modern battleships, fast armored cruisers (for running down commerce raiders), and torpedo boat-destroyers. They also adopted a "two-power standard" whereby the Royal Navy would be maintained at a strength equal to that of the next two greatest naval powers combined. This extraordinary action precipitated the decline of the *jeune école*, which by 1914 few people even in France remembered.[40]

Mahan provided the big-navy prophets with a bible, however crudely written, that has endured to this day. The immediate international success that greeted his works must be attributed nonetheless to the temper of the times. In arguing that oceanic power determined world power, Mahan rode the crest of a popular and powerful wave of navalism and imperialism. Historical accuracy and interpretation aside, his books appeared to justify the wisdom of decisions that in many instances had already been taken. In the case of the Royal Navy, it reinforced the perception that decisive actions like Trafalgar and Tsushima were of paramount importance. As suggested by Ivo Lambi, Admiral Tirpitz also viewed Mahan's theory as confirmation of his own practically developed thoughts. In the United States the technologically oriented navalism of President Theodore Roosevelt superseded Mahan's historically based philosophy. One can only speculate that when the Japanese adopted *The Influence of Sea Power upon History* as a text, they too saw within its pages something of themselves. Perhaps because of the ease and speed with which his concepts and principles were subsumed within such "blue water" naval doctrines, Mahan escaped being branded a heretic. His pioneering achievements in an era when lessons from the age of sail were beginning to be looked upon as technologically irrelevant[41] seem to have placed him firmly in the orthodox camp.

Richmond, who owed more to Corbett than Mahan, inherited the former's view of the place of naval strategy in the grand scheme of things. That he insisted on drawing distinctions between ends and means, not surprisingly, led him to take issue with the air power apostles of the interwar years. He opposed the massive bombing of large cities and industrial centers on both economic and moral grounds, believing that such measures could prove detrimental to British national interests in the long term. He suspected that strategic doctrine was to an unhealthy degree being shaped by an excessive reaction to technological imperatives. In voicing such concerns, Richmond earned the enmity of the Royal Air Force and an undeserved reputation for downplaying air power. When accused during the war that, like most senior naval officers, he failed to appreciate the value of air forces, he replied:

I do not think any of us can boast very much of our prescience.... I have a lively recollection, for instance, of a theory that was constantly proclaimed to the effect that as "offence is the best defence" so we did not need fighters to defend ourselves against bombing: the proper defence was to bomb the enemy. But it was the fighters of the R.A.F. that saved England in 1940. We should, I think, be wise enough to admit that none of us were free from error. Among my own however, I do not include two. I opposed constantly and without relaxation, a view presented to me at the Imperial Defence College that the principles of war do not apply to the Air—a doctrine stated to me categorically by Trenchard . . . and another according to which the Air staff would make its own plans of war, irrespective of the other two services. I preached the "oneness" of war.[42]

Like Mahanian dogma in its time, the seeds of strategic bombing theory fell on fertile ground from 1916 onward. To politicians and publics wearied by Great War bloodletting, the air arm appeared to offer a unique technological means of avoiding the carnage of trench stalemate and even war itself. With the publication of Giulio Douhet's *Command of the Air* in 1921, which did not attract attention outside Italy until after Douhet's death in 1930, strategic bombing received its first coherent and comprehensive treatment as a theory of war. Like Trenchard, who held similar ideas but wrote little, Douhet considered the airplane the offensive weapon *par excellence* because it would always get through. In his view it offered the best hope of overcoming what he perceived to be the permanent ascendancy of the surface defense. The first task of the air offensive was to gain command of the air by aggressively striking enemy air bases and production facilities with bombers protected by combat planes. Thereafter massed bombers operating independently beyond static trench lines could directly gas or pulverize with impunity the vital centers of enemy population and industry, thereby precipitating a collapse of civilian morale and rapid national disintegration. Neither Douhet nor Trenchard favored diverting planes from this primary mission of strategic bombardment; the defensive was a form of warfare best left to armies and navies. The role of the independent air force was to inflict the greatest damage in the shortest time and win the race against annihilation.[43]

Though Douhet has often been referred to as "the Mahan of airpower," it would be erroneous to assume that he exerted an equivalent influence. In fact, he was court-martialed and imprisoned for criticizing the Italian high command in 1917. Although Italy was the first major power to devote its greatest effort to the air arm, it reputedly derived its official air doctrine from Britain and the Great War independent bombing force commanded by Trenchard. As pointed out by Scot Robertson, moreover, the latter's strategic unorthodoxy fast became orthodoxy within an RAF fearful to the point of paranoia about its future chances of survival. Trenchard was by then a true believer in strategic bombing, and that belief offered the RAF a role that ensured, if not entirely justified, its continued independence. At the same time, the outstanding success enjoyed by "the father of the RAF" in impressing his views on British politicians responsible for defense planning casts him more in the mold of a masterful empire-builder than a heretic. By crushing opposition to his dogma within the service, he furthermore strikes one as a high priest of convention. Likewise, the seemingly futuristic air philosophy espoused by the ahistorical Douhet appears less than revolutionary in light of Fuller's comment that the former artillerist was really "a tactical reactionary, because he harked back to the great artillery bombardments of World War I, which were purely destructive operations, and tilted them from an horizontal into a vertical position."[44]

Across the Atlantic, Brigadier-General William Mitchell donned the air crusader's surcoat, becoming the spokesman and idol of the American Army Air Service. An able and flamboyant regular officer who had risen to prominence in the Great War, Mitchell was a rebel and maverick by nature. One of his plans for 1919 proposed dropping a parachute division behind enemy lines. As a young major he had also met Trenchard, whom he admired greatly. Although Douhet probably influenced him indirectly, Mitchell differed from both men in arguing the case not just for strategic bombing but for a balanced centralized air force that could dominate surface warfare. He seriously believed that armies were in a state of arrested development and navies in a period of rapid decline. When Mitchell returned from Europe he energetically campaigned for an independent air force using his considerable flair for publicity. As an extraordinarily vocal propagandist for air power, he produced a steady stream of largely polemical testimony, articles, and books on the subject. In 1921, in what seemed more a publicity stunt than scientific experiment, his bombers sank an anchored German prize ship, the dreadnought *Ostfriesland*, a feat that gained the attention of Trenchard and Douhet. What he and his crusaders really aimed to show, however, was that land-based air power could replace the navy altogether in coastal defense. In 1925 Mitchell issued an outrageously insubordinate press statement deliberately intended to provoke a court-martial; he was found guilty of discreditable service conduct and forced to resign. Mitchell's sensational trial and willing martyrdom nonetheless served to embed his ideas more deeply in the dogma of the air force faith. In 1946 Congress canonized him with a special medal.[45]

Obviously, there are many shades and hues of the cloth from which the military heretic is cut. It seems clear, however, that such an individual is invariably distinguished by his profound sense of vocation. Fuller and Richmond, especially, were above all officers deeply committed to the serious study of their profession. They developed reformist outlooks precisely because they had studied war in greater depth and breadth than their fellows, who even as a collectivity experienced difficulty in rationally refuting many of their arguments. Although Fuller and Richmond were both basically practical men who had fulfilled the demanding requirements of service life, they also manifested a rare capacity to think conceptually and to put their thoughts into words. In doing so they manifested perhaps the most enduring characteristic of the military heretic: that of demonstrating extraordinary competence and bequeathing lasting knowledge to the profession of arms. They not only preached but produced their own scriptures. Like the more pedestrian Mitchell, though in less sensationalist fashion, they also suffered service martyrdom. In the final analysis, they were not prepared to recant their beliefs in order to save their careers.

In contrast, the writings of Mahan and Douhet were embraced so quickly and enthusiastically in certain quarters as to elevate their authors to sainthood and their doctrines to dogma. Liddell Hart and Corbett, on the other hand, were civilian students of war who attempted to reform the service establishment from outside as well as from within. Though not military heretics in the mold of Fuller and Richmond, they probably came closer to the mark than those serving professionals who either vacuously jumped through career hoops or cunningly maneuvered to advance their personal promotion prospects. This is not to suggest that there were not principled regular officers who thought long and hard about the profession of arms. As Brian Bond and John Winton have both shown, many senior British officers of more orthodox stamp possessed a reasonable understanding of the shortcomings of their respective services and actively worked toward their resolution with varying degrees of success.[46] The charge most often leveled against Liddell Hart and Fuller is that they failed to take sufficient account of financial, industrial, and practical technological constraints in the formulation of their theories. In their defense, it can be countered that too much attention paid to peacetime realities would have perpetuated bureaucratic inertia at the expense of progressive military thought and conceptualization.

The value of the uniformed heretic is that he ensures the existence of that dialectic so critical to the continued advancement of learning and professional progression of the service. By challenging fundamental assumptions and proposing alternative solutions, even to the extreme, he can actively promote serious military thought through productive debate and shake those servicemen who are more principled than careerist out of their complacency. That military service can legally oblige its members to place themselves in harm's way, of course, underscores the need for an authoritarianism that places a premium on obedience and discipline.[47] The natural tendency of such a system is nonetheless to proliferate mindless bureaucracy that, especially in peacetime, often spouts a party line and breeds apathy of the rankest kind. The suggestion that juniors ought to disguise their intelligence until they become more senior is but a pernicious manifestation of this malaise. Presumably, the opposite practice of the German general staff in engaging youthful brilliance at the earliest opportunity reflects the assumption that clever ideas are not in themselves deleterious to professional military establishments.

The harsh reality nonetheless remains: no military force or general staff is ever entirely immune from mental atrophy and professional stagnation. For this reason, a definite requirement for uniformed critics daring enough to question military policies and offer fresh approaches within defense establishments continues to exist. This is a role that cannot be fulfilled by outsiders. As Fuller's biographer wisely stated, without "continuing and informed debate within the Services themselves about the development of tactics and strategy and technological advances . . . [they] shall have no influence at all . . . in the development of defence policy."[48] If the military profession "is to avoid enslavement to unreasoning orthodoxy," observed the late great Canadian naval historian, Barry D. Hunt, "the vital role of 'heretics' in preserving any community from 'mental crystallization'" has to be appreciated. For his own service with and on behalf of the Canadian Forces, which he so personally enriched, Hunt fully perceived the essential truth of Admiral Richmond's assertion: "that it is they that keep a service alive in peace, that every innovator is an innovator because he has given thought to his subject and nourished it with discussion, and that every great captain in war has owed his success to the fact that he was an innovator to whom tradition was a valuable servant, not a tyrannical master."⁴⁹

NOTES

1. Arthur O'Shaughnessy, "The Music-makers," *Other Men's Flowers,* ed. A. P. Wavell (New York, 1945), 40.
2. *The Oxford Book of Quotations* (London, 1966), 181.
3. According to Colonel Harry G. Summers, when the Albigensian heresy was crushed in 1250, the military commander asked the bishop, "How do you tell the heretics from the true believers?" The response was, "Kill them all! God will know his own." See his *On Strategy II: A Critical Analysis of the Gulf War* (New York, 1992), 67.
4. According to Field Marshal Erich von Manstein, "the German Army would not have had the Panzer arm without the perseverance and the striving temperament of Guderian"; Robert J. O'Neill, "Doctrine and Training in the German Army 1919–1939," *The Theory and Practice of War,* ed. Michael Howard (Bloomington, IN, 1975). Major-General F. W. von Mellenthin likewise calls Guderian the "creator of th[e] Panzer force" in his *German Generals of World War II: As I Saw Them* (Norman, OK, 1977), 86. On T. E. Lawrence's heresy, see his brilliant Chapter XXXIII in *Seven Pillars of Wisdom* (London, 1940), 193–202; and John A. English, "Kindergarten Soldier: The Military Thought of Lawrence of Arabia," *Military Affairs,* 1 (1987), 7–11.
5. On Charles de Gaulle, see Brian Bond and Martin Alexander, "Liddell Hart and De Gaulle: The Doctrines of Limited Liability and Mobile Defense," Peter Paret, ed., *Makers of Modern Strategy: From Machiavelli to the Nuclear Age* (Princeton, NJ, 1986), 598–623. De Gaulle advocated a mechanized professional army of long-term career specialists. His book *Vers l'Armée de métier* (Paris, 1934) was long on history and politics, but offered few specifics on military theory and practice. Alistair Horne, *To Lose a Battle: France 1940* (London, 1979), 101–4. Orde Wingate, an ardent Zionist, believed in the efficacy of guerrilla-style long-range penetration groups as opposed to conventional fighting methods. His personal and intellectual influence on the fledgling Israeli army was profound. Major Evans F. Carlson spent six months with the Communist Chinese army in North China in 1937 and was most responsible for implanting its unique "fire team" concept of basic infantry organization within the United States Marine Corps. See John A. English, *On Infantry* (New York, 1984), 164–65, 180, 188–89, 208; and John Masters, *The Road Past Mandalay* (New York, 1979), 159–66.
6. Peter Paret, *Clausewitz and the State: The Man, His Theories, and His Times* (Princeton, 1985), 68–71, 125, 137–46, 287–88; Gordon A. Craig, *The Politics of the Prussian Army 1640–1945* (London, 1955), 45, 63, 78–79, 193–95; Hajo Holborn, "The Prusso-German School: Moltke and the Rise of the General Staff," and Gunther E. Rothenberg, "Moltke, Schlieffen, and the Doctrine of Strategic Envelopment," in Paret, *Makers of Modern Strategy,* 281–325; Masters, *Mandalay,* 87–88; see also "The Staff Caste" in John A. English, *The Canadian Army and the Normandy Campaign: A Study of Failure in High Command* (New York, 1991), 89–106 and Colonel T. N. Dupuy, *A Genius for War: The German Army and the General Staff, 1807–1945* (London, 1977).

7. Theodore Ropp, *War in the Modern World* (New York, 1962), 155–58; Holborn, "Prusso-German School," 291; and Michael Howard, *The Franco-Prussian War: The German Invasion of France, 1870–1871* (London, 1981), 23–29. Every general staff officer had to be able, at any time, to take over the work of another and apply to it the same body of basic ideas and principles of operational and tactical thought. Oberst i. G. Christian O. E. Millotat, *Understanding the Prussian-German General Staff System* (Carlisle, PA, 1992), 37. An example of early Prussian doctrine that remains with us today is the tenet, probably first advocated by General Gustav von Hindersin, that artillery formations should never be held in reserve since the weapon of artillery is the shell not the gun, and the artillery's reserve is therefore in its ammunition. Dupuy, *Genius*, 90.

8. Millotat, *General Staff System*, 1, 27–31, 41–43; and William H. McNeill, *The Pursuit of Power* (Chicago, 1982), 218, 248–49. In 1938 it was decreed that the commander alone was responsible externally and internally, but that the general staff officer remained accountable for the relevance of his advice, which he was to offer as if he were jointly rather then just internally responsible himself; see Millotat, 46.

9. Millotat, *General Staff System*, 19–21, 23, 43, 46, 59–60; Major-General J. F. C. Fuller, *The Conduct of War 1789–1961* (London: 1979), 159; Ropp, *War*, 241; and Craig, *Prussian Army*, 301. The younger German general staff officer seems also to have retained the respect of the ordinary *frontschwein*, whereas those wearing the red-tabs of the British general staff appear to have had the same effect upon front-line soldiers as a red flag before a bull; see English, *Normandy*, 93.

10. Timothy T. Lupfer, *The Dynamics of Doctrine: The Changes in German Tactical Doctrine during the First World War* (Fort Leavenworth, KS, 1981), 7–35, 41–58. Captain Hermann Geyer, one of about a dozen general staff officers of the Army High Command operations section responsible for the Western Front, went on to become a lieutenant-general in World War II, but he exercised more influence in the Great War as an author of doctrine; Ibid., 57.

11. See also Michael Geyer, "German Strategy in the Age of Machine Warfare, 1914–1945," Paret, *Makers of Modern Strategy*, 527–97. Geyer argues that when Ludendorff "combined function with efficiency instead of hierarchy" and when "captain's wrote manuals for generals," they effected a "transition to a military-machine culture." In his view, "the displacement of the well-tried hierarchical control of men over men in favour of a functional organization of violence" produced a new paradigm in which "the optimal use of weapons alone shaped command and deployment. The use of weapons even organized the coordination and cooperation among units." Geyer further speculates that the Allies "resisted the development of new forms of tactics and organization of forces," and that the British in particular "used technological innovation, tank warfare, in order to bypass a reform of the structure . . . of fighting forces and to preserve the existing hierarchies within the army"; Ibid., 541–43. More detailed studies, and different views, are contained in two excellent works: Bill Rawling, *Surviving Trench Warfare: Technology and the Canadian Corps, 1914–1918* (Toronto, 1992); and Bruce I. Gudmundsson, *Stormtrooper Tactics: Innovation in the German Army, 1914–1918* (New York, 1989).

12. Shelford Bidwell and Dominick Graham, *Fire-Power: British Army Weapons and Theóries of War 1904–1945* (London, 1982), 15–16; Lupfer, *Dynamics of Doctrine*, 56–58; Gudmundsson, *Stormtrooper Tactics*, 173; and T. H. E. Travers, *The Killing*

Ground: The British Army, the Western Front and the Emergence of Modern Warfare 1900-1918 (London, 1987), 254-56.

13. Bidwell and Graham, *Fire-Power*, 1-3, 14-19; and Travers, *Killing Ground*, 43, 54, 66-67, 254-55.

14. Travers, *Killing Ground*, 86, 96-97, 102-6, 255. During the last "Hundred Days" of the Great War, the armies of the British Empire made spectacular advances against the Germans employing tanks, artillery, infantry, engineers, and airplanes in highly sophisticated combination. See Rawling, *Trench Warfare*, 188-215.

15. Major-General J. F. C. Fuller, *Memoirs of an Unconventional Soldier* (London, 1936), 434; and English, *Normandy*, 91-92.

16. Anthony John Trythall, *"Boney" Fuller: Soldier, Strategist, and Writer* (New Brunswick, NJ, 1977), 1, 5-23, 95.

17. Brian Holden Reid, *J. F. C. Fuller: Military Thinker* (London, 1987), 10-12.

18. Trythall, *Fuller*, 23, 29-31, 132; and Reid, *Fuller*, 2, 16, 19, 26-28.

19. John I. Alger, *The Quest for Victory: The History of the Principles of War* (Westport, CT, 1982), 105-6, 113-15, 135, 145, 187, 190; and Reid, *Fuller*, 27-28.

20. McNeill, *Power*, 334; Trythall, *Fuller*, 35-75; and Reid, *Fuller*, 31, 48-56.

21. Trythall, *Fuller*, 86-91; and Reid, *Fuller*, 58, 64-65, 223. Fuller's article was entitled, "The Application of Recent Developments in Mechanics and Other Scientific Knowledge to Preparation and Training for Future War on Land." Much to the disgust of the Admiralty, Fuller also won the Royal United Service Institution (RUSI) Naval Gold Medal Prize Essay for 1921. On the discovery that the author of the anonymous entry was a soldier (and perhaps Fuller), the medal was not awarded.

22. Trythall, *Fuller*, 75, 105-6, 116. Fuller described Cavan as "a little rabbit of a man . . . only 800 years out of date"; see Reid, *Fuller*, 88, 182.

23. Trythall, *Fuller*, 120-30, 134-43; and Bidwell and Graham, *Fire-Power*, 168.

24. Trythall, *Fuller*, 141, 145; Reid, *Fuller*, 82, 151. The brigade was withdrawn within two months.

25. Trythall, *Fuller*, 162.

26. Trythall, *Fuller*, 165, 175, 177, 178, 203, 209-11, 243, 268; Reid, *Fuller*, 87, 96, 123-25, 126-27, 175; and Steve E. Dietrich, "The Professional Reading of General George S. Patton, Jr.," *Journal of Military History*, 1 (1989), 400.

27. Trythall, *Fuller*, 179.

28. Reid, *Fuller*, 175.

29. Trythall, *Fuller*, 75, 98, 107, 178; and Reid, *Fuller*, 3, 16, 29, 152, 175. In 1929, Fuller wrote to Liddell Hart: "Ridicule is . . . the only weapon, for reason is impotent against the bastioned ignorance and stupidity of our army—'muddleization' in place of 'modernization' is the order of the day"; from Reid, *Fuller*, 152.

30. Trythall, *Fuller*, 169; Reid, *Fuller*, 3, 150, 152, 225.

31. Brian Bond, *Liddell Hart: A Study of His Military Thought* (London, 1977), 9, 16-22, 27, 38-59, 61, 65-115, 119-59; Robert H. Berlin and Christopher R. Gabel, eds., "The Fuller-Liddell Hart Lecture: A Dialogue Held at the RUSI on 12 October 1978 between Brigadier A. J. Trythall, MA, and Mr. Brian Bond MA, FRHistS," *Modern Military Thought* (Fort Leavenworth, KS, 1980), 243-46; Michael Howard, "Liddell Hart," *Encounter*, 6 (June, 1970), 37-41; Jay Luvaas, *The Education of an Army: British Military Thought, 1815-1940* (Chicago, 1964), 376-424; and Bond and Alexander, "Liddell Hart and De Gaulle," 598-623.

32. Ibid.

33. Barry D. Hunt, *Sailor-Scholar: Admiral Sir Herbert Richmond 1871–1946* (Waterloo, Ontario, 1982), 2. Richmond authored nine books, among them *Statesmen and Sea Power* (Oxford, 1946) and *The Navy as an Instrument of Policy* (Cambridge, 1953), both of which are still studied today.

34. Hunt, *Sailor-Scholar*, 1, 25, 28, 100, 149; and D. M. Schurman, *The Education of a Navy: The Development of British Naval Strategic Thought, 1867–1914* (Chicago, 1965), 112–15.

35. Hunt, *Sailor-Scholar*, 3, 19, 51, 93–94; and Schurman, *Education*, 122, 125.

36. Hunt, *Sailor-Scholar*, 69.

37. Hunt, *Sailor-Scholar*, 58, 190–94; and Barry D. Hunt, "The Outstanding Naval Strategic Writers of the Century," *Naval War College Review*, 5 (1984), 95–96.

38. D. M. Schurman, *Julian S. Corbett: Historian of British Maritime Policy from Drake to Jellicoe* (London, 1981), 22, 53–56; Lt. Col. Ky L. Thompson, "Theory before Praxis: Sir Julian Corbett and The Maritime Strategy," *Marine Corps Gazette*, 12 (December, 1988), 73–78; Hunt, "Writers," 89–91, 96; and Schurman, *Education*, 156, 160, 165, 187–88.

39. Schurman, *Education*, 188; and his "Mahan Revisited," *Sartryck ur Kungl Krigsvetenskapsakademiens Bihafte—Militarhistorisk Tidskrift* (1982), 40–41; Hunt, "Writers," 89–91; and Philip A. Crowl, "Aldred Thayer Mahan: The Naval Historian," *Makers of Modern Strategy*, 455–61.

40. D. M. Schurman, *Corbett*, 45, 58, 168–69; and Schurman, *Education*, 150, 183; Larry H. Addington, *The Patterns of War since the Eighteenth Century* (Bloomington, IN, 1984), 103–6; Hunt, "Writers," 87, 92; and Ropp, *War*, 208–10.

41. Crowl, "Mahan," 447–49, 471–74; Commander Michael T. Corgan, "Mahan and Theodore Roosevelt: The Assessment of Influence," *Naval War College Review*, 6 (1980), 89–93; Schurman, "Mahan Revisited," 34; and Hunt, "Writers," 88. Mahan's reputation rests on two "Influence" books; the second, *The Influence of Sea Power upon the French Revolution and Empire, 1793–1812*, was published in 1892.

42. Hunt, *Sailor-Scholar*, 160–61.

43. Giulio Douhet, *Command of the Air*, trans. Dino Ferrari (New York, 1942), 3–92; Ropp, *War*, 248, 292–93; David MacIsaac, "Voices from the Central Blue: The Air Power Theorists," Paret, *Makers of Modern Strategy*, 629–30; J. F. C. Fuller, *The Conduct of War* (London, 1979), 240–42; Walter Millis, *Arms and Men* (New York, 1956), 227; Bernard Brodie, *Strategy in the Missile Age* (Princeton, 1971), 71–101. The British War Cabinet and public were badly scared by German bomber raids in 1917. Sydney Wise, "The Royal Air Force and the Origins of Strategic Bombing," *Men at War: Politics, Technology and Innovation in the Twentieth Century*, eds. T. H. E. Travers and Christon I. Archer (Chicago, 1982), 149–172. Teachings at the U.S. Air Corps Tactical School emphasized industrial warfare rather than breaking enemy morale; see Ropp, *War*, 309–10.

44. Fuller, *Conduct*, 240; and Ropp, *War*, 248, 294. See also Gavin Lyall, "Marshal of the Royal Air Force The Viscount Trenchard," in Field Marshal Sir Michael Carver, ed., *The War Lords* (Boston, 1976), 176–87.

45. Major Alfred F. Hurley, *Billy Mitchell: Crusader for Air Power* (New York, 1964), 25–36, 57–70, 75–79, 93–107, 116, 129, 139–40; Millis, *Arms and Men*, 224–32; Ropp, *War*, 279, 292; and Brodie, *Missile Age*, 71, 77, 107.

46. Bond, *Liddell-Hart*, 107, 113; and John Winton, *To Change an Army: General Sir John Burnett-Stuart and British Armoured Doctrine* (Lawrence, KS, 1988), 3–5, 166–67,

207–9, 232–38. Burnett-Stuart was instrumental in having Fuller nominated to command the Experimental Mechanized Force. In 1926 he wrote the War Office: "It is no use just handing it over to an ordinary Divisional Commander like myself. You must connect directly with it as many enthusiastic experts and visionaries as you can; it doesn't matter how wild their views are if only they have a touch of the divine fire"; in Winton, 76.

47. Winton, *Burnett-Stuart*, 7.
48. "The Fuller–Liddell Hart Lecture," 248, 251.
49. Hunt, "Writers," 105–6, 211.

Bibliography

"Able Generalship." *Army and Navy Gazette* 1 (11 July 1863).
Addington, Larry H. *The Patterns of War since the Eighteenth Century.* Bloomington: Indiana University Press, 1984.
Alamán, Lucas. *Historia de México desde los primeros movimientos que preparon su independencia en el año de 1808 hasta la época presente* IV. México: Imprenta de J. M. Lara, 1851.
Alfaro, Xavier Tavera. "Calleja, represor de la insurgencia." In *Repaso de la Independencia*, ed. Carlos Herrejón Peredo. Zamora: El Colegio de Michoacán, 1985.
Alger, John I. *The Quest for Victory: The History of the Principles of War.* Westport: Greenwood, 1982.
Allen, W. E. D., and Paul Muratov. *Caucasian Battlefields: A History of the Wars on the Turco-Caucasian Border 1828–1921.* Cambridge: Cambridge University Press, 1953.
Ambert, J. *Equisses historiques, psychologiques et critiques de l'Armée Françaises.* Saumur: Degouy, 1851, 18–37.
Anderson, Col. George S. "Practical Military Instruction." *Journal of the Military Service Institution of the United States* 47 (1910).
Anna, Timothy E. *The Fall of the Royal Government in Mexico City.* Lincoln: University of Nebraska Press, 1978.
"Answers to Correspondence." *Army and Navy Gazette* 1 (6 June 1863).
"Antietam Impressions." *Blue and Gray Magazine* 3 (November 1865).
Archer, Christon I. *The Army in Bourbon Mexico, 1760–1810.* Albuquerque: University of New Mexico Press, 1977.

———. "The Counterinsurgency Army and the Ten Year's War." In *The Independence of Mexico and the Creation of the New Nation*, ed. Jaime E. Rodríguez. Los Angeles: UCLA Latin American Center, 1989.

———. "The Royalist Army of New Spain: Militarism, Praetorianism, or Protection of Interests?" *Armed Forces and Society* 17:1 (Fall 1990).

"Army of the Potomac—General Hooker." In *Report of the Joint Committee on the Conduct of the War*. Washington, DC: 1865.

Asada Sadao. "Japanese Admirals and the Politics of Naval Limitation: Katō Tomosaburō vs. Katō Kanji." In *Naval Warfare in the Twentieth Century*, ed. Gerald Jordan. London: Croom Helm, 1977, 141–66.

———. "Japan's 'Special Interests' and the Washington Conference, 1921–22." *American Historical Review* 67 (1961), 62–70.

———. "Nihon kaigun to gunshuku: Tai-Bei seisaku o meguru seiji katei." In *Washinton taisei to Nichi-Bei kankei*, eds. Hosoya Chihiro and Saitō Makoto. Tokyo: Tokyo Daigaku Shuppankai, 1978.

Bailes, Howard. "Patterns of Thought in the Late Victorian Army." *Journal of Strategic Studies* 4 (1981).

"Ball's Bluff." In *The Rebellion Record*, Vol. III, ed. Frank Moore. New York: 1864.

Barak, Major-General Ehud. "In the Field He Was at Home." *Yediot Achronot* Special Supplement (22 September 1991).

Barker, A. J. *The Vainglorious War, 1854–56*. London: Weidenfeld and Nicolson, 1970.

Barnett, C. *The Desert Generals*, new ed. Bloomington: University of Indiana Press, 1982.

Barras, T. C. "Vice-Admiral Lord Nelson's Lost Eye." *Transactions of the Ophthalmological Societies of the United Kingdom* 105 (1986).

"Battles between Officers." *Army and Navy Journal* 1 (16 April 1864).

Beauregard, G. T. "The First Battle of Bull Run." In *Battles and Leaders of the Civil War*, Vol. I, eds. C. C. Buel and Robert U. Underwood. New York: Century Co., 1888.

Berghahn, Volker R. *Der Tirpitz-Plan. Genesis und Verfall einer innenpolitischen Krisenstrategie unter Wilhelm II*. Dusseldorf: Droste-Verlag, 1971.

———. "Zu den Zielen des deutschen Flottenbaus unter Wilhelm II." *Historische Zeitschrift* 210 (1970).

Berlin, Robert H., and Christopher R. Gabel, eds. "The Fuller–Liddell Hart Lecture: A Dialogue Held at the RUSI on 12 October 1978 between Brigadier A. J. Trythall, MA, and Mr. Brian Bond, MA, FRHistS." In *Modern Military Thought*. Fort Leavenworth: Combat Studies Institute, 1980.

Bernhardi, Friedrich von. *How Germany Makes War*. London: 1914.

Bialer, Uri. *The Shadow of the Bomber: The Fear of Air Attack and British Politics, 1932–1939*. London: Royal Historical Society, 1980.

Bidwell, Shelford. "Wingate and the Official Historians: An Alternative View." *Journal of Contemporary History* 15 (1980).

Bidwell, Shelford, and Dominick Graham. *Fire-Power: British Army Weapons and Theories of War 1904–1945*. London: Allen and Unwin, 1982.

Boguslawski, A. von. *Tactical Deductions from the War of 1870–71*, 3d ed. London: H. S. King, 1874.

Bond, Brian. *British Military Policy between the Two World Wars.* Oxford: Clarendon, 1980.
―――. *Liddell Hart: A Study of His Military Thought.* London: Cassell, 1977.
Borg, Dorothy, and Shumpei Okamoto, eds. *Pearl Harbor as History: Japanese American Relations, 1931-1941.* New York: Columbia University Press, 1973.
Boyle, Andrew. *Trenchard.* London: Collins, 1962.
Brett, M. V., and Viscount Esher. *Journals and Letters of Reginald, Viscount Esher.* Vol. I. London: Nicholson and Watson, 1934-1938.
Brodie, Bernard. *Sea Power in the Machine Age.* Princeton, NJ: Princeton University Press, 1941.
―――. *Strategy in the Missile Age.* Princeton: Princeton University Press, 1971.
Brusilov, A. A. *Mémoires du General Broussilov. Guerre 1914-1918.* Paris: Hachette, 1929.
―――. *Moi vospominaniia,* 6th ed. Moscow: Voenizdat, 1983.
―――. *A Soldier's Note-Book. 1914-1918.* London: Macmillan, 1930; reprinted Westport, CT: Greenwood, 1971.
Bulow, Bernhard von. *Denkwurdigkeiten,* Vol. I. Berlin: 1930.
Bustamante, Carlos María de. *Cuadro histórico de la revolución mexicana,* Vol. I. Mexico: 1961.
Capelluti, Frank J. *The Life and Thought of Giulio Douhet.* Ph.D. diss., Rutgers University, 1967.
Carell, P. *The Foxes of the Desert.* London: Macdonald, 1960.
Carrias, Eugene. *La pensée militaire française.* Paris: Presses Universitaires de France, 1960.
Carver, Field Marshal Sir Michael, ed. *The War Lords.* Boston: Little, Brown, 1976.
Cecil, Lamar. *Wilhelm II. Prince and Emperor, 1859-1900.* Chapel Hill and London: University of North Carolina Press, 1990.
"The Central Principle." *Army and Navy Gazette* 1 (4 April 1863).
Chester, Captain James. "Military Misconceptions and Absurdities." *Journal of the Military Service Institution of the United States* 14 (1893).
Clausewitz, Carl von. *On War,* Book 3, eds. and trans. Michael Howard and Peter Paret. Princeton: Princeton University Press, 1984.
Coffin, Charles Carleton. *The Boys of '61; or, Four Years of Fighting.* Boston: Estes and Laurent, 1881.
Colin, J. *The Transformations of War.* London: Rees, 1912.
Colville, J. R. *Wavell, Scholar and Soldier: To June 1941.* London: Collins, 1964.
―――. *Wavell, Supreme Commander, 1941-1943.* London: Collins, 1969.
"The Competency of Our Officers." *Army and Navy Journal* 1 (10 October 1863).
Cooper, Malcolm. *The Birth of Independent Air Power.* London: Allen and Unwin, 1986.
―――. "Blueprint for Confusion: The Administrative Background to the Formation of the Royal Air Force 1912-1919." *Journal of Contemporary History* 22 (1987).
―――. *The German Army, 1933-1945.* London: Macdonald and Jane's, 1978.
Coox, A. D. *Nomonhan. Japan against Russia, 1939.* Palo Alto, CA: Stanford University Press, 1985.

Corbett, Julian. *Some Principles of Maritime Strategy.* London: Longmans, Green, 1911.
Corgan, Commander Michael T. "Mahan and Theodore Roosevelt: The Assessment of Influence." *Naval War College Review* 6 (1980).
Cox, Jaffna L. "A Splendid Training Ground: The Importance to the Royal Air Force of Its Role in Iraq 1919–1932." *Journal of Commonwealth and Imperial History* 13 (1985).
Craig, Gordon A. *The Politics of the Prussian Army 1640–1945.* London: Oxford University Press, 1955.
Crefeld, Martin van. *Command in War.* Cambridge, MA: Harvard University Press, 1985.
———. *Supplying War: Logistics from Wallenstein to Patton.* Cambridge: Cambridge University Press, 1977.
Crowell, Lorenzo. "The Illusion of the Decisive Napoleonic Victory." *Defence Analysis* 4 (1988).
Crowley, James B. *Japan's Quest for Autonomy.* Princeton: Princeton University Press, 1966.
———. "A New Deal for Japan and Asia: One Road to Pearl Harbor." In *Modern East Asia: Essays in Interpretation,* ed. J. B. Crowley. New York: Harcourt, Brace & World, 1970.
Davis, Burke. *The Billy Mitchell Affair.* New York: Random House, 1967.
Dayan, Moshe. *Breakthrough: A Personal Account of the Egypt-Israel Peace Negotiation.* New York: Knopf, 1981.
———. *Diary of the Sinai Campaign.* New York: Shocken Books, 1967.
———. "Israel's Borders and Security Problems." *Foreign Affairs* 33 (1955).
———. *Living with the Bible.* Jerusalem: Edanim, 1978.
———. *Moshe Dayan: Story of My Life.* New York: William Morrow, 1976.
———. *Yoman Vietnam.* Tel Aviv: Dvir, 1977.
Dayan, Ruth, and Helga Dudman. *. . . Or Did I Dream and Dream.* Jerusalem: Steimazky's Agency with Weidenfeld and Nicolson, 1973.
Dayan, Yael. *My Father, His Daughter.* New York: Farrar, Straus and Giroux, 1985.
———. *The New Face in the Mirror.* London: Weidenfeld and Nicolson, 1959.
de Gaulle, Charles. *The Army of the Future.* London: Hutchinson, 1940.
———. *Vers l'Armée de métier.* Paris: Berger-Levrault, 1934.
Dean, Sir Maurice. *The Royal Air Force and Two World Wars.* London: Cassell, 1979.
Diest, Wilhelm. *The Wehrmacht and German Rearmament.* London: Macmillan, 1981.
Dietrich, Steve E. "The Professional Reading of General George S. Patton, Jr." *Journal of Military History* 1 (1989).
"Don Félix María Calleja del Rey: Actividades anteriores a la guerra de independence." *Boletín del Archivo General de La Nación,* Mexico, I (segunda serie, no. 1, 1960), 57–86; (no. 2), 253–97; and (no. 4), 553–81.
Doughty, Robert A. *The Seeds of Disaster: The Development of French Army Doctrine, 1919–1939.* Hamden, CT: Archon, 1985.
Douhet, Giulio. *Command of the Air,* trans. Dino Ferrari. New York: Coward-McCann, 1942.

Dupuy, Colonel T. N. *A Genius for War: The German Army and the General Staff, 1807–1945.* London: Macdonald and Jane's, 1977.
"The Education of Generals." *Army and Navy Journal* 1 (5 September 1863).
English, A. D. *The RAF Staff College and the Evolution of the RAF Strategic Bombing Policy, 1922–1929.* Master's thesis, Royal Military College of Canada, 1987.
English, John A. *The Canadian Army and the Normandy Campaign: A Study of Failure in High Command.* New York: Praeger, 1991.
———. "Kindergarten Soldier: The Military Thought of Lawrence of Arabia." *Military Affairs* 1 (1987).
———. *On Infantry.* New York: Praeger, 1984.
Erikson, Erik H. *Young Man Luther: A Study in Psychoanalysis and History.* New York: W. W. Norton, 1962.
Erikson, John. *The Soviet High Command.* London: Macmillan, 1962.
Falk, Avner. *Moshe Dayan: Ha'Ish Ve Ha'Agada.* Jerusalem: Cana, 1985.
———. "Moshe Dayan: The Infantile Roots of Political Action." *Journal of Psychohistory* 11 (1983).
———. "Moshe Dayan: Narcissism in Politics." *Jerusalem Quarterly* (Winter 1984).
Farwell, Byron. *The Great Anglo-Boer War.* New York: Harper and Row, 1976.
ffrench Blake, R. L. V. *The Crimean War.* London: Leo Cooper, 1971.
Fiske, Bradley. *From Midshipman to Rear-Admiral.* New York: Century, 1919.
Fitère, J. M. *Panzers en Afrique: Rommel et l'Afrikacorps.* Paris: Presses de la Cité, 1980.
Foerster, Stig. "Facing 'People's War': Moltke the Elder and German Military Options after 1871." *Journal of Strategic Studies* 10 (1987).
Freud, Sigmund, and William C. Bullitt. *Thomas Woodrow Wilson: A Psychoanalytical Biography.* Boston: Houghton Mifflin, 1967.
Fuller, J. F. C. *The Conduct of War 1789–1961.* London: Methuen, 1979.
———. *Memoirs of an Unconventional Soldier.* London: Ivor Nicholson and Watson, 1936.
Gat, Azar. *The Origins of Military Thought from the Enlightenment to Clausewitz.* Oxford: Clarendon, 1989.
Gavin, William Gilfillan, ed. *Infantryman Pettit: The Civil War Letters of Corporal Frederick Pettit.* New York: Avon Books, 1990.
Gazit, Shlomo. "He Made No Excuses." *Ma'ariv* Special Supplement (22 September 1991).
———. *Yediot Achronot* Special supplement (September 1991).
Gemzell, Carl-Axel. *Organization, Conflict, and Innovation: A Study of German Naval Strategic Planning, 1880–1940.* Lund: Esselte Studium, 1973.
George, Alexander L., and Juliette L. George. *Woodrow Wilson and Colonel House: A Personality Study.* New York: Dover, 1964.
Glatthaar, Joseph T. *Forged in Battle: The Civil War Alliance of Black Soldiers and White Officers.* New York: Free Press, 1990.
Golovin, N. N. "The Brusilov Offensive, 1916." *Slavonic and East European Review*, n.d.
Grant, Ulysses S. *The Personal Memoirs of Ulysses S. Grant.* New York: Charles L. Webster Co., 1885.
"Great Generals." *Army and Navy Gazette* 1 (4 April 1863).

Griffith, Paddy. *Military Thought in the French Army, 1815–51*. Manchester: Manchester University Press, 1989.
Gudmundsson, Bruce I. *Stormtrooper Tactics: Innovation in the German Army, 1914–1918*. New York: Praeger, 1989.
Hamegbi, Hayim. "Our Brother Moussa." *Hadashot* (17 September 1991).
Hamilton, C. E. "The Royal Navy, *la Royale*, and the Militarisation of Naval Warfare, 1840–1870." *Journal of Strategic Studies* 6 (1983).
Handel, Michael I. *Israel's Political-Military Doctrine*. Occasional Papers in International Affairs, No. 30. Cambridge, MA: Harvard Center for International Affairs, 1973.
———. *Masters of War: Sun Tzu, Clausewitz and Jomini*. London: Cass, 1992.
———. *Perception, Deception and Surprise: The Case of the Yom Kippur War*. Jerusalem: Jerusalem Papers on Peace Problems, No. 19, 1976.
———. *War, Strategy and Intelligence*. London: Cass, 1988.
Harris, J. P. "British Armour and Rearmament in the 1930s." *Journal of Strategic Studies* 11 (1988).
———. "The British General Staff and the Coming of the War, 1933–1939." *Bulletin of the Institute of Historical Research* 59 (1986).
Hassell, Ulrich von. *Tirpitz. Sein Leben und sein Wirken mit Berucksichtigung seiner Beziehungen zu Albrecht von Stosch*. Stuttgart: 1920.
Hastings, Max. *Bomber Command*. New York: Dial Press, 1979.
Hattendorf, John B., and Lynn C. Hattendorf, eds. *A Bibliography of the Works of Alfred Thayer Mahan*. Newport, RI: Naval War College, 1986.
Hattendorff, John B., and R. Jordan, eds. *Maritime Strategy and the Balance of Power: Britain and America in the Twentieth Century*. New York: St. Martin's Press, 1989.
Heckmann, W. *Rommels Krieg in Afrika*. Garden City, NY: Doubleday, 1981.
Herwig, Holger H. "The Failure of German Sea Power, 1914–1945: Mahan, Tirpitz, and Raeder Reconsidered." *International History Review* 10 (1988).
———. *Luxury Fleet: The Imperial German Navy 1888–1918*. London, Boston, and Sydney: George Allen & Unwin, 1980.
Higginson, Thomas W. "Regular and Volunteer Officers." *Atlantic Monthly* 14 (September 1864).
Higham, R. *Air Power: A Concise History*, rev. ed. Manhattan KS: Sunflower University Press, 1984.
Hoffsommer, Robert, ed. "The Rise and Survival of Private Mesnard." *Civil War Times Illustrated* 24 (January 1986).
Hohenlohe-Ingelfingen, Kraft Carl zu. *Letters of Infantry*. London: E. Stanford, 1889.
Holmes, Richard. *The Road to Sedan: The French Army, 1866–70*. London: Royal Historical Society, 1984.
Horne, Alistair. *To Lose a Battle: France 1940*. London: Penguin, 1979.
Howard, Michael. *The Franco-Prussian War: The German Invasion of France, 1870–1871*. London: Methuen, 1981.
———. "Liddell Hart." *Encounter* 6 (June 1970).
———, ed. *The Theory and Practice of War*. Bloomington: Indiana University Press, 1975.
Howe, M. A. DeWolfe, ed. *The Home Letters of General Sherman*. New York: Scribner's Sons, 1905.

Hunt, Barry D. "The Outstanding Naval Strategic Writers of the Century." *Naval War College Review* 5 (1984).
———. *Sailor-Scholar: Admiral Sir Herbert Richmond 1871–1946*. Waterloo, Ontario: Wilfrid Laurier University Press, 1982.
Huntington, Samuel P. *The Soldier and the State*. Cambridge, MA: Harvard University Press, 1956.
Hurley, Major Alfred F. *Billy Mitchell: Crusader for Air Power*. New York: Franklin Watts, 1964; Bloomington: University of Indiana Press, 1975.
Hyde, H. M. *British Air Policy between the Wars, 1918–1939*. London: Heinemann, 1976.
Ikeda Kiyoshi. *Kaigun to Nihon*. Tokyo: Chūōkōronsha, 1981.
———. "Rondon kaigun jōyaku hiroku: Ko kaigun taishō Katō Kanji ikō, Showa 13-nen." *Hōgaku zasshi* 16 (1969), 123–42.
———. "Rondon kaigun jōyaku to tōsuiken mondai." *Hōgaku zasshi* 15 (1968).
Irvine, D. D. "The Origin of Capital Staffs." *Journal of Modern History* 10 (1938).
Janis, Irving L. *Victims of Groupthink*. Boston: Houghton Mifflin, 1972.
Japan. Gaimusho [Foreign Office]. *Nihon gaikō bunsho: Junevu kaigun gunbi seigen kaigi*. Tokyo: 1982.
———. *Nihon gaikō bunsho: Rondon kaigun kaigi, yobi kōshō, jōyaku setsumeisho*. Tokyo: 1982.
———. *Nihon gaikō bunsho: Washinton kaigi*, 2 vols. Tokyo: 1977–1978.
———. *Nihon gaikō bunsho: Washinton kaigi, Gunbi seigen mondai*. Tokyo: 1974.
Jomini, Baron. *The Art of War*, trans. Capt. G. H. Mendell and Lt. W. P. Craighill. Philadelphia: J. B. Lippincott, 1862.
Jones, Neville. *The Origins of Strategic Bombing: A Study of the Development of British Air Strategic Thought and Practice up to 1918*. London: Kimber, 1973.
Karpin, Michael. "Longing for Moshe Dayan." *Davar Ha'Shavua* (7 September 1991).
Kennedy, Paul M. "The Development of German Naval Operations against Britain, 1896–1914." *English Historical Review* 89 (1974).
———. "German World Policy and the Alliance Negotiations with England." *Journal of Modern History* 40 (1973).
———. *The Rise of Anglo-German Antagonism. 1860–1914*. London, Boston, and Sydney: Allen and Unwin, 1980.
———. "Strategic Aspects of the Anglo-German Naval Race." In *Strategy and Diplomacy 1870–1945. Eight Studies*, ed. Paul M. Kennedy. London: Fontana Paperbacks, 1984.
———. "Tirpitz, England and the Second Navy Law of 1900: A Strategical Critique." *Militargeschichtliche Mitteilungen* 2 (1970).
Knorr, Klaus, and Patrick Morgan, eds. *Strategic Military Surprise: Incentives and Opportunities*. New Brunswick, NJ: Transaction Books, 1983.
Knox, General Alfred W. F. *With the Russian Army, 1914–1917*, Vol. II. London: Hutchinson, 1921.
Lambi, Ivo Nikolai. *The Navy and German Power Politics, 1862–1914*. Boston, London, and Sydney: Allen and Unwin, 1984.
Lautenschlager, Karl. "Technology and the Evolution of Naval Warfare." *International Security* 8 (1983).

Lawrence, T. E. *Seven Pillars of Wisdom*. London: Jonathan Cape, 1940.
LeMay, Curtis, with Mackinlay Kantor. *Mission with LeMay: My Story*. New York: Doubleday, 1965.
Lemoine Villicaña, Ernesto. *Morelos: su vida revolucionaria a travós de sus escritos y de otros testimonios de la época*. Mexico: UNAM, 1965.
Levitskii, A. "General Brusilov." *Voennaia by'*, No. 89 (January 1968).
Liddell Hart, B. H. *The Ghost of Napoleon*. London: Faber, 1933.
Lieven, Dominic. *Russia's Rulers under the Old Regime*. New Haven, CT: Yale University Press, 1989.
Linderman, Gerald F. *Embattled Courage: The Experience of Combat in the American Civil War*. New York: Free Press, 1987.
Lupfer, Timothy T. *The Dynamics of Doctrine: The Changes in German Tactical Doctrine during the First World War*. Fort Leavenworth, KS: Combat Studies Institute, 1981.
Luvaas, Jay. *The Education of an Army: British Military Thought, 1815–1940*. Chicago: Chicago University Press, 1964.
———. "European Military Thought and Doctrine, 1870–1914." In *The Theory and Practice of War*, ed. M. E. Howard. Bloomington: Indiana University Press, 1975.
Lyman, Theodore. *Meade's Headquarters, 1863–1865: Letters of Colonel Theodore Lyman*, ed. by George R. Agassiz. Boston: Atlantic Monthly Press, 1922.
Mack, John E. *A Prince of Our Disorder: The Life of T. E. Lawrence*. Boston: Little Brown, 1976.
Mahan, Alfred Thayer. *The Influence of Sea Power upon History 1660–1783*. London: Methuen University Paperpacks, n.d.
———. *Retrospect and Prospect: Studies in International Relations Naval and Political*. London: S. Low, 1902.
Marder, A. J. *From Dreadnought to Scapa Flow*, Vol. I. Oxford: Oxford University Press, 1961.
Masters, John. *The Road Past Mandalay*. New York: Bantam, 1979.
Mazzetti, Massimo. *La politica militare italiana fra le due guerre mondiali (1918–1940)*. Rome: 1982.
McNeill, William H. *The Pursuit of Power*. Chicago: University Press, 1982.
Mead, Peter. "Orde Wingate and the Official Historians." *Journal of Contemporary History* 14 (1979).
Mead, Peter, and Shelford Bidwell. "Orde Wingate: Two Views." *Journal of Contemporary History* 15 (1980).
Meade, George, Jr., ed. *The Life and Letters of George Gordon Meade*. New York: Scribner's Sons, 1913.
Mearsheimer, John. *Liddell Hart and the Weight of History*. Ithaca, NY: Cornell University Press, 1988.
Mellenthin, Major-General F. W. von. *German Generals of World War II: As I Saw Them*. Norman: University of Oklahoma Press, 1977.
Menning, Bruce W. "Deep Strike in Russian and Soviet Military History." *Journal of Soviet Military Studies* 1 (1988).
Merlier, M. G. "De Grandmaison—penseur et écrivain militaire." *Actes du quatre-vingt-septième congrés national des savantes: Poitiers 1962*. Paris: Congrés national des savantes, 1963.

BIBLIOGRAPHY

Michie, Peter Smith, ed. *The Life and Letters of Emory Upton.* New York: D. Appleton & Co., 1885.
Millett, A., and W. Murray, eds. *Military Effectiveness*, Vol. I. Boston: Allen and Unwin, 1988.
Millis, Walter. *Arms and Men.* New York: Mentor, 1956.
Millotat, Oberst i. G. Christian O. E. *Understanding the Prussian-German General Staff System.* Carlisle, PA: U.S. Army War College Strategic Studies Institute, 1992.
Mitcham, S. W. *Rommel's Last Battle: The Desert Fox and the Normandy Campaign.* New York: Stein and Day, 1983.
———. *Triumphant Fox: Erwin Rommel and the Rise of the Afrikakorps.* New York: Stein and Day, 1984.
More, Hadassa. *Derakhim Lohatot.* Tel Aviv: Kotz, 1963.
Morimatsu Toshio. *Dai Honnei.* Tokyo: Kyōikusha, 1980.
Morley, James W. *Japan Erupts: The London Naval Conference and the Manchurian Incident 1928–1932.* New York: Columbia University Press, 1984.
Morrison, James L., Jr. *"The Best School in the World": West Point, the Pre-Civil War Years, 1833–1866.* Kent, OH: Kent State University Press, 1986.
Murray, Penelope, ed. *Genius: The History of an Idea.* New York: Basil Blackwell, Inc., 1989.
Murray, Williamson. *Strategy for Defeat: The Luftwaffe, 1933–1945.* Maxwell, AL: Air University Press, 1983.
Mysyrowicz, L. *Autopsie d'une défaite: Origines de l'effondrement militaire française de 1940.* Lausanne: L'Age d'Homme, 1973.
Nevins, Allan, ed. *A Diary of Battle: The Personal Journals of Colonel Charles S. Wainwright, 1861–1865.* New York: Harcourt, Brace & World, 1962.
Nihon Kokusai Seiji Gakkai, Taiheiyō Sensō Gen'in Kenkyūbu, ed. *Taiheiyō sensō e no michi*, 7 vols., 1 supp. Tokyo: Asahi Shimbunsha, 1962–1963.
Nish, Ian H. *Alliance in Decline: A Study in Anglo-Japanese Relations 1908–1923.* London: Athlone Press, 1972.
———. *Japanese Foreign Policy, 1869–1942: Kasumigaseki to Miyakezaka.* London: Routledge & Kegan Paul, 1977.
Nomura Minoru. *Rekishi no naka no Nihon kaigun.* Tokyo: Hara Shobo, 1980.
Nuñez y Domínguez, José de J. *La virreina mexicana: Doña María Francisca de la Gándara de Calleja.* Mexico: Imprenta Universitaria, 1950.
O'Neill, Robert J. "Doctrine and Training in the German Army 1919–1939." In *The Theory and Practice of War*, ed. Michael Howard, Bloomington: Indiana University Press, 1975.
O'Shaughnessy, Arthur. "The Music-makers." In *Other Men's Flowers*, ed. A. P. Wavell. New York: G. P. Putnam's Sons, 1945.
Ostrovskii, B. *Admiral Makarov, 1848–1904.* Leningrad: `Molodaia gvardiia, 1951.
"Our Military Past and Future." *Atlantic Monthly* 44 (November 1879).
Pail, Meir. "The Most Successful Chief of Staff until Today." *Ma'ariv* Special Supplement (22 September 1991).
Pakenham, T. *The Boer War.* London: Weidenfeld and Nicolson, 1979.
Palmer, Bruce. *The 25-Year War: America's Military Role in Vietnam.* Lexington: University of Kentucky Press, 1978.

Paret, Peter. *Clausewitz and the State: The Man, His Theories, and His Times.* Princeton: Princeton University Press, 1985.

———, ed. *Makers of Modern Strategy from Machiavelli to the Nuclear Age.* Princeton: Princeton University Press, 1986.

Patterson, A. T., ed. *The Jellicoe Papers,* Vol. I. London: Navy Records Society, 1966.

Peden, George. *British Rearmament and the Treasury.* Edinburgh: Scottish Academic Press, 1979.

Pelz, Stephen E. *Race to Pearl Harbor: The Failure of the Second London Naval Conference and the Onset of World War II.* Cambridge, MA: Harvard University Press, 1974.

Polastro, Walter. "La marina militare italiana nel primo dopoguerra (1918–1925)." *Il Risorgimento,* Pt. 3 (1977).

"Political Attacks on West Point." *Blue and Gray Magazine* 9 (December 1861).

"Popular Appreciation of Military Education." *Army and Navy Gazette* 1 (21 November 1863).

Porch, Douglas. *The March to the Marne: The French Army, 1871–1914* (Cambridge: Cambridge University Press, 1981).

Powers, Barry. *Strategy Without Slide-Rule: British Air Strategy, 1914–1939.* London: Croom Helm, 1976.

Raleigh, Sir Walter, and H. A. Jones. *The War in the Air,* 6 vols. Oxford: Clarendon Press, 1922–1937.

Ranft, B., ed. *The Beatty Papers,* Vol. I. London: Navy Records Society, 1989.

Rapoport, Vitaly, and Yuri Alexeev, eds. *High Treason: Essays on the History of the Red Army, 1918–1939.* Durham, NC: Duke University Press, 1985.

Rawling, Bill. *Surviving Trench Warfare: Technology and the Canadian Corps, 1914–1918.* Toronto: University Press, 1992.

Reardon, Carol. *Soldiers and Scholars: The U.S. Army and the Study of Military History, 1865–1920.* Lawrence: University Press of Kansas, 1990.

Reid, Brian Holden. *J. F. C. Fuller: Military Thinker.* London: Macmillan, 1987.

"The Removal of Generals." *Army and Navy Journal* 1 (28 May 1864).

Report of the Joint Committee on the Conduct of the War. Washington: Government Printing Office, 1865.

Richmond, Herbert. *The Navy as an Instrument of Policy.* Cambridge: Cambridge University Press, 1953.

———. *Statesmen and Sea Power.* Oxford: Clarendon, 1946.

Robertson, James I., ed. *The Civil War Letters of General Robert McAllister.* New Brunswick, NJ: Rutgers University Press, 1965.

Rohl, J. C. G. "Admiral Muller and the Approach to War, 1911–14," *Historical Journal* 123, no. 4 (1969).

Rom, Sharit. "The Organ of the State." *Hadashot* Special Yom Kippur Supplement (17 September 1991).

Ropp, Theodore. *War in the Modern World.* New York: Collier, 1962.

Rostunov, I. I. *General Brusilov.* Moscow: Voenizdat, 1964.

Salewski, Michael. *Tirpitz Aufstieg—Macht—Scheitern.* Gottingen, Zurich, Frankfurt: 1979.

Samuels, Martin. *Command or Control? Command, Training and Tactics in the German and British Armies, 1864-1918.* Ph.D. Diss., Manchester University, 1992.

Saundby, Air Marshal Sir Robert. *Air Bombardment: The Story of Its Development.* London: Chatto and Windus, 1961.

Saward, Dudley. *Bomber Harris: The Story of Marshal of the Royal Air Force, Sir Arthur Harris.* London: Cassells, 1984.

Schafer, Joseph, ed. and trans. *The Intimate Letters of Carl Schurz, 1841-1869.* Madison: State Historical Society of Wisconsin, 1928.

Schifman, Alex. "Missing the Commander." *Hadashot* Special Yom Kippur Supplement (September 1991).

Schofield, John M. *Forty-Six Years in the Army.* New York: Century Company, 1897.

Schottelius, Herbert, and Wilhelm Diest, eds. *Marine und Marinepolitik im Kaiserlichen Deutschland 1871-1914.* Dusseldorf: Drost Verlag, 1972.

Schurman, D. M. *The Education of a Navy: The Development of British Naval Strategic Thought, 1867-1914.* Chicago: Chicago University Press, 1965.

———. *Julian S. Corbett, 1854-1922: Historian of British Maritime Policy from Drake to Jellicoe.* London: Royal Historical Society, 1981.

———. "Mahan Revisited." *Sartryck ur Kungl Krigsvetenskapsakademiens Bihafte—Militarhistorisk Tidskrift* (1982).

Sears, Stephen W. *George B. McClellan: The Young Napoleon.* New York: Ticknor & Fields, 1988.

Semanov, Sergei. *General Brusilov. Documental'Noel povestovanie.* Moscow: Voenizdat, 1986.

———. *Makarov.* Moscow: "Molodaia gvardiia," 1972.

Shapiro, Carolyn. "Napoleon and the Nineteenth Century Concept of Force." *Journal of Strategic Studies* 11 (1988).

Sharon, Ariel. "This Myth Should Not Be Destroyed." *Yediot Achronot* (3 October 1991).

Sheridan, Philip H. *Civil War Memoirs of Philip H. Sheridan*, reprint ed. with intro. by Paul Andrew Hutton. New York: Bantam Books, 1991.

Sherman, William T. *The Memoirs of General W. T. Sherman*, Vol. 1. New York: D. Appleton & Co., 1875.

Sherry, Michael S. *The Rise of American Airpower: The Creation of Armageddon.* New Haven, CT: Yale University Press, 1987.

Shimshoni, Jonathon. *Israel and Conventional Deterrence: Border Warfare from 1953 to 1970.* Ithaca: Cornell University Press, 1988.

Showalter, Dennis E. "Army and Society in Imperial Germany: The Pains of Modernization." *Journal of Contemporary History* 18 (1983).

———. *Railroads and Rifles: Soldiers, Technology, and the Unification of Germany.* Hamden, CT: Archon, 1975.

Silliker, Ruth L., ed. *The Rebel Yell and the Yankee Hurrah: The Civil War Journal of a Maine Volunteer.* Camden, ME: Down East Books, 1985.

Simpkin, Richard. *Deep Battle: The Brainchild of Marshal Tukhachevskii.* London: Brassey's, 1987.

Slater, Robert. *Warrior Statesman: The Life of Moshe Dayan.* New York: St. Martin's Press, 1991.

Smith, Malcolm. *British Air Strategy between the Wars.* Oxford: Clarendon Press, 1984.
Snyder, Jack. *The Ideology of the Offensive: Military Decision Making and the Disasters of 1914.* Ithaca: Cornell University Press, 1984.
Speidel, H. *Invasion 1944: Ein Beitrag zu Rommels und des Reichs Schicksal.* Tubingen: Wunderlich, 1949.
Spiers, Edward M. *The Army and Society, 1815–1914.* London: Longman, 1980.
Spires, David N. *The Making of the German Officer, 1921–1933.* Westport, CT: Greenwood Press, 1983.
Stefani, Filippo. *La storia della dottrina e degli ordinamenti dell'esercito italiano,* Vol. I. Rome: Ufficio Storico dello Stato Maggiore, 1984.
Steinberg, Jonathan. *Yesterday's Deterrent: Tirpitz and the Birth of the German Battle Fleet.* London: Macdonald, 1965.
Stone, Norman. *The Eastern Front, 1914–1917.* London: Hodder & Stoughton, 1975.
Storr, Anthony. *Churchill Revisited.* New York: Dial Press, 1969.
———. *Churchill's Black Dog.* London: Collins, 1989.
Strachan, Hew. "Soldiers, Strategy, and Sebastopol." *Historical Journal* 21 (1978).
———. *From Waterloo to Balaclava: Tactics, Technology and the British Army, 1815–1854.* Cambridge: Cambridge University Press, 1985.
Sullivan, Brian R. *A Thirst for Glory: Mussolini, the Italian Military, and the Fascist Regime, 1922–1936.* Ph.D. diss., Columbia University, 1984.
Summers, Harry. *On Strategy: A Critical Analysis of the Vietnam War.* San Francisco: Presidio Press, 1982.
———. *On Strategy II: A Critical Analysis of the Gulf War.* New York: Dell, 1992.
Sweetman, John. "The Smuts Report: Merely Political Window Dressing?" *Journal of Strategic Studies* 4 (1981).
Sykes, Christopher. *Orde Wingate.* London: Collins, 1959.
Tapert, Annette, ed. *The Brothers' War.* New York: Vintage Books, 1988.
Teveth, Shabtai. *Moshe Dayan.* Tel Aviv: Shocken, 1971.
———. *Moshe Dayan: The Soldier, The Man, The Legend.* Boston: Houghton Mifflin, 1973.
Thomas, Charles S. *The German Navy in the Nazi Era.* London: Unwin Hyman, 1990.
Thompson, Lieutenant-Colonel Ky L. "Theory before Praxis: Sir Julian Corbett and The Maritime Strategy." *Marine Corps Gazette* 12 (1988).
Thompson, Sir Robert, and Peter Mead. "Wingate—The Pursuit of Truth." *Army Quarterly and Defense Journal* 108 (1981).
Tirpitz, Alfred von. *Erinnerungen.* Leipzig: v. Halfe und Roeblen Verlag, 1919.
———. *Politische Dokumente,* Vol. I. *Der Aufbauer deutschen Weltmacht.* Stuggart: Cotta, 1924.
Toyama Saburō. *Nihon Kaigun Shi.* Tokyo: Kyōikusha, 1980.
Travers, T. H. E. *The Killing Ground: The British Army, the Western Front and the Emergence of Modern Warfare 1900–1918.* London: Allen and Unwin, 1987.
———. "A Particular Style of Command: Haig and the GHQ, 1916–1918." *Journal of Strategic Studies* 19 (1987).
Travers, T. H. E., and Christon I. Archer, eds. *Men at War: Politics, Technology and Innovation in the Twentieth Century.* Chicago: Precedent, 1982.

Trythall, Anthony John. *"Boney" Fuller: The Intellectual General.* London: Cassell, 1977.
Tzu, Sun. *The Art of War.* New York: Oxford University Press, 1963.
Unno Yoshirō. "Rondon kaigun gunshuku kaigi: Nihon no tachiba to shuchō." *Kokusai seiji* (1960), no. 11: *Nihon gaikoshi kenkyu-Showa jidai*, 36–49.
Venturi, Franco. "Le avventure del generale Henry Lloyd." *Rivista storica italiana* 91 (1979).
"Volunteer Officers." *Army and Navy Journal* 2 (24 September 1864).
Warner, P. *The British Cavalry.* London: Dent, 1984.
Wavell, W.P. "The Army and the Prophets." *Journal of the Royal United Service Institution* 75 (1930).
Webster, Sir Charles, and Noble Frankland. *Strategic Air Offensive against Germany,* Vol.1. London: Her Majesty's Stationery Office, 1961.
Wedemeyer, Albert C. *Wedemeyer Reports!* New York: Holt, 1958.
Weigley, Russell. *The Age of Battles: The Quest for Decisive Warfare from Breitenfeld to Waterloo.* Bloomington: Indiana University Press, 1991.
Weir, Gary E. "Tirpitz, Technology, and Building U-boats, 1897–1916." *International History Review* 6 (1984).
Whaley, Barton. *Strategem: Deception and Surprise in War.* Cambridge, MA: MIT Center for International Studies, 1969.
Willett, John. *Popski: A Life of Lt. Col. Vladimir Peniakoff.* London: Macgibbon & Kee, 1954.
Williams, T. Harry. *Lincoln and His Generals.* New York: Vintage Books, 1952.
Winton, John. *To Change an Army: General Sir John Burnett-Stuart and British Armoured Doctrine.* Lawrence: University of Kansas Press, 1988.
Winzen, Peter. *Bulow Weltmachtkonzept. Untersuchungen zur Fruhphase seiner Aussenpolitik 1897–1901.* Boppard am Rhein: 1977.
Zárate, Julio. "La guerra de independencia." In *México a través de los siglos,* Vol. II, ed. Vicente Riva Palacio. Mexico: Editorial Cubre, 1967.

Index

Abdallah, King of Jordan, 171
Abrams, Colonel Creighton, 177
Admiralty. *See* Royal Navy
Agadir crisis (1911), 91–92
Agranat Commission, 175
Aguirre, Matías de, 53
Alamán, Lucas, 33, 35–36
Aldama, Juan de, 48
Alexander I of Russia, 103, 106
Alexander II of Russia, 103, 106, 110
Alfaro, Xavier Tavera, 34
Algiers, 36
Allenby, General Sir Edmund, 22
Allende, Ignacio, 48
Allon, Yigal, 175, 194 n.36
Ambert, General, 14
André, General, 17
Anglo-French entente (1904), 89
Anglo-Japanese alliance (1902), 148, 150
Apaches, 37
Ardagan, Battle of (1877), 113
Aristotelian neoclassicism, 12
arme blanche, 18

Armijo, Gabriel, 53
art of command in war, 60
Asada Sadao, 145, 146, 148, 153, 162
Austria-Hungary, 89–90, 95; Galicia, 7, 119
Austro-French war (1859), 14
Azanza, Miguel José de, 39

Baconian ideas, 12
Baltic Sea, 91–92, 94
Bar Lev line, 171
Barlow, Francis C., 64
Barragón, Luis Miguel, 53
Baudisson, Count Friedrich von, 91–93
Baum, Abraham, 177–78
Beatty, Admiral Sir David, 21
Beauregard, General P.G.T., 69
Behncke, Paul, 93
Bellemere, Carey de, 17
Bendemann, Felix von, 89
Ben Gurion, David, 168, 172, 180
Beresford, Admiral Lord Charles, 50
Bernhardi, General Friedrich von, 1
Bismarck, Prince Otto von, 5, 95

Boer War. *See* South African War
Bomber Command. *See* Royal Air Force
Boulangisme, 24
Boutakoff, Admiral, 18
Brabazon, Major-General, 18
Branciforte, Marqués de, 37–38
Brusilov, Boris, 103–5
Brusilov, General Aleksei Alekseevich, 6–7, 21–22, 101, 107–9, 111–12, 115–16, 117–18; background and character, 103–7, 109–10; Corps of Pages, 104–6, 108–9, 111; early military campaigns, 112–15, 118; test of combat, 114
Brusilov, Lev Alekseevich, 103
Brusilov, Nadezhda, 117
Buell, Don Carlos, 71
Bulow, Prince Bernhard von, 89–91
Burnside, General Ambrose, 58, 66–67, 71
Bustamante, Anastasio, 53
Bustamante, Carlos María de, 33, 35
Butterfield, Daniel, 66

Cadorna, General Luigi, 21
Cady, Rush, 61
Cairo conference (1921), 129–30
Calleja, Félix, 3, 38–41, 42–44, 46–49, 52–53; background and character, 36–38; controversy about, 33–35, 44–45; military policies of, 54; success of, 34, 44–46, 50–52, 54
Capelle, Eduard von, 87
Carlson, Evans, 198
Casey, Silas, 61–62, 64, 69
Catherine the Great, 103
Caucasus, 7, 103–4, 107, 109–10, 112–13, 115, 117–18; wars in, 105, 112
Cavan, Field Marshal Lord, 205
Cecil of Chelwood, Viscount, 154
Central Asia, 3, 7
Chamberlain, Neville, 27
China, 148, 150
Churchill, Sir Winston, 129–30
Churchill, Winston (grandson), 183

Civil War, American (1861–1865). *See* United States of America
Clausewitz, General Karl von, 13, 16–17, 133, 176; doctrines of, 13, 126, 137, 139, 170, 173
Coerper, Carl, 87
Colegio Militar (Puerto de Santa María), 36
command of the sea, 19–21, 96, 209–13, 215, 217
Confederate States of America, 4, 59, 65, 70. *See also* United States of America
Conger, Captain Arthur L., 78
Corbett, Sir Julian, 19–20, 210–12, 215
Corcoran, Michael, 60
Cortés, Hernan, 33, 35
Crimean War (1854–1856), 1, 16, 104
Crowder, Enoch, 78
Crowley, James, 144, 145
Cullum, George W., 68
Custance, Rear-Admiral Reginald, 20

Dahnhardt, Harald, 87–88
Daniels, Josephus, 151–52
Dayan, Hanita, 168
Dayan, Moshe, 4, 6, 167–69, 174–76, 178, 181–83, 185, 194 n.36; background and character, 167–73, 176, 177, 187–90, 191 n.1; controversy about, 165–67; writings, 169–71
Dayan, Ruth, 194 n.2
Dayan, Shmuel, 169
Decatur, Stephen, 57
Delafield, Richard, 70
Dewar, Rear-Admiral Kenneth, 20, 21
Dingman, Roger, 145–46
Disraeli, Benjamin, 197
Dodge, R.J., 68
Dogger Bank incident (1904), 91
Dostoevsky, Fyodor, 109
Douglas, Admiral Archibald, 150
Douhet, Giulio, 26–27, 131, 213–14, 215
Dragomirov, M.I., 7, 13, 117
Dreadnought, HMS, 209
dreadnoughts, 91

Eisenhower, Dwight, 180
Elizabeth I of Russia, 106
Eshkol, Levi, 168, 182
Estrada, Francisco de, 40

Fischel, Max von, 93–94, 96
Fisher, Admiral Sir John, 20–21, 88, 209
Fiske, Bradley, 19
Foch, General Ferdinand, 201
France, 14, 16–17, 23–25, 27, 41, 85, 87–90, 92, 95, 198, 200–201, 207. *See also* French army; French navy
Franco-Prussian war (1870–1871), 13, 15
Frederick the Great, 5, 34
Fremont, John C., 58, 71
French, Field Marshal Sir John, 21
French army, 14–15, 17, 23, 50, 198, 207; École Militaire, 17
French navy, 18, 25, 85, 87, 89; naval maneuvers (1913), 93; and Revolution, 12, 16, 24; Empire, 12; Second Empire, 13; Third Republic, 24
Freycinet, Charles de, 13
Fuller, J.F.C., 7–8, 11, 23–24, 177, 202–7, 208, 209, 215–16, 217
Fushimi, Prince Admiral, 147, 159, 163

Gagemeister, Genrietta Antonova, 104, 110
Gagemeister, Karl Maksimovich, 104–5
Galster, Karl, 86
Gambetta, Leon, 13, 86
Gamelin, General Maurice, 23
Gandara, Dona Maria Francisca de la, 38–39
Garibaldi, Giuseppe, 15
Gaulle, Charles de, 17, 24–25, 198, 207
Geneva naval conference (1927), 5, 147, 152–53, 155, 162
German army: of Prussia, 5, 14; of Germany, 7–8, 13, 22, 25, 96; and High Command, 84, 92; and General Staff, 199–200, 217
German navy, 20, 22, 85–87, 88–94, 95, 96, 148; blockade of British coast, 93; deterrent function of, 89; High Command, 85; High Seas Fleet, 5, 83, 91–93; Imperial Naval Office, 84–85, 87, 89, 90, 92, 94; Kriegsakademie, 25; operational planning against Britain, 93–94; strategic air offensive, 126, 138; Tirpitz's battleship doctrine, 96. *See also* Tirpitz, Admiral Alfred von
Germany, 5, 8, 16–18, 20, 22, 25–26, 27, 83, 85, 87–93, 95–96, 125, 136, 138; Foreign Office, 89; naval laws (first), 87; (second), 87–88, 94; Prussia, 5, 14; Reichstag, 83–84, 86; wars of unification, 13; *Weltpolitik*, 90
Gibson, Hugh, 153
Gneisenau, Field Marshal Count August von, 199
Göemes Pacheco, Lieutenant General Juan Vicente de, 36
Goodyear, R.B., 66
Gorostiza, Brigadier Pedro de, 36–37
Grant, General Ulysses S., 4, 71, 73–75, 77
Great Britain, 3, 5, 7–9, 11, 14–15, 17–18, 20, 23, 24, 26, 36–37, 39, 57, 83, 85–86, 87, 90, 92, 94–95, 131–32, 137, 148, 151, 200–202; national security, 88; strategic air offensive, 123–25, 126–27, 130–32, 134–36; world power, 89. *See also* Royal Air Force; Royal Army; Royal Navy
Greeley, Horace, 58
Guderian, General Heinz, 8, 25, 198
guerre de course, 211–12

Hagana, 168
Haig, Field Marshal Sir Douglas, 12, 127
Hale, Lonsdale, 18
Hamaguchi Osachi, 154, 162
Hara Kei, 149

Heeringen, August von, 93
Heinrich of Prussia, Prince, 91
Heligoland, 85, 91
Henderson, G.F.R., 18
Hentsch, Lieutenant-Colonel Richard, 200
Heraclitus, 207
heresy, 2–3, 12, 14, 24–25, 27, 96, 156, 187, 197–98, 216–17; in military terms, 1–2, 6, 7–8, 20, 27, 96, 123, 125, 133, 145, 157, 187, 214, 216–17. *See also* orthodoxy
Hidalgo, Father Miguel, 38, 46, 47–48, 52; and rebellion, 38, 41–42, 43
Higginson, Thomas, 77
Hitler, Adolf, 3, 26
Holabird, J.B., 68
Holland, 84, 95
Hollman, Friedrich, 20, 86
Holtzendorff, Henning von, 92, 94
Holy Roman Empire, 84
Hooker, General Joseph, 57–58, 65–66, 71, 74–75
Hore-Belisha, Leslie, 208
Hughes, Charles Evans, 152
Hunt, Barry D., 216–17
Hurlburt, Stephen, 75

Imperial Japanese Army, 5, 157, 159
Imperial Japanese Navy, 5, 143–44, 157, 161–63; factions within: Administrative (*Gunsei-ha*), 161–62, Command (*Gunrei-ha*), 161–62, Fleet (*Kantai-ha*), 145, 149, 161, Hard-line (*Kyooko-ha*), 161, Moderate (*Onken-ha*), 161, Treaty (*Jōyaku-ha*), 161; and General Staff, 143–44, 145, 147, 150, 155, 156, 157–58, 159, 161, 163; and Navy Ministry, 144, 157, 158, 160, 161, 163
Imperial Military Tribunal of the Far East, 144
Imperial policing (Britain), 129–30
Ironside, General Sir Edmund, 207

Israel, 6, 166, 173–74, 181–82; War of Independence (1948), 170
Israeli Defense Forces (IDF), 6, 166, 172, 176–77, 182, 183, 185–86, 187–90
Italian navy, 22
Italy, 13, 16, 23, 27, 89; Fascist, 23, 25
Iturriagaray, José de, 39, 41

Jackson, Andrew, 60
Jackson, General Thomas "Stonewall," 65–66
Japan, 5–6, 89, 116, 143, 146–47, 149, 157, 161–63; grand strategy of, 6. *See also* Imperial Japanese Navy; Imperial Japanese Army
Jellicoe, Admiral Sir John, 21
jeune école, 84, 212
Jimenez, Mariano, 48
Joffre, General Joseph, 17, 21
Johnston, General Joseph E., 59
Jomini, General Antoine Henri, Baron de, 13, 60–61, 176; doctrines of, 15, 69, 170
Julius Caesar, 69, 71
Jutland, Battle of (1916), 22, 83

Kaiser Wilhelm Canal, 90
Kars, (Turkish) fortress of, 113–15
Katō Kanji, Admiral, 4–6, 143–44, 146–47, 149–51, 159, 163–64; and arms limitation, 143, 145, 147, 150, 152–53, 154–55, 156, 158, 160, 162–63; background and character, 146–47, 154; controversy about, 144–46, 148, 153, 162
Katō Tomosaburō, Admiral, 149, 152, 153, 158
Kearny, Philip, 64
Kiel Canal, 90
Kitchener, Field Marshal Lord, 13
Knorr, Admiral Eduard von, 85
Knox, Colonel Alfred, 116; and view of Brusilov, 106, 110
Kobayashi Seizō, Admiral, 154
Korem, Rachel, 192 n.4

Las Cruces, Battle of (1810), 43
Lawrence, T.E., 21–22, 198
Lee, General Robert E., 59, 72
Lermontov, Mikhail, 112
Liddell Hart, Captain Sir Basil, 7–8, 11, 23–24, 177, 208–9, 215–16
Lincoln, Abraham, 59–60
Llano, Ciriaco de, 51
Lloyd, E.H., 12
Lloyd, Selwyn, 181
London naval conferences: (1930), 5, 143, 145, 147, 154–55, 156, 158, 160, 162–63; (1934), 147
Luce, Stephen, 19
Ludendorff, General Erich, 22, 200
Lynden-Bell, Major-General A.L., 205

Machiavelli, Niccolo, 12
Maginot, André, 23
Mahan, Captain Alfred Thayer, 5, 18–19, 27, 84, 89, 95–96, 209; doctrines of, 20, 22, 27, 211–12
Makarov, S.O., 117, 119
Maltzahn, Curt, 86
Mannerheim, General Carl, 23
Marion, Francis, 60
Marlborough, Duke of, 12
Marquina, Félix Berenguer de, 39
Maurice, J.F., 18
McAllister, Robert, 76
McClellan, General George, 58, 65–67, 71, 75; as "the Young Napoleon," 71–72
Meade, General George, 67, 71–72, 76
Meir, Golda, 175
Metaxas, General John, 23
Mexican army, 34, 37, 50
Mexico, 3, 33, 36–39, 40, 42, 44–45, 46, 47–48, 50–52, 59; independence, 53; militia forces, 37; revolution, 53; society, 34; Spanish rule in, 54. *See also* New Spain
Miliutin, D.A., 106
Milne, General Sir George, 205
Miranda, Francisco, 37
Mitchell, Brigadier-General William, 27, 214–15
Mollet, Guy, 181

Moltke the elder, General Helmut von, 13, 199
Moltke the younger, General Helmut von, 90
Montgomery, General Sir Bernard, 198, 207
Montgomery-Massingberd, General Sir Archibald, 206, 207
Monts, Anton von, 95
Mora, José María Luis, 35
More, Hadassa, 192 n.4
Morelos, José María, 44, 46, 49–52
Morgan, Daniel, 60
Muller, Georg Alexander von, 91–92

Napoleon, 3, 12–13, 15, 17, 58, 62, 69, 71–72, 116, 176, 178, 185, 198
Nelson, Admiral Lord, 57, 198
New Spain, 38, 41–42, 52. *See also* Mexico
Newtonian ideas, 12
Nicholas I of Russia, 103
Nivelle, General Robert, 201
Nootka Sound controversy (1789), 37
North Sea, 88–89, 92–93
North Sea Strategy, 94
Northrup, Charles, 61

Okada Keisuke, Admiral, 158, 162–63
Orrantia, Francisco de, 53
orthodoxy, 2, 4, 8–9, 13–15, 21–23, 25, 96, 156, 159; in military terms, 15, 20–24, 26, 27, 123, 125, 133, 139, 214. *See also* heresy

Patton, General George, 8, 196, 207
Pedraza, Manuel Gomez, 53
Pelz, Stephen, 145–46, 148, 162
Persius, Lothar, 86
Peskov, S.V., 108
Pétain, General Henri, 17, 27, 201
Pohl, Hugo von, 93
Pokrovskii, N.S., 108
Pope, General John, 58, 67
Port Arthur, 119
Prasca, Visconti, 23

Prussia. *See* Germany
Pushkin, Alexander, 112

Raeder, Admiral Erich, 26, 96
Revillagigedo, Conde de, 36–38
Revollo, Ignacio Garcia, 42
Richmond, Admiral Sir Herbert, 7–8, 20–21, 209–13, 215, 217
Robertson, General Sir William, 210
Rommel, General Erwin, 178, 179, 184, 185, 198
Roosevelt, Theodore, 212
Rostonov, I.I., 102–3
Royal Air Force (RAF), 3–4, 27, 123–24, 125, 131–32, 134–36, 137, 139–40, 209, 213–14; Air Ministry, 129; Air Staff, 125, 127–28, 130–31, 132–33, 134–36, 137–38; Bomber Command, 124–25, 129–30, 136–37; interwar period, 127–29, 132–35; strategic air offensive, 123–25, 130–32, 134–36, 138; during World War I, 124, 126–27, 132, 133, 136, 213; during World War II, 139–40. *See also* Trenchard, Air Marshal Sir Hugh
Royal Army, 11, 14–15, 21, 129–30, 201–2, 215–16; Imperial General Staff, 9; War Office, 131
Royal Navy (RN), 5, 21, 25, 27, 89–90, 208, 209–12; Admiralty, 88, 93, 131; blockade of German North Sea coast, 92–93; distant blockade, 93, 96
Royal United Services Institution, 11
Russia, 7, 21, 23, 64, 85, 88–90, 95, 102, 104, 107–9, 111, 115, 148; Bolshevik coup d'état (1917), 102, 111; school of war, 117
Russian army, 16, 116; Caucasian, 103, 111, 115; Cavalry of the Line, 106; "Kerenskii offensives," 102; Imperial Guards, 106, 110–11, 116; Nikolai Cavalry School, 106; Officers' Cavalry Station, 78, 118–19; tsarist, 7, 103, 113, 116; tsarist General Staff Academy, 102, 111, 115–16; Red, 102–3

Russian navy, 18, 85, 87, 89
Russo-Japanese war (1904–1905), 5, 89, 116, 147, 148
Russo-Turkish war (1876–1878), 113, 118
Rust, Franz, 86

Sadeh, Yitzhak, 176–77
Saitō Makoto, Admiral, 153–54
Salmond, Geoffrey, 129
Saxe, Hermann Maurice de, 12
Scharnhorst, General Gerhard von, 198
Scheer, Admiral Reinhard von, 83
Schiller, Friedrich, 72
Schleinitz, Vice-Admiral von, 86
Schlieffen Plan, 201
Schurz, General Carl, 65
Scott, General Winfield, 57, 59
Seeckt, General Hans von, 8, 25
Semanov, Sergei, 102
Semper, José María, 47
Sharon, Ariel, 171
Sharon, Colonel Arik, 172, 173, 186
Sheridan, General Philip, 4, 73
Sherman, General William, 4, 73–75, 78–79
Shidehara Kijūrō, 162
Sigel, Franz, 60
Sinai Campaign (1956), 166, 171–72, 173–74, 180–82, 184, 185, 186
Six-Day War (1967), 166, 168, 181, 182, 185, 186
Skobelev, M.D., 118
South African War (1899–1902), 202–3; British efforts in southern Africa after 1880, 3; Royal Commission on, 18
Spain, 3, 9, 36, 39, 41, 45, 51, 52
Spanish army, 34, 36; of the center, 43–45, 48–49; of New Spain, 42; European Spanish expeditionary, 49
Stembok, Iulii Ivanovich, 107
Stembok family, 105, 107–9
Stimson, Henry, 19
strategic air offensive. *See* Germany; Great Britain; Royal Air Force
Strong, William K., 75
Sturdee, Admiral Sir Frederick, 21

INDEX

submarines, 22, 25, 91, 93
Suez crisis (1956). *See* Sinai Campaign
Sun Tzu, 180
Suvorov, Aleksandr, 7, 116–17
Suzuki Kantarō, 155–56, 158
Swift, Captain Eben, 78
Szogyeny, Count Ladislaus, 90

Takarabe Takeshi, Admiral, 158–59
technology: and change, 12; developments in, 22; military, 4; and threatened orthodoxies of land war, 25
Ten-Year Rule, 128
Tirpitz, Admiral Alfred von, 4–6, 20, 22, 83–94, 96, 212; emphasis on offensive naval warfare, 92; risk theory, 88–90, 94. *See also* German navy
Togo, Admiral, 147
Tokugawa, Prince, 152
Tolstoy, Leo, 104, 112
Treitschke, Heinrich von, 84
Trenchard, Air Marshal Sir Hugh, 3–4, 26–27, 123–24, 127–28, 131, 213–14, 215; air power and, 123–24, 132–33. *See also* Royal Air Force
Trumball, Lyman, 59
Tsunoda Jun, 145, 146
Tukhachevsky, General Mikhail, 23
Turkey, 7, 103–4, 113–14, 117–18

U-boats, 22, 25, 91, 93
United States Army, 27, 58–59, 70, 78; and Colored Troops, 62; and Confederacy, 51; and military education, 63, 79; of the Potomac, 65–66; tactical pragmatism in, 16; and the Union, 4, 57–58, 61, 63–64, 65–66, 70, 73–75
United States Army Air Service, 214–15
United States Army Artillery School, 78
United States Army War College, 78
United States Naval War College, 19
United States Navy, 22, 27, 211–12; and interwar arms limitation, 5, 143, 145, 147, 149, 152–53, 155, 156, 158, 160, 162, 210
United States of America, 5, 27, 39, 47, 72, 77, 87, 148, 151, 212; Antietam, 61; Bull Run, 67, 70; Chancellorsville, 65–66; Civil War (1861–1865), 4, 9, 57–58, 59, 65–66, 68, 72–73, 75, 77–79; Fredericksburg, 57; Vicksburg, 58, 76; Virginia campaign (1864), 74, 77; world interests, 84
Upton, Colonel Emory, 77–78

Valois, Victor, 86
Venegas, Javier de, 43, 45–48, 52
Vollerthun, Waldenmar, 89
Voltaire, 14

Wadsworth, James, 59
Wagner, Captain Arthur, 78
Washington, George, 57, 62
Washington naval conference (1921–1922), 5, 145–46, 147–48, 149, 151–52, 160, 210; and treaty, 145, 148
Wavell, General Sir Archibald, 8–9
West Point, 58–59, 61, 68–74, 78
Weygand, General Maxime, 23
Wilhelm II of Germany, 5, 83, 85–87, 90, 92–93
Wilkinson, Spencer, 18
Wingate, Orde, 6, 177, 184, 187, 192 n.3, 198
World War I, 5–9, 21, 23–24, 26, 78, 83–84, 102–3, 124, 126–27, 132, 133, 136, 138, 148, 157–58, 200, 208; Ainse offensive, 21; Caporetto, 21; Passchendaele, 21
World War II, 8, 96, 124–25, 139–40

Yamamoto Gombei, Admiral, 157
Yarnell, Admiral H.E., 154
Yom Kippur War (1973), 166, 171, 174–75, 186

Zarate, Julio, 33, 35
Zavala, Lorenzo de, 35
Zeppelin aircraft, 126–27

About the Editors and Contributors

CHRISTON I. ARCHER is Professor of History and former Head of the Department of History at the University of Calgary. His publications include *The Army in Bourbon Mexico, 1760–1810* (1977). He is currently preparing a book on the Royalist Army and counterinsurgency in Mexico during the wars of independence.

JOHN A. ENGLISH served as a career officer in the Canadian armed forces. He has written extensively on infantry and command problems. Among his books are *On Infantry* (1984) and *The Canadian Army and the Normandy Campaign: A Study of Failure in High Command* (1991).

JOHN GOOCH is Professor of History at the University of Leeds. He has written numerous articles on British military affairs; among his books is the classic study: *The Plans of War: The General Staff and British Military Strategy* (1974). His most recent writing includes *Army, State, and Society in Italy, 1870–1915* (1989). He is also a founder and editor of the *Journal of Strategic Studies*.

IAN GOW is NatWest Professor of Japanese Business Studies and Director of the Centre of Japanese Studies, Stirling University, Scotland. He has published widely in three areas of expertise: Japanese small businesses, current Japanese defense problems, and Japanese naval history. His publications regarding defense problems include J. W. M. Chapman, R. Drifte, and I. T. M. Gow, *Japan's Quest for Comprehensive*

Security: Defence, Diplomacy, and Dependence (1983). He is now completing a study of Admiral Katō Kanji.

MICHAEL I. HANDEL is Professor in the Department of Strategy at the Naval War College, Newport, Rhode Island. He has written extensively on Clausewitz and also on military intelligence; his recent publications include *War, Strategy, and Intelligence* (1989) and the edited book *Intelligence and Military Operations* (1990). He is a senior editor and founder of *Intelligence and National Security*.

A. HAMISH ION is Associate Professor of History at the Royal Military College of Canada. He is the author of *The Cross and the Rising Sun: The Canadian Protestant Missionary Movement in the Japanese Empire, 1827–1931* (1990).

DAVID R. JONES has held a number of university appointments in Canada and the United States, including Visiting Research Fellow, Naval War College, Newport, Rhode Island. He has written numerous articles on the Imperial Russian Army and on Tsar Nicholas II.

IVO LAMBI is Professor of History at the University of Saskatchewan. He is a founder and member of the editorial board of the *Canadian Journal of History/Annales Canadiennes d'histoire*. He is the author of *The Navy and German Power Politics, 1862–1914* (1984). Currently he is preparing a book on Bismarck's diplomacy 1870–1890.

B.J.C. MCKERCHER is Associate Professor of History at the Royal Military College of Canada. He is the author of *The Second Baldwin Government and the United States, 1924–1929* (1984) and *Esme Howard: A Diplomatic Biography* (1989) and editor of *Arms Limitation and Disarmament* (Praeger, 1992).

CAROL REARDON is Associate Professor in the Department of History, Pennsylvania State University. A former assistant editor of the journal *Diplomatic History*, she has recently published *Soldiers and Scholars: The U.S. Army and the Uses of Military History, 1865–1920* (1990).

SCOT ROBERTSON is a Defence Scientist with the Department of National Defence in Ottawa, Ontario. He has published numerous articles relating to defense subjects in the Government of Canada ORAE (Operations Research and Analysis Establishment) series. He is a well-known authority on the strategic bombing offensive during World War II.